# Academic Writing

## AN INTRODUCTION

# Academic Writing

## AN INTRODUCTION

**Janet Giltrow**

*with*

Daniel Burgoyne

Richard Gooding

Marlene Sawatsky

broadview press

brary and Archives Canada Cataloguing in Publication

iltrow, Janet, 1949-
    Academic writing : an introduction / Janet Giltrow ; with Daniel
urgoyne, Richard Gooding, Marlene Sawatsky.

ncludes bibliographical references and index.
SBN 1-55111-724-X

    1. Academic writing. 2. Report writing. 3. English language--Rhetoric.
. Burgoyne, Daniel, 1966-  II. Gooding, Richard Alan, 1960-  III. Sawatsky,
Marlene IV. Title.

PE1408.G54 2005      808'.042      C2005-902619-7

Broadview Press Ltd. is an independent, international publishing house, incorporated in 1985.
Broadview believes in shared ownership, both with its employees and with the general public; since
the year 2000 Broadview shares have traded publicly on the Toronto Venture Exchange under the
symbol BDP.

We welcome comments and suggestions regarding any aspect of our publications–please feel free to
contact us at the addresses below or at broadview@broadviewpress.com.

*North America*

PO Box 1243, Peterborough, Ontario, Canada K9J 7H5
3576 California Road, Orchard Park, NY, USA 14127
Tel: (705) 743-8990; Fax: (705) 743-8353
email: customerservice@broadviewpress.com

*UK, Ireland, and continental Europe*

NBN Plymbridge
Estover Road, Plymouth  PL6 7PY
Tel: + 44 (0) 1752 202301; Fax: + 44 (0) 1752 202331
Fax Order Line: + 44 (0) 1752 202333
Customer Service: cservs@nbnplymbridge.com
Orders: orders@nbnplymbridge.com

*Australia and New Zealand*

UNIREPS, University of New South Wales
Sydney, NSW, 2052
Tel: 61 2 9664 0999; Fax: 61 2 9664 5420
email: info.press@unsw.edu.au

www.broadviewpress.com

Broadview Press Ltd. gratefully acknowledges the financial support of the Government of Canada
through the Book Publishing Industry Development Program for our publishing activities.

PRINTED IN CANADA

# Contents

# Preface

Consider *Academic Writing: An Introduction* your invitation to join the scholarly community.

Possibly you consider this course of studies a requirement — and maybe it is. Or at least an obligation: people should pay attention to their writing. Everybody says it's important. But instead of thinking of this course as a requirement or an obligation — or a last chance to fix your grammar — try thinking of it as an invitation to participate in the knowledge-making activities of research communities.

Should such a direct invitation be necessary? After all, you are (probably) already admitted to university and enrolled in your courses. That should be invitation enough. Unfortunately — or not entirely unfortunately, as we will see in a minute — students' undergraduate situation is not always entirely hospitable. Lectures and readings can make assumptions which you may feel are unwarranted: taking for granted principles and ways of reasoning which are not familiar to you or are quite unlike those you are used to from secondary school or from everyday experience. Moreover, you are probably enrolled in courses in several different disciplines. What is assumed in one discipline differs from what is assumed in another discipline. What your history professor likes and expects in an essay is different from what your sociology professor likes and expects. These can seem like inhospitable conditions — not very inviting.

Fortunately, these very conditions of difference — the distinctiveness of scholarly habits of reasoning, the differences amongst the disciplines — have also produced rich resources: styles of writing, ways of asking and addressing questions, habits of attending to the voices of others. These resources are available to you, and they are means for you to take part in the work that research communities do.

Getting access to these resources, you will find that many of the problems that bother the traditional writing classroom will be silenced. The intimidating problem of "plagiarism," for example: once you get the habit of scholarly attentiveness to the voices of others, and appreciation for the scholarly exchange of ideas, the plagiarism monster will be a mere wisp, nothing. So too the problem of your "own opinion": where do you get to state your own views? Once you join the scholarly conversation, and learn how to orchestrate that conversation, your own position will emerge, commanding attention. And the problem of your role as a writer: in the traditional classroom you might read an essay by Carl Sagan on the galaxy, or by George Orwell on his shooting of an elephant: what are you supposed to write? Something about another galaxy or another elephant? An argument in favour of galaxies or elephants, calling for their protection? In this course of studies, your reading is your writing: just as the research authors associated with this course of study have read other research, and represent their reading, you too, as a research author, will represent your reading, and thereby yourself as a scholar.

As you will soon find, this book refers to a theory of language based in rhetorical study of *genre*. Without attempting to define "genre" here (see Chapter 1), I will say that a genre-based approach to academic writing sees the disciplines not as accumulations of facts in history or in anthropology or in other fields but as "forms of life": ways of doing things together. As such, disciplines are teeming with attitudes, values, interests — and motives. Scholars are moved to research, to read, to write; they identify with their disciplines. In some ways, the writing you do at university — and in this course — may be the most demanding you have ever done. But, in other ways, the writing you do in this course may be the easiest. For it will be motivated: there is a reason for it, a use for it. It is for making knowledge. And you will be the one making knowledge — asking questions, advancing proposals, indicating possibilities.

*Janet Giltrow*
*University of British Columbia*
*April 2005*

# 1

# Introducing genre

## 1A Hearing Voices

The seven passages below are in English. The observation that they are all written in English may be less important than the grounds on which they differ. As you read them, think about what they have in common and how they differ from one another. Issuing from decidedly different moments in North American life, each passage voices a different **cultural situation**. No one could say which of these passages is "best," or which is proper English and which is not. But we can think about how each voice — each style of expression — serves the situation from which it arises.

### PASSAGE 1

Eugenics theory powerfully influenced late nineteenth- and early twentieth-century U.S. policies concerning the groups then known as "the dependent, defective, and delinquent classes" (Henderson 1901, U.S. Department of the Interior 1883). In essence, eugenicists held that the "fit" should be encouraged to reproduce ("positive" eugenics) and the "unfit" prevented from doing so ("negative" eugenics). Historians generally agree that between 1900 and 1920 this doctrine formed the basis for a full-fledged social movement with research centers, propaganda vehicles, and strong middle-class support (Haller 1963, Kevles 1985, Ludmerer 1972, Pickens 1968). Less commonly acknowledged is the fact that eugenics theory affected public policy for decades before becoming the social movement's foundation and that eugenic ideas long outlived the movement it-self, in ways that a new generation of historians is just starting to explore (Dann 1991, Noll 1990, Reilly 1991). Even today, eugenics arguments occasionally make their way into debates about such matters as population growth and crime control (e.g., Wattenberg 1987, Wilson 1989; for a recent analysis see Duster 1990).

Nicole H. Rafter 1992 "Claims-making and socio-cultural context in the first U.S. eugenics campaign." *Social Problems* 39 (1): 17.

## PASSAGE 2

TALENTED, successful, good looking male, 30's, seeks attractive, in-telligent, petite female, who knows authentic gems are rare. Toronto area. Box 000.

## PASSAGE 3

My husband and I spent a recent vacation driving along the spec-tacular California coast. One morning we stopped at Big Sky Cafe in San Luis Obispo for breakfast. Their menu includes a hash with delicious "glazed" eggs. What's the secret to the eggs?

Eileen Gilbert
Casper, Wyoming

## PASSAGE 4

Vokey and Read (1992) further extend their findings by applying a regression analysis to the general familiarity and memorability com-ponents to predict recognition discrimination, criterion, and hit and false alarm rates. They reason that if the effect of typicality on recog-nition is a function of both general familiarity and memorability, each of these should be a significant predictor of recognition per-formance. To do this, they derived a regression equation composed of differential additive weightings of the general familiarity and mem-orability components to predict discrimination performance. In fact, they found that both familiarity and memorability were significant predictors of discrimination performance, but not of criterion.

Alice J. O'Toole, Kenneth A. Deffenbacher, Dominique Valentin and Hervé Abdi 1994 "Structural aspects of face recognition and the other-race effect." *Memory and Cognition* 22 (2): 209.

## PASSAGE 5

PANORAMIC VIEW! Super 2 yr old 1 bedroom apartment in prime South Slopes, features 180 degree Gulf Island view, 9' ceilings, in-suite laundry, 6 appliances, fantastic kitchen with oak cabinets, track lighting, balcony off living room & bedroom, gas f/p & more. Comes with 2 parking places. Unit located at 0000 Station Hill Court. Call now, priced to sell $147,900. Barry Wilson, Viewtime Realty.

## PASSAGE 6

PROVIDED that the Mortgagor, when not in default hereunder, shall have the privilege of prepaying, at any time and without notice or bonus, the whole or any part of the Principal Amount. Where any such additional payment is made the Payment Dates of all remaining monthly instalments, if any, of the Principal Amount and interest thereon shall thereupon be advanced so that the Mortgagor shall pay the Amount of Each Periodic Payment in each and every month commencing with the month immediately following the month in which the additional principal is repaid and continuing until all the monies secured by this Mortgage shall have been fully paid.

## PASSAGE 7

"Memories give me the strength I need to proceed, the strength I need to believe." Puff Daddy. This babygirl faced many challenges & brings with her wisdom, strength & sweet memories. Much luv to God & her loving parents. FM's: B&E's, YB '95-97 crew, Vox/R#17, fireworks, 290 guy (Minty? Sarah!), car races (boom!) eject'n seat/ Chungism w/Mike, killing 007/starfish w/Ho, who's Paul?, Summer Jam, jon z's w/evil one & STM grad/ 101 w/Brian. Shouts: my girl 2107 (&pops), Jenn, Geoff, Ang, Bear (you're mine! 112 hugs), all my buddies & bad boyz [sic]! FP: skydive, be happy & live the good life!

---

*Exercise 1*
Name the types of writing exemplified in Passages 1–7 and the cultural situation which each serves.

## 1B Hearing Genres

The passages above not only serve the cultural situations in which they arise, they also embody them. They represent distinct occasions in our culture; at the same time, people recognize and respond to them in ways that are generally seen as typical. So, when we hear these different voices, we also "hear" the setting in which they operate. The sounds of these passages indicate typical moments which culture has produced: occasions of professional publication, mating, property transaction, or legal agreement. In each case, situation has left its mark on, or *imprinted*, English. It has pressed into the general shape of the language features which mark it for use in particular contexts. The **imprint** makes language characteristic: something we recognize as typical.

To name the **types** and **situations** for each of these passages, you have to call on your knowledge of North American culture. Perhaps Passage 3 escaped you: your life experience may not have included contact with the situation which has produced a type of writing which we could call "request for recipe" and which appears in cooking magazines. Or, if you are not from North America, you may be surprised by the boastfulness of the author of Passage 2, and by his search for a person of a certain size. Hearing and speaking, reading and writing, we enact our experience of the world as that experience has been shaped by culture.

As the diversity of the seven passages shows, language is sensitive to situation. Moreover, the way we use language changes as new situations arise. For example, new technologies have given rise to new situations and new ways of using language, such as instant messaging. In this situation, instead of using conventional spelling and full sentences, we often use single letters, numbers, and emoticons; and our friends recognize this way of writing as a typical, not incorrect, use of English. In recent years, this sensitivity has been captured and studied in new ways of thinking about genre. This book takes advantage of new reasoning about **genre**.

See page 281 for a list of readings on **genre theory**.

Before sketching the new ideas about genre, let us glance at the old ones. Chances are that when you hear the word "genre," you think of music or movies. For example, you may think of the difference between hip hop and classical music, or between slasher movies and psychological thrillers. Or you heard the word in the high school classroom in connection with literary studies. Genre was, for instance, a way of saying that poems, novels, and plays are different: they are different genres. So the notion of genre helped school boards make their curriculum orderly and helped English departments keep courses separate. For these purposes, genre was a useful concept, tending towards traditional ideas about literary form.

But then, at the end of the twentieth century, more and more scholars began to think of genre in terms of the social and political contexts of knowledge. Scholars considered the ways in which the quality of statements about the world depended on who was making the statement. Alert to new opportunities, genre offered itself as a way of thinking about the context-dependency of language — the ways in which language depends upon and responds to the social and political contexts that produce it.

While old ideas of genre had slipped into regarding only **form**, the new ideas insisted that it was not form alone that constituted genre, but situation and form:

**situation + form = genre**

Or, to put it another way, the situations that writers find themselves in *give rise* to genres.

This new understanding of genre gave researchers a way of talking about these similarities not as rules but as signs of common ground among communities of readers and writers: shared attitudes, practices and habits, positions in the world. Forms of speaking are connected to social contexts where people *do* things — like selling a house, or finding a mate. Different routines of social behaviour — habits of acting in the world — create different genres of speech and writing.

In this light, consider the thank-you note as a genre. People who know this genre not only know how to compose the note — what to mention, how much to say, how to begin, how to conclude, what kind of writing materials to use — but also *when* to do all this: soon after receipt of a certain type of gift from a person in a certain relation to the recipient. (So, in all probability, you would not send a thank-you note to your parents for the gift of a laptop computer or to the Students' Union for the so-called gift of a daily planner or student handbook. And if you delay sending a thank-you note where one is called for, you will feel — consciously or unconsciously — that you are failing to comply with the genre's norms, no matter how perfectly you compose the note itself.) The thank-you note genre is made up not only of a characteristic type of written expression but also of the situation in which it occurs. It is a way of acting in the world. People with know-how in this genre understand not only its form but also its situation. We could even say that, at some deep, unconscious level, these people also share an understanding of the role of the genre in larger social or cultural situations — systems of relationship amongst kin and friends, symbolized by the exchange of commodities (in particular, gifts) and expressions of recognition (ways to say thank you).

Once scholars began to consider genre outside traditional literary studies, it became clear that English classes weren't its only, or even its best, place of work. Increasingly, other kinds of writing began to be thought of in terms of genre: auditors' reports, news accounts of violent crime, case reports in publications in veterinary medicine, architects' proposals, primary school show-and-tell sessions, and — most important to our interests — academic writing. At all these sites, genre was a means to investigate similarities in documents occurring in similar situations.

Genre theory gave researchers a way of talking about these similarities not as rules but as signs of common ground among communities of readers and writers: shared attitudes, practices and habits, positions in the world. So the style of Passage 5 comes about not because somebody followed rules, but because it embodies a widely recognized situation — property transaction in a market economy — through its typical, list-like naming of qualities that the users of this genre recognize as valued and translatable into dollars. Views are good, so is newness, and so is oak finishing on kitchen cabinets. The document assumes that readers recognize the value of parking spaces and the desirability of laundering clothes at home. It assumes that readers will not interpret "6 appliances" as a sign of overcrowding in a small apartment, and that readers don't need to be told what these appliances are, or what they do. It also assumes that readers are familiar with the customary practice of buying and selling a dwelling — contacting a broker specializing in this kind of transaction. Note that such knowledge is not universal but **cultural**. In another culture, where people inherit their homes from their parents, or share them with co-workers, such a genre would not exist at all. Or some culture, somewhere, might value a home not for its appliances or parking spaces but for its human history: while in our culture we exchange homes with strangers, dwellings in some other place might be identified with their residents. Then the genre accompanying property transactions might develop techniques for describing the dwelling's current occupant in appealing or prestigious terms. In either case, the genre suits the cultural situation.

Perhaps, a hundred years from now, scholars will examine personal ads or requests for recipes or mortgage documents to piece together vanished systems of association amongst people. Or they will look at the genres which report research in social history or cognitive psychology to understand the systems of relationship and production which held academic communities together at the end of the twentieth century and the beginning of the twenty-first.

## 1C High School vs. University Writing

Genre theory predicts that diversity of expression will reflect the complexities of social life, whether that life takes place in a chat room or on a hockey rink or in a university classroom. Because people interact for a lot of different purposes, they write and speak in a lot of different ways. And, as the world changes, so too will ways of writing and speaking change. If we apply genre theory to the kinds of writing that take place in a university, we can better understand what communities of scholars do and how they typically communicate with one another. The benefits for the student just beginning a university career are inestimable.

Writing *instruction*, however, has tended to focus on one type of writing: the schoolroom essay. Different kinds of assignments may produce slightly different versions of the essay — the "argument" essay, for example, or the "expository" essay — but, generally, when students arrive at college or university, they are experienced in producing a form of writing which serves schoolroom situations. Along with this experience, they absorb — from teachers, from handbooks, from public sentiments — ideas about writing. It should be "clear" and "concise," for example; it should not be "vague" or "wordy." Writing should also be "logical" and "well organized."

But then, at university, students encounter writing that would not be "clear" to most people (consider Passage 4), and writing that most people would not call "concise" (consider the fourth sentence of Passage 1). And what seems to be "logical" in one **discipline** is not thought to be "logical" in another discipline. For example, a physics student, recording findings from an experiment, may be expected to privilege unbiased observation and objective recording of data, while an anthropology student, writing a report on the behaviour of a community, may be asked to recognize that the community needs to accept and even edit results. A course in Victorian poetry may ask a student to come up with a thesis on a writer's use of metaphor, while a philosophy course in logic may apply rules that seem to defy common sense. "Organization" in a book review for history is not "organization" in a psychology lab report, and neither resembles "organization" in an "argument" essay learned in high school. After long experience in the schoolroom essay, and long contact with maxims about good writing, university students face many examples of expression which contradict the schoolroom tradition.

Genre theory tells us that the schoolroom essay — in its style — serves its situation. (Inspecting the situation, we might look for connections between the kinds of features prized in student essays and the larger function of the schoolroom itself. We might consider the schoolroom's role in socializing youth, in controlling the time of young people, in accrediting some and discrediting others, in scheduling some students for further education — in well-paid occupations that structure and regulate social life — and scheduling others for poorly paid or low-prestige occupations.) Since the essay is a persistent genre, it must be doing an adequate job of serving and maintaining and defining schoolroom situations.

But the schoolroom situation and the university classroom situation are different. Accordingly, the kind of writing that suits the schoolroom tends not to suit the university classroom. That is, they represent two different genres (in both situation and form) of writing.

## 1D The University as Research Institution

The most important distinction between high school situations and university situations is that the latter are located in research institutions. While students may see themselves as learners rather than researchers, they nevertheless do their learning under the direction of people who are trained as researchers and who read and write research publications. The knowledge that university students acquire is the kind of knowledge that comes from the techniques of inquiry developed by the various academic disciplines. We could go so far as to say that the very wording of the facts and concepts students must absorb derives from research practice: the routines, habits, and values which motivate scholars to do the work they do.

This wording represents research communities' beliefs and their members' shared techniques for interpreting the world. At the same time, such wording is also the medium in which students must work.

If university students are not writing schoolroom essays, what are they writing? What wordings will represent the student's position in the university situation? While it would be too much to say that students should write research articles, it is not too much to say that their writing shares features of the research genres. After all, one goal of the undergraduate curriculum is to prepare students for graduate work so that they can eventually assume positions as researchers in the university and other research institutions. The style of the information students encounter in their university courses is shaped by the research situations that produced it. So, as students work with a particular type of research information, the style of that research genre becomes the most appropriate for them to adopt. And while the wording of research writing shares some features with the schoolroom essay — both are, after all, English — the differences are perhaps more meaningful than the similarities. (Equally, the styles of the different disciplines share many features, but the differences can be meaningful, and can have consequences.)

This book puts student writers in touch with the wording of the research genres. It shows student writers what the salient, or distinguishing, features of scholarly expression are — features which distinguish the scholarly genres and which we recognize as typical of academic situations. At the same time, it encourages students to develop informed perspectives on scholarly styles and situations. As sites for shared understandings, and shared means of interpreting the world, genres can seem like worlds unto themselves — self-justifying, "natural," immemorial. But the research genres (like any others) are not in fact worlds unto themselves. They are involved in all the social and political complexities of their times.

---

### Exercise 2

The styles of expression in Passages 1 to 7 differ in many respects. In the chapters which follow, you will acquire means of identifying and using salient features of 1 and 4 — the two passages from research genres. But you might begin to develop your awareness of style here by inspecting and comparing all seven samples. First, and most broadly, what distinguishes 1 and 4 from the others? Second, and more narrowly, can you distinguish between the styles of 1 and 4? (Passage 1 is the first paragraph of the article's introduction; Passage 4 is the sixth paragraph of the article's introduction.) In approaching these tasks, you might take into account these features:

- ways the writers are represented in the text (most obviously, do they mention themselves?);
- words — their commonness (would they show up in, for example, conversation between neighbours?), their recurrence (to what degree do these writers repeat the same words?); and sentences — their length, completeness;
- capitals, parentheses, names, numbers.

How would you describe the relation between writer and reader in each of these passages?

From what you know (or can guess) about the ways of life which surrounded each of these samples, estimate how each of the writers learned to write this way (on the job? in class? on a weekend seminar?).

### Exercise 3

Each of these passages was apparently written by a different person. But say this were not the case. Which passages could have been written by the same people? What are your reasons for thinking so?

### Exercise 4

In this chapter we have used the term "cultural situation" to refer to, among other things, circumstances that define the relationship between writer and reader. What other factors are part of a "cultural situation"? Generate a list of five cultural situations that have specific types of writing associated with them. In each case, consider how the cultural situation imprints language, creating particular types of communication.

# 2

# Citation and summary

In the next two chapters we head for **summary** — an important feature of the research genres. Summary may not seem, at first, an attractive destination. Or a serious one. With its schoolroom role as a check to see if you've done assigned reading, or its role in exams in seeing if you understand what you read ("List the three main points the author makes. Write in complete sentences."), summary can appear to be a mechanical exercise. But for scholarly writers — researchers and professors — summary fulfils quite different functions. In summarizing, academics identify with a community of researchers, establish what positions have been taken by others, and take a **position** themselves. All of these activities allow them to construct new knowledge. In this sense, summary is a central activity of scholarly life.

So, to put summary in the context of research itself and to show how summary is part of the scholarly community of practice, we are going to begin by examining examples of **citation** from different disciplines. We will also look at how citation in scholarly discourse differs from citation in everyday conversation and other situations.

## 2A Introducing Scholarly Citation

Here is a way of writing which somebody unaccustomed to scholarly writing might find peculiar:

## PASSAGE 1

Increasing concern over the possibility of global climate change has heightened interest in the factors that affect clouds in climatically pivotal areas such as the Arctic (e.g., Goody 1980; Abelson 1989; Ackerman *et al.* 1986). Changes in either the areal coveral or radiative properties of arctic layer clouds could modify the arctic climate and ice pack and potentially affect global climate (e.g., Schlesinger 1986; Walsh and Crane 1992; Curry *et al.* 1996).

Information on the structures of arctic clouds is relatively scant. Most previous microstructural measurements for summer were obtained in June 1980 during the Arctic Stratus Experiment (ASE) (e.g., Tsay and Jayaweera 1984; Herman and Curry 1984; Curry and Ebert 1992) when stratocumulus clouds were widespread (Warren *et al.* 1988). Cloud measurements in the Arctic at other times of the year by Witte (1968) and Jayaweera and Ohtake (1973) suggest that cloud structures are fairly simple and homogeneous over large areas, with cloud liquid-water content (LWC) generally increasing above cloud base.

Peter V. Hobbs and Arthur L. Rangno 1998 "Microstructures of low and middle-level clouds over the Beaufort Sea." *Quarterly Journal of the Royal Meteorological Society* 124: 2035–2071, 2035.

But this kind of citation isn't peculiar to meteorologists. Other people — sociologists, for instance — write this way, too:

## PASSAGE 2

Initial skepticism over the impact of neighborhood conditions and neighborhood contexts on the behavior of adolescents and young adults (Jencks and Mayer 1990) has spurred considerable research purportedly documenting such effects (Aneshensel and Sucoff 1996; Billy, Brewster, and Grady 1994; Corcoran et al. 1992; Duncan 1994; Duncan, Connel, and Klebanov 1997; Elliott et al. 1996; Entwisle, Alexander, and Olson 1994; cf. Evans, Oates, and Schwab 1992). Grounded primarily in Wilson's (1987) prominent treatise on *The Truly Disadvantaged,* several recent studies have examined the impact of neighborhood disadvantage on family-related events, including the timing of first sexual activity (Billy et al. 1994; Brewster 1994; Brewster, Billy, and Grady 1993), first marriage (Hoffman,

Duncan, and Mincy 1991; Massey and Shibuya 1995), and nonmarital and/or teenage childbearing (Billy and Moore 1992; Brooks-Bunn et al. 1993; Crane 1991).

Scott J. South and Kyle D. Crowder 1999 "Neighborhood effects on family formation: Concentrated poverty and beyond." *American Sociological Review* 64: 113–32, 113–14.

Weather and neighbourhoods are familiar topics, but here they are being talked about in rather unfamiliar ways. Besides somewhat rare wordings (e.g., "radiative properties" and "the impact of neighbourhood disadvantage on family-related events"), there are some conspicuous formal features — long parenthetical interruptions to the sentences, with only names and years in them. Why do South and Crowder write "the timing of first sexual activity (**Billy et al. 1994; Brewster 1994; Brewster, Billy, and Grady 1993**), first marriage (**Hoffman, Duncan, and Mincy 1991; Massey and Shibuya 1995**), and nonmarital and/or teenage childbearing (**Billy and Moore 1992; Brooks-Bunn et al. 1993; Crane 1991**)"? What kind of writing is that?

These parenthetical patches are a condensed, concentrated way of telling us that somebody other than the present writer has said something: they signal citation.

Other writers in different research disciplines use different citing strategies. They unpack the clumps of names and dates, show us that these statements have been uttered by other speakers, and even permit us to hear their actual words. In Passage 3, Ann Taylor Allen, an historian, is beginning a discussion of what others have said about moods of uncertainty at the turn of the previous century (people feeling insecure, alienated). Bold type is used to emphasize the **reporting expressions** which attribute statements about those moods to writers other than Allen.

### PASSAGE 3

**Most of the literature on European and North American intellectual history at the turn of the century emphasizes** the problematic and disorienting effects of (**as Everdell puts it**), "the impossibility of knowing even the simplest things that the nineteenth century took for granted."[1] In fact, **the characterization of** the period from 1890 to 1914 as an era of pessimism, alienation, and anxiety has become a cliché of intellectual history. In German political thought, **Fritz Stern describes** a mood of "cultural despair";[2] for the social

sciences, **writes Lawrence Scaff**, "the central problem appears to be
the same in every case: a sense that unified experience lies beyond
the grasp of the modern self and that malaise and self-conscious
guilt have become inextricably entwined with culture."[3] **Eugen
Weber remarks** that, in France at the turn of the century, "the dis-
crepancy between material progress and spiritual dejection reminded
me of my own era."[4] In Britain, **the literary critic Terry Eagleton
refers to** a "cataclysmic crisis of Victorian rationality."[5]

*Notes*
1   William R. Everdell, *The First Moderns: Profiles in the Origins of Twentieth-
    Century Thought* (Chicago, 1997), 10–11.
2   Fritz Stern, *The Politics of Cultural Despair: A Study in the Rise of the Germanic
    Ideology* (1961; rpt. edn., New York, 1965).
3   Lawrence A. Scaff, *Fleeing the Iron Cage: Culture, Politics, and Modernity in the
    Thought of Max Weber* (Berkeley, Calif., 1989), 80.
4   Eugen Weber, *France: Fin de Siècle* (Cambridge, Mass., 1986), 3. For other
    examples, see […].
5   Terry Eagleton, "The Flight to the Real," in *Cultural Politics at the Fin de Siècle*,
    Sally Ledger and Scott McCracken, eds. (Cambridge, 1995), 13.

Ann Taylor Allen 1999 "Feminism, social science, and the meanings of modernity: The debate on the origin of the family in Europe and the United States, 1860–1914." *The American
Historical Review* 104 (4): 1085–1113, 1085–86.

Citation — the attributing of a statement to another speaker — produces one of the distinctive sounds (and looks) of scholarly writing. The
distinctiveness of this way of writing could lead to one or two views of
scholarly writing which, while not necessarily unfounded, may be misleading. The first is that only scholars repeat the words and ideas of others. The second is that scholarly citations are a shortcut to "authority,"
simply a way to support an argument, and that scholarly writing is a platform for those who have a knack for repeating the words of others. We
discuss each of these views below.

## 2B Is Citation Unique to Scholarly Writing?

So commonly do people in everyday conversation repeat the sayings of
others that specialists in language studies investigate this speech habit.
For example, Wallace Chafe (1994) focuses on how speakers' representations of others' words involve awareness of contexts distant from the setting of the conversation; Patricia Mayes's study of citation in spoken

English finds that "at least half of the direct quotations are not authentic renditions, and many are the invention of the speaker" (1990:358); and Greg Myers (1999) proposes methods to classify the many functions of citation, showing that the speech technique of representing the words of others involves complex purposes and, on the listener's part, subtle interpretive schemes. These are all studies of citation in commonplace settings: people telling about their experiences and feelings, explaining themselves or passing on information about others.

And, if we consult our own experience, we too can readily tune into citation in our daily encounters:

(a)  So this guy comes over and says is that your car and I'm like yeah and he goes you gonna leave it there and I'm like — *what???*

(b)  So they say the urban coyotes are getting pretty bad

(c)  The weatherman says showers in the morning but then clearing

Compare the secondhand report in Passage (d) with the thirdhand report in Passage (e):

(d)  Judy — you know, from Student Loans — she called me the other day, and she says they haven't received my cheque. And I say, I sent it last week. And she says, Oh.

(e)  Pat's friend Sally is breaking up with her boyfriend. Apparently Sally is very upset and phones Pat all the time, and Pat is getting really tired of this. I guess Sally is always saying, Why me? So Pat finally said, Why not you? I think Pat's getting a bit frustrated.

In (d) a speaker ("I") reports a conversation between herself and another speaker (Judy). In (e), a speaker ("I") says what her friend (Pat) said her friend (Sally) said, and what she (Pat) said she said to her friend (Sally).

In Passage (f) below, a speaker, telling a dog-bites-man story, says what her mother said she said, and what her mother said someone else said (notice how the daughter quotes the mother directly, but the stranger's words are swallowed by descriptions of his attitude, e.g., "this man was going absolutely mad"):

> (f) [My mother] took — she's got these two Dobermans who are really unruly but very sweet. She took them for a walk on the beach one day, and this was at the height of the Rottweiler scare, and this jogger's running along the beach at Liverpool, and Sophie, her dog that she can't control, decided to run along after the jogger and bit him on the bottom. And this man was going absolutely mad, and my mother started off by being nice to him and saying, "I'm terribly sorry; she's only a pup and she was just being playful," and so on, and he got worse, so the more she tried to placate him, the more he decided he was gonna go to the police station and create a scene about it. So she said, "Let me have a look", and she strode over to him and pulled his <LAUGHS> pulled his tracksuit bottoms down, and said, "Don't be so bloody stupid, man, there's nothing wrong with you, you're perfectly all right". At which point he was so embarrassed he just jogged away.
>
> Cited in Jennifer Coates 1996 *Women Talk: Conversation between Women Friends.* Cambridge, MA: Blackwell, 100–01.

Why is citation so common in everyday conversation? Possibly because much of what we know about the world we learn only from what others have said, and because conveying this knowledge as coming from a particular source gives us a chance to take a position in relation to other people's positions in the world. For example, the speakers in (a) and (d) take an oppositional stance vis-à-vis the other speaker they cite, and cite their own speech to confirm this position. Mentioning coyotes, the conversationalist in (b) cites a consensus he has detected in news reports of the day; the speaker in (c) uses citation to show the source of his prediction about the weather. (It seems rare, in Western culture, to hear a weather prediction without at least an implicit citation of weather professionals, e.g., "it's supposed to rain then clear up."). In (f), the story about the jogger and the dog, the storyteller manages the speech of others in such a way as to lead us to sympathize with the dog owner rather than with the man who was bitten.

Sometimes writers in non-academic genres — in (g), a writer of a letter to the editor of a small-town newspaper — use citation to **typify** what they take to be a general message from other sources (in this case, sources with which the writer strongly disagrees) by putting words in others' mouths:

> (g) Disincentives are everywhere for drivers .... "take transit so we can clog our arteries with fuel-hogging buses." I don't like it, and there is nothing I can do about it.

> Letter to the editor, *Tri-City News* 26 April 2000.

In (h), the speaker is one of a group of British "working-class men" who are on probation after having been convicted of money-related crimes. Like the speaker in (i), he puts words in others' mouths:

> (h) They can rip off millions and pay nothing, then someone gets caught, twenty, thirty pounds DSS an' "they're a criminal scum-bag".

> Sara Willott and Chris Griffin 1999 "Building your own lifeboat: Working-class male offenders talk about economic class." *British Journal of Social Psychology* 38: 445–60, 451.

Notice that the speaker is *not* stating that small-time thieves are criminal scum-bags. He is stating that *others* (what we might call Big Interests) *say* that small-time thieves are criminal scum-bags, and he aligns himself in opposition to these others: his citation distinguishes his interests from the interests of those he perceives as embezzling and pillaging on a large scale. On the other hand, the next speakers (from the same group) self-cite not to oppose others but to establish solidarity amongst themselves:

> (i) Mark: always said, right, you don't take from somebody who's just as bad off as you. I'd rather take from somebody who could *afford* to lose.
> Andy: What you say, "you don't take off your own kind."
> Mark: Exactly.
> Steve: Your own doorstep.
> Andy: Yup, your own doorstep ...

> Willott and Griffin 1999: 456.

Sometimes in everyday conversation, we simply repeat what we have heard, sewing it with invisible stitches into our utterances. Someone who has himself conducted no studies of climate change and has not visited South Asia could say —

(j)   There are droughts in South Asia ... global warming

— and his listeners could infer that he read this somewhere, or heard it on television.

Other times, a view of our own gets a boost from citing a source people consider authoritative.

(k)   He was black and blue from head to toe, the doctor says it was a miracle he survived.

Much of our performances as speakers is citation — repeating what others have said, attributing statements to those with authority, or those with whom we disagree: naming some of our sources ("Barb," "my mother"), typifying others ("the doctor," "the weatherman"), leaving some anonymous ("they say"), or leaving some cited claims unattributed. Some citation is verbatim; some is paraphrase; some is invented.

Seeking recognition and sympathy for our position, or spreading the news or playing our part in rumour and hearsay, we repeat what others have said.

---

**Exercise 1**

Locate the speaker (or source of information) and the reported speech in the examples above. For instance, Passage (a) above can be worked out as follows: "So this guy (speaker) comes over and says (reporting expression) is that your car (reported speech) and I (speaker)'m like (reporting expression) yeah (reported speech) and he (speaker) goes (reporting expression) you gonna leave it there (reported speech) and I'm (speaker) like (reporting expression) — *what???* (reported speech)"

**Exercise 2**

Citation in everyday conversation: Without offending anyone's privacy, listen to discussions which you overhear or in which you participate: listen for, and record, two or three instances of citation in everyday conversation. How does this speaker (who might be you) attribute his or her cited statement to a source? Is the source named ("Barb," "Prince Charles"), typified ("the Registrar's Office," "the vet"), anonymous ("I heard ...," "they")? What role did the citation play in the conversation?

**Exercise 3**

Citation in news genres: Citation not only plays a part in many conversational situations, it also has a major function in newspaper reports, in Western cultures especially. To get a sense of its characteristic operation in constructing public information, inspect the passage below. Identify those statements which are citations. Which are paraphrase? Which are presented word for word? Which cited speakers are fully identified? Which are typified or anonymous? What would the passage sound like if we removed the expressions which attribute statements to others? For example, removing both reporting expressions from the first sentence —

> Outgoing U.S. Ambassador to Canada Paul Cellucci said American officials were given the direct impression that Canada was going to participate in the U.S.-led ballistic missile-defence plan.

— we would get:

> Canada was going to participate in the U.S.-led ballistic missile-defence plan.

Speculate on the function of citation in the news genres generally — and in this article in particular.

> Outgoing U.S. Ambassador to Canada Paul Cellucci said American officials were given the direct impression that

Canada was going to participate in the U.S.-led ballistic missile-defence plan.

"We were given that impression in a very direct way for a long time," Cellucci said, appearing on CTV's *Question Period*.

He said Americans were "perplexed" at the decision not to participate because "we've been pretty much assured for a long time that Canada wanted to participate, that this was in Canada's sovereign interest to participate."

He said the decision was Canadians' loss "because they will not have a seat at the table."

"We have this odd situation where the Canadians will participate at NORAD, detecting when the missile is launched, determining where it's heading, and even if they determine it's heading towards Canada, it's at that point they will have to leave the room, because they're not participating.

"In the United States we'll decide what to do about the missile."

Speaking to reporters from the Liberal policy convention on Sunday, Prime Minister Paul Martin denied that Canada ever guaranteed it was on onboard.

Martin said that Canadian officials finally chose to opt out of the plan last month because they never got answers about what participation would entail.

"The missile shield is a project in evolution," Martin said in French.

"It will continue evolving. And we don't know what the demands will be, for a project that is evolving because it will change."

"And we know well that when you participate in something, the demands can come. There's no one who can explain or quantify them today."

Martin also said that the Canadian government told the U.S. last summer that "we were not prepared to go further at that time." [...]

"Cellucci says Canada reneged on missile plan," <www.ctv.ca>, 7 March 2005.

## 2c Why Do Scholars Use Citation?

In the last section we saw that citation is a feature of everyday conversation; it is therefore not peculiar to scholarly writing. It is nevertheless *conspicuous* in this kind of writing. It is a salient feature: it sticks up or stands out; it makes academic research recognizable from a distance. Citation is a feature which these genres don't seem to be able to do without.

But what about the claim — or, as it's sometimes expressed, the *accusation* — that scholarly writers repeat others simply to support their claims or sound impressive? Do citations merely serve the purpose of making the writer sound authoritative — learned and important?

Let's look again at Passage 2, from the beginning of the chapter, starting with the first sentence:

> Initial skepticism over the impact of neighborhood conditions and neighborhood contexts on the behavior of adolescents and young adults (Jencks and Mayer 1990) has spurred considerable research purportedly documenting such effects (Aneshensel and Sucoff 1996; Billy, Brewster, and Grady 1994; Corcoran et al. 1992; Duncan 1994; Duncan, Connel, and Klebanov 1997; Elliott et al. 1996; Entwisle, Alexander, and Olson 1994; cf. Evans, Oates, and Schwab 1992).

Notice that South and Crowder don't claim that neighbourhoods have good or bad effects or no effects on the young people who live in them. Instead, they report that someone (Jencks and Mayer) has said that neighbourhoods may not have much effect on young people, and that some skeptical researchers (the remaining citations) reacted and set out to test this possibility. Are South and Crowder skeptical themselves? No, they attribute the skepticism to these other researchers. But then the adverb "purportedly" suggests that they do not necessarily occupy the same **position** as those whose work has challenged that skepticism.

In the next sentence, South and Crowder interpret the eight clusters of speakers (appearing at the end of the sentence) as having been influenced by yet another speaker — the author of what they call a "prominent treatise":

> Grounded primarily in Wilson's (1987) prominent treatise on *The Truly Disadvantaged*, several recent studies have examined the impact of neighborhood disadvantage on family-related events, including the timing of first sexual activity (Billy et al. 1994; Brewster 1994; Brewster, Billy, and Grady 1993), first marriage (Hoffman,

Duncan, and Mincy 1991; Massey and Shibuya 1995), and nonmarital and/or teenage childbearing (Billy and Moore 1992; Brooks-Bunn et al. 1993; Crane 1991).

So, why do scholars use citation? Have South and Crowder got "authority" by citing others? So far, they have told a story of others speaking, and they have taken a reserved position, neither disputing nor accepting others' statements. In fact, rather than imparting an authoritative status, the citations seem to cultivate a stance of uncertainty, which is elaborated as the discussion continues:

> While a general consensus appears to be emerging that, net of individual and family attributes, at least some neighborhood characteristics significantly influence these and other life-course events, thus far these studies have generated inconsistent findings regarding the existence, strength, and functional form of neighborhood effects on marriage and nonmarital childbearing.

South and Crowder don't say that neighbourhoods *do in fact* influence young people's "family-related" behaviour, but that, from a certain position (theirs), you can see that researchers might be beginning to agree that some aspects of neighbourhoods *can* have some effect. Note how the use of "while," "appears," and "at least some" casts doubt on the "general consensus" and prepares the reader for an alternative position. Then, in the second part of the sentence, the writers make a claim of their own — and it turns out to be not about neighbourhoods, but about the **state of knowledge** about neighbourhoods. What they claim is that findings are "inconsistent": taken together, these studies do not provide a clear answer to questions about the influence of neighbourhoods on young people growing up in them. They continue with more assertions of their own:

> More important, several key elements in Wilson's theory relating neighborhood socioeconomic disadvantage to family formation patterns have been treated only cursorily, if at all. And virtually all prior studies of neighborhood effects on marriage and childbearing suffer from one or more methodological deficiencies that limit their contribution to our knowledge in this area.

What is South and Crowder's position on this topic? Neither embracing nor disputing any of the studies they refer to, South and Crowder assemble the findings of a group of speakers and, taking these findings together, estimate the state of knowledge on a topic: in this case they find a deficit in the current state of knowledge — a **knowledge deficit**. Moreover, at the same time they position their own voice amongst these other voices — they *identify with* this deficit: "**our** knowledge in this area" (emphasis added). Collectively, all these speakers, including the present authors, own the knowledge (such as it is).

> See Chapter 10 (page 247) and Chapter 11, Sections 11D and 11E (pages 253–259) for further discussion of **state of knowledge** and **knowledge deficit**.

Someone looking for answers to questions about "good" neighbour-hoods and "bad" ones, desirable behaviour and undesirable, might be disappointed. Experts seem to be less sure of these things than non-experts.

Examining Passage 3 above, we find, in the first sentence, that Allen does not say that it is impossible to know "even the simplest things," but that people *now say* that (other) people *thought* this way at the end of the nineteenth century and beginning of the twentieth. She goes on to bring other speakers to the page who seem to agree that, at that time, people felt that way. While she arranges for these voices to converse with one another, and come to an agreement, she positions herself at some distance from these views, referring to them as "a cliché of intellectual history." Although in this passage Allen does not explicitly identify a deficit in our understanding of this period of Western thought, we can anticipate that she will show that, despite this apparent agreement amongst experts, something has been missed. (Later, she will show us what it is.)

Do scholarly writers acquire authority by citing? Few (if any) of the citations we've looked at here "back up" the writer who refers to others, or who repeats the words of others. Moreover, the citations can add up to uncertainty rather than authority.

We will find cases, though, where scholarly writers do position themselves beside an important figure and share his or her authority or prestige. It would be wrong to say that scholarly writers don't acquire some status — and a right to speak — by citing others. By convening fellow scholars, and arranging for conversation amongst them, the writer gets to

- take a position in relation to the other voices;
- identify himself or herself as a member of a group collectively;

- take a turn in the conversation;

- construct knowledge.

In the research genres, citation represents and enables certain actions: listening to the statements of others; identifying the position from which the statement comes; evaluating established knowledge and paying attention to the possibility that it may be incomplete, contradictory, or even wrong; watching for opportunities to improve the state of knowledge.

---

**Exercise 4**

Consider Passages 1 and 2 from the beginning of the chapter as attempts at identifying the state of knowledge about arctic clouds and children's negative emotions. What specific wordings do the writers use to attribute assertions to others? What specific wordings do they use to indicate uncertainty?

**Exercise 5**

(1)   In this passage, those expressions which attribute a statement to another speaker have been emphasized.

Within the context of the tecato subculture, **previous researchers have linked** machismo almost exclusively to hypermasculine aspects of drug use and aggression. Thus **Bullington (1977:108, 115) regards** machismo as both an adaptive, efficacious attitude in navigating through prison experience and an underlying variable related to the expression of criminal behavior. Likewise **Casavantes (1976), in his study of "el tecato" [the male Mexican heroin addict], emphasizes** the hypermasculine aspects of this model. **He notes that** "... machismo in its exaggerated form [includes] fighting, drinking, performing daring deeds, seducing women, asserting independence from women, and ... bragging about escapades" (Casavantes, 1976:149).

Gilbert A. Quintero and Antonio L. Estrada 1998 "Cultural models of masculinity and drug use: 'Machismo,' heroin, and street survival on the U.S.-Mexican border." *Contemporary Drug Problems* 25: 147–65.

What happens when we remove those expressions?

Within the context of the tecato subculture, machismo is connected with hypermasculine aspects of drug use and aggression. Machismo is both an adaptive, efficacious attitude in navigating through prison experience and an underlying variable related to the expression of criminal behavior. Machismo in its exaggerated form includes fighting, drinking, performing daring deeds, seducing women, asserting independence from women, and bragging about escapades.

(2)  Identify the reporting expressions in this passage, and rewrite the passage removing these reporting expressions.

The problem of teenage parenthood, acknowledged to be a significant social problem in the United States since the late 1960s, has been the subject of much study (Alan Guttmacher Institute, 1985; Chilman, 1980; Furstenberg, Lincoln, and Menken, 1981; Lancaster and Hamburg, 1986; Hayes, 1987). Efforts to understand its causes have generally focused on the issue of individual choice regarding the decision to engage in sexual behavior (Chilman, 1978; Pete and DeSantis, 1990) and to use contraceptive devices (Finkel and Finkel, 1975; Goldsmith, Gabrielson, 1972). The association of teenage motherhood with dropping out of school prematurely (Gray and Ramsey, 1986; Roosa, 1986), not being employed (Trussell, 1976), and becoming dependent on government subsidies (Klerman, 1986; Moore, 1978) is well-documented. In general, consideration of how schools and educational policies contribute to the high rate of teenage motherhood has been limited to how dropping out affects the likelihood of a girl becoming pregnant, how pregnancy affects the probability of dropping out, and the relationship between education aspirations and pregnancy rates (Moore, Simms, and Betsey, 1986).

Helen Rauch-Elnekave 1994 "Teenage motherhood: Its relationship to undetected learning problems." *Adolescence* 29 (113): 91–103, 91–92.

# 3

# Summary

At the beginning of the last chapter we mentioned that we needed to examine citation in order to understand summary. This is because we can look at each of the cited statements in our passages as tiny **summaries**. In a single sentence from a passage we examined at the beginning of Chapter 2, South and Crowder present the gist of one report (that type of neighbourhood may not affect young people's behaviour) as well as the gist of what eight others have said (that neighbourhoods do affect behaviour). Each repetition represents an aspect of the cited work which is relevant to the current discussion:

> Initial skepticism over the impact of neighborhood conditions and neighborhood contexts on the behavior of adolescents and young adults (Jencks and Mayer 1990) has spurred considerable research purportedly documenting such effects (Aneshensel and Sucoff 1996; Billy, Brewster, and Grady 1994; Corcoran et al. 1992; Duncan 1994; Duncan, Connel, and Klebanov 1997; Elliott et al. 1996; Entwisle, Alexander, and Olson 1994; cf. Evans, Oates, and Schwab 1992).

Sometimes the summaries are tiny (one sentence); sometimes they're much longer. South and Crowder go on to summarize more extensively the "prominent treatise" by Wilson. (The expressions that attribute, characterize, and evaluate the statements about neighbourhoods are emphasized.)

> **Perhaps the most prominent and influential theoretical explanation** of how neighborhoods influence the life course of young adults

comes from **Wilson (1987; 1996)**. To some extent, **Wilson's thesis subsumes** the main causal mechanisms linking disadvantaged neighborhoods to undesirable behavioral outcomes **described by Jencks and Mayer (1990:115)**. These include the *epidemic* (or contagion) *model*, which emphasizes the role of peer influence, the *collective socialization perspective,* which emphasizes the positive impact of successful adult role models (and **which is Wilson's main focus**), and the *institutional model*, which focuses on how adults from outside the community, such as teachers and police officers, affect the behavior of children and young adults. **The thrust of all these models — and Wilson's argument —** is that the presence of disadvantaged neighbors (or the relative absence of advantaged neighbors) increases the likelihood that young persons will engage in nonnormative or otherwise undesirable behaviors, such as dropping out of school, committing crimes, eschewing marriage, and bearing children out of wedlock.

Without summary, South and Crowder would not be able to introduce Wilson, Jencks and Mayer into their article. With summary, South and Crowder arrange for these different writers to take their turn — and go on, in this article, to report and discuss their inquiries into the influence of concentrated poverty on "nonmarital fertility." In this way, South and Crowder create a type of scholarly conversation.

Just as conversations in daily life differ, so do scholarly conversations. And we might predict that summaries will change accordingly. South and Crowder are not the only sociologists to summarize Wilson. Looking at another summary of Wilson, this time by Quillian, will prepare you to appreciate (a) how important summary of even well-known works is to scholarly discussion (South and Crowder may read Quillian, and Quillian may read South and Crowder), and (b) how each summary is a *new* version for *new* purposes and emphases.

William Wilson's book *The Truly Disadvantaged* (1987) first pointed out that, starting in the 1970s, areas of concentrated urban poverty increasingly took on a different character than they had earlier in the century. Like the ethnic ghettos that have long interested urban sociologists, dwellers in modern poor urban neighborhoods are almost all members of minority races or ethnicities. Unlike older ethnic ghettos, however, Wilson argues that the minority-populated urban neighborhoods of the 1970s and 1980s contained an especially high concentration of poor families. He hypothesizes that one cause of this trend is that middle-class blacks in the 1970s and 1980s increasingly relocated to predominately white suburbs, leaving behind neighborhoods composed largely of poor or new poor families.

Lincoln Quillian 1999 "Migration patterns and the growth of high-poverty neighborhoods, 1970-1990." *American Journal of Sociology* 105 (1): 1–37, 1.

Summary isn't just for researchers and professors; it also provides students with a means to join scholarly conversations. While you may not be ready to cite 18 sources in two sentences, as South and Crowder do at the beginning of their article, you can compose the kinds of summaries we see above, bringing to the page the voices you read. This chapter is devoted to developing your skills as a summarizer of scholarly material, and becoming involved in the kinds of activities that are enabled by and represented in the research genres. In the next two sections, you will study related methods for approaching summary: the first notes for **gist** as you read; the second explores the original as an arrangement of **levels** — levels of generality and detail, of abstract and concrete reference.

## 3A Noting for Gist

In this method, we write as we read, noting what we predict should be remembered in preparation for writing. The notes answer this question: if I were reading this with the intention of going on to write, what would I estimate as important from each paragraph? Avoiding full sentences and straight copying, the notes capture the gist — the point or basis — of each section in a form that is temporary, pliable, ready for other uses.

| | |
|---|---|
| Social practices, norms, and institutions are designed to meet heterosexual systems' need to produce sex/gender dimorphism — masculine males and feminine females — so that desire can then be heterosexualized. Gendered behavioral norms, gendered rites of | *heterosexual systems: social norms → the masc. & fem. genders* |

passage, a sexual division of labor, and the like, produce differently gendered persons out of differently sexed persons. Prohibitions against gender crossing (e.g., against cross-dressing, effeminacy in men, mannishness in women) also help sustain the dimorphism necessary to heterosexualize desire.

Children and especially adolescents are carefully prepared for heterosexual interaction. They are given heterosexual sex education, advice for attracting the opposite sex, norms of heterosexual behavior, and appropriate social occasions (such as dances or dating rituals) for enacting desire. Adult heterosexuality is further sustained through erotica and pornography, heterosexualized humor, heterosexualized dress, romance novels, and so on.

*children: social customs → preparation for heterosexuality*

*adults: gendered attitudes, clothes → sustain heterosexual desire*

Heterosexual societies take it for granted that men and women will bond in an intimate relationship ultimately founding a family. As a result, social conventions, economic arrangements, and the legal structure treat the heterosexual couple as a single, singularly important, social unit. The couple is represented linguistically (boyfriend-girlfriend, husband-wife) and is treated socially as a single unit (e.g., in joint invitations or in receiving joint gifts). It is legally licensed and legally supported through such entitlements as communal property, joint custody or adoption of children, and the power to give proxy consent within the couple. The couple is also recognized in the occupational structure via such provisions as spousal healthcare benefits and restrictions on nepotism. Multiple practices

*expected, socially, legally, econ.: men & women in intimate couple, for family*

*social, linguistic convention: M/F couple*

*law: M/F couple*

*economic & institutional structures: M/F couple*

and institutions help heterosexual individuals to couple and create families and support the continuation of those couples and couple-based families. These include dating services, match-makers, introductions to eligible partners, premarital counseling, marriage counseling, marriage and divorce law, adoption services, reproductive technologies, family rates, family health care benefits, tax deductions for married couples and so on.

*all this ( "multiple") → privilege for heterosexual couple seems normal, natural*

The sum total of all the social, economic, and legal arrangements that support the sexual and relational coupling of men with women constitutes heterosexual privilege. And it is privilege of a peculiar sort. Heterosexuals do not simply claim *greater* socio-political-legal standing than nonheterosexuals. They claim as natural and normal an arrangement where *only* heterosexuals have socio-political-legal standing. Lesbians and gay men are not recognized as social beings because they cannot enter into the most basic social unit, the male-female couple. Within heterosexual systems the only social arrangements that apply to nonheterosexuals are eliminative by nature. The coercive force of the criminal law, institutionalized discrimination, "therapeutic" treatment, and individual prejudice and violence is marshalled against the existence of lesbians and gay men. At best, lesbians and gay men have negative social reality. Lesbians are not-women engaged in nonsex with nonrelationships that may constitute a nonfamily.

*the privilege makes non-heterosexuals unrecognizable...*

*...except as something to be "fixed"*

*only negative social standing for non-heterosexuals*

Cheshire Calhoun 1994 "Separating lesbian theory from feminist theory." *Ethics* 104: 558–82, 579–80.

Reading for gist, we produce a set of wordings that partly depend on the original wordings but are also partly free of the original, too. These wordings prepare for a new version of what has been said by someone else, incorporating ties to the first speaker but also putting a new accent on those words.

## 3B Recording Levels

We could write a summary from these gists alone. But, doing so, we might be missing an opportunity to get a better picture of the original, or leaving to chance some of our recollection of that original when we write the summary.

You might notice that our gist notes eliminate details — "cross-dressing," for example, "dances," "romance novels," "family rates." In our everyday conversational "summarizing," we also eliminate details. For example, we'd probably say —

A. How was the tour?
B. Excellent, very well organized, good food and tours at each port.

— instead of —

A. How was your cruise?
B. On the third night I had a delicious salmon terrine with juniper berries, followed by a peach sorbet garnished with a sprig of mint. Paul had the .... In Copenhagen we went on a bus to Tivoli, there were two buses, we got on the second one, the buses were waiting when we went ashore ... and then ...

— although some people tend towards the detail technique, and may encounter social disapproval as a result. If we don't eliminate details, the summary would be too long, and risk not being a summary at all. (Imagine if the traveller told every detail — then the answer to the question might be as long as the cruise itself!) Yet, still, some details seem to be important, since they give specific examples of more abstract ideas.

> **Abstraction**
>
> Cutting across the high levels of generality are planes of abstraction. "Prohibition" is an abstraction — an abstract reference. Men-

tion of the stop sign at the bottom of my lane, prohibiting me from rolling down the lane and directly out into the road, is a concrete reference. I can touch the sign, and locate it in the physical world, the way I cannot "touch" *prohibition*, although I experience the abstract phenomenon *prohibition* each time I encounter the stop sign. (On the plane of *generality*, the stop sign would be a "detail," or "specific.")

At a *general level*, the first paragraph of the Calhoun passage is about something like *the heterosexualization of desire* through *sex/gender dimorphism* — what *is that*? At a less general level, we encounter "prohibitions against gender crossing" ... and "gender crossing" would be ... *what*? At a still less general and more specific level, we get the answer, finding prohibitions "against cross-dressing" as an example. Now we have a grasp on "sex-gender dimorphism" (probably).

The second paragraph begins at a high level, too — "Children and especially adolescents are carefully prepared for heterosexual interaction" — and then *goes down* to the level of specifics: dating, dances, and so on.

We could create a diagram of the gists that traces the process of reading, the up and down shifts in **levels of generality**. Such a diagram would show the levels in action, descending and rising. Or we could create a diagram that deliberately ignores the process of the passage, and that just shows the overall organization of generality and detail (see Figure 3.1, p. 34).

What might we learn from this pattern? *As readers*, if we find the beginning claims of a scholarly paragraph difficult (what *is* "dimorphism"?), we might be patient, and wait to see if these high-level claims are demonstrated with examples or instances that might link the claim to our concrete experience; *as writers*, we might anticipate that our readers will look for these lower levels, so they can get a firmer grasp of what we're talking about. Notice how the diagram in Figure 3.1 shows how higher-level generalizations relate to one another, and how certain details are significant.

## 3C Using Gist and Levels of Generality to Write Summary

Taking the clusters of gist produced by reading-and-noting Calhoun's passage, and keeping an eye on the structure of generality and detail, a one-sentence summary of these four paragraphs can be written.

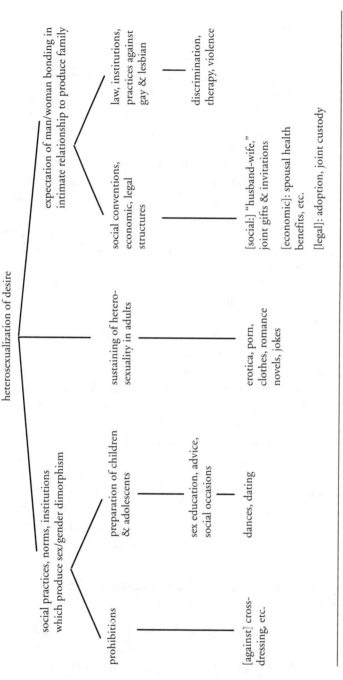

**Figure 3.1.** Diagram of the levels of generality in the Calhoun passage. Read from top to bottom, the diagram shows high to low levels of generality. The columns show how mid-level generalizations provide a context for higher-level abstractions, and how they are in turn supported by low-level details. The diagram, like a snapshot or a portrait, captures an analysis of Counts and Counts' reasoning in the passage.

> To explain the means by which heterosexual society produces het-
> erosexuality as "natural," and produces "negative social reality" for
> lesbians and gay men, Calhoun (1994) catalogues the social prac-
> tices (e.g., dating, sex education, erotica) which construct sex/gen-
> der dimorphism, and the social conventions (e.g., joint gifts and
> invitations to husband-and-wife) and legal and economic structures
> (e.g., adoption procedures, spousal health benefits) which produce
> the "single unit" of intimately bonded man and woman.

As well as representing content, the summary:

- attributes these statements as originating with another writer
  ("Calhoun (1994)");
- characterizes the action of the original ("To explain" how society has come to view heterosexuality as natural); and
- describes the development of the discussion (it "catalogues" examples).

Including select details in a summary allows a reader to understand it: to
grasp what the abstractions mean. Calhoun's persuasiveness depends at
least partly on the way she summons so many examples of the practices
and norms which heterosexualize desire: the summary preserves this quality
of the original. Similarly, when South and Crowder summarize Wilson,
they also recover some details from the original:

> These include the *epidemic* (or contagion) *model*, which emphasizes
> the role of peer influence, the *collective socialization perspective*, which
> emphasizes the positive impact of successful adult role models (and
> which is Wilson's main focus), and the *institutional model*, which
> focuses on how adults from outside the community, **such as teach-
> ers and police officers**, affect the behavior of children and young
> adults. (Bold-face added for emphasis)

While noting-for-gist is a means of recording compactly — or "remembering" — a spread of details which might otherwise escape your recollection,
you might also think of it as a "forgetting": once the high-level gist is transferred to the summary, it "forgets" the details which accompanied it. By
reintroducing select details, as South and Crowder do above, you can help
generalities "remember" their origins, and show them to your reader.

With each of these moves — identifying the speaker-who-is-not-me,
characterizing the action of the original, and describing its development
— a writer takes a **position** in relation to the original.

This position might be developed by saying what larger phenomenon this one is part of; for example:

> Calhoun's discussion reminds us that what we view as "natural" can often be traced not to nature but to social custom. She takes a social constructionist view of ...

The position could also be developed by estimating the commonness or uncommonness of the claims made by the original. For example, saying:

> Summoning arguments established by feminist reasoning, Calhoun ...

locates Calhoun in current, and fairly common, claims about the social construction of gender.

It also secures a position for the writer of the summary and makes this an independent version by not sticking to the order of the original. By beginning with points from the last paragraph — heterosexuality produced as "natural," "negative social" reality for gays and lesbians — the summary takes a reader to this element of the original first, thereby thematizing this aspect of Calhoun's discussion. This is not to say that it is more correct to do so, only that for the purpose of *this* summary — perhaps an emphasis on the naturalizing effects of social norms — this order is good. With *other* intentions, or another perspective on the topic, a writer might have started at another point — for example:

> Calhoun (1994) describes legal and institutional discrimination against gays and lesbians (adoption and custody laws, for example, spousal benefits in the workplace), but also brings to light the array of social habits which extend such discrimination: we learn what is "natural" and expected — and what is "unnatural" — not only from laws and policy but also from everyday practice — routines of socializing like dating and dances among adolescents, for instance, and, among adults, social invitations to the man-woman couple.

Other summaries might arrange for still other emphases by selecting another point at which to begin, and another order to follow.

While there are no rules for recording and manipulating these "gists," it can be a good idea to arrange them on a single page or to write them on separate slips of paper and rearrange them in different patterns so you can see them all at once. In the same way, creating a diagram of the levels of generality clarifies relations between abstractions and the details that

they organize. That way, you can escape the order of the original, and design your own. And by arranging gists in a non-linear way, you can induce them to make new connections with one another. By making new connections amongst claims, you offer new perspectives on the original. That is, *even if* the reader of the summary had already read the original, the summarized version is *new*: it is reconfigured for the present purposes. Your arrangement of the materials of the original is an expression of your position *vis-à-vis* the original, and, however familiar readers are with the original, the summary will be new to them.

---

### Exercise 1

Here is a passage from an article reporting an anthropological study of "RVers." RVers are people who spend much of their year in recreational vehicles: motorhomes, truck-campers, trailers. In the field-work reported below, researchers found, amongst RVers, sub-categories: "boondockers," who park their "rigs," usually for free and unofficially, on (US) federal lands; and "private-park RVers," who stay in organized, commercial facilities.

Use the reading-and-noting technique to capture the passage's gists, and the mapping technique to survey its range from generality to detail. Write a two- or three-sentence summary of the passage.

In one sense shared territory does not create community for RVers who treasure their mobility and their ability to turn on the key and be gone if they don't like their neighbours. In another sense it does. As Davis observes, "People cluster together for protection, contact, organization, group integration, and for the purpose of exploitation of a particular region and the community is the smallest territorial group that can embrace all aspects of social life" (Davis 1949:312). As we have said, RVers choose different sorts of places to cluster and they define themselves and are defined by others by where they park. These definitions reinforce the sense of community among RVers who cluster together, but also emphasize differences that alienate RVers from each other. We look first at the way in which their choice of place separates RVers and then turn to a discussion of how space unites them through common values, interests and experience.

When RVers select a place to park their rigs they are also making a choice about lifestyle and about identity. Some choose private resort parks where their personal space is limited but where they feel safe and comfortable. They seek the protection of walls and guards; they enjoy the luxury of water and sewer hookups, electricity and cable TV; their space is organized into streets and blocks where each RV has its own "pad";[1] and leisure activities are organized by professionals who encourage and promote contact among park residents. Many private resort parks have strictly enforced rules about how a rig may be parked, where dogs may be walked, the conditions under which residents may have guests, and for how long and under what circumstances children and grandchildren may visit. Many of the people who choose this lifestyle see themselves holding standards of affluence, respectability and orderliness and they particularly appreciate the fact that the other park residents are similar to themselves in age, social standing, consumption level and interests. In thinking about private parks one is reminded of the distinction made by Bellah et al. between "lifestyle enclaves" and communities. Lifestyle, they point out, "brings together those who are socially, economically, or culturally similar, and one of its chief aims is the enjoyment of being with those who 'share one's lifestyle'" (Bellah et al. 1985:72). In their terms, groups such as retirement "communities,"organized around a common lifestyle, are "lifestyle enclaves," not communities. A community is inclusive and focusses on the interdependence of private and public life while recognizing and tolerating the differences of those within it. In contrast, "lifestyle is fundamentally segmental and celebrates the narcissism of similarity. It usually explicitly involves a contrast with others who 'do not share one's lifestyle'"

(Bellah et al. 1985: 72). Resort park residents make a sharp distinction between their standard of living and lifestyle and that of boondockers. Our non-boondocking informants advised us that, as part of our research, we should go to one of the boondocking areas. "You should spend one night there, just to see it, but you won't want to stay longer," one couple said about Slab City. Another marvelled that boondockers "sit out there on the desert, happy as clams," adding, "but I couldn't do it."

Boondockers agree that they are unlike the folks who live in resort parks and many of them treasure the difference. They are not a homogeneous lot, for people from all social classes, level of education and degrees of affluence can be found boondocking. They opt for economy and simplicity, the absence of rules and organization and unlimited external space. They particularly want to avoid the crowding — what one person calls sites "like cemetery plots" and another referred to as being "crammed in like sardines" — that they see as characteristic of private parks. Boondockers often used the term "freedom" to describe their way of life and many of them said that resort park residents had simply exchanged the restriction and crowding of urban life for an RV version of the same thing.

Boondockers are regarded by others (and sometimes they regard each other) with considerable ambivalence. On the one hand, the lives of boondockers epitomize the values on which America was founded: they are independent of rules and regulations, they live simply with a minimum of luxury and expense, they embody the qualities of individualism and ingenuity and they co-operate on their own terms for mutual security and to share resources. On the other hand, they are marginal to North American society. Many of them have no fixed address — not even a mail box in an RV park. Many, particularly those who are flea marketers, participate in an underground economy that avoids regulations and taxes — a fact that is not lost on officials of nearby towns. Most instructive and, we think, representative of the attitude of civic officials toward boondocking flea marketers, is a letter cited by Errington that expresses the resentment of a small-town businessman towards transient vendors (1990:642). He bitterly resents the fact that they pay no taxes and little rent and face none of the risks and costs endured by town retailers. "Let's tax 'em," he says. "Let's set up a licensing procedure that will discourage the money hounds" (Errington 1990:642).

*Note*
1   A pad is a private space that includes the place where the RV is parked and an area round it that is usually only a few feet wide.

Dorothy Ayers Counts and David R. Counts 1992 "'They're my family now': The creation of community among RVers." *Anthropologica* 34: 153–82, 168–70.

## 3D Establishing the Summarizer's Position

We have identified several ways in which summarizers take a position in relation to the writer whose ideas they are representing.

They can use **reporting expressions** ("Counts and Counts (1992) examine"; "Wilson argues"). By doing so, they characterize the action of the original — in this case, as an examination or an argument. Or the original might be characterized as an analysis, or some observations, or a commentary on something, or a review of research on something, or an explanation.

Summary can also mention what kind of study produces the knowledge: field research, for example, or statistical analysis, or experimental or theoretical inquiry.

Summarizers can also take a position by pointing to larger issues not mentioned in the original but whose wider applications the original suggests. By taking such a position, summarizers can estimate the generalizability or limits of the statements presented in the original. For example, Counts and Counts employ Bellah et al.'s distinction between "lifestyle enclaves" and communities: could this distinction be applied to other groups of people living together, such as gated communities, kibbutzim, or residents of inner cities? At the same time, Counts and Counts argue that boondockers "epitomize the values upon which America was founded": a summarizer might mention this limitation to the discussion, and suggest difficulties that might arise in discussion of Canadian, British, or French RVers.

**Exercise 2**

Write a two- to three-sentence summary for each of the passages below. Practice the reading-and-noting technique, producing gists whose order you can arrange or re-arrange according to the perspective you want to offer your reader. To get a feel for the structure of each passage, attempt a rough sketch of its levels: pick out the lowest level of detail, and the higher levels of generality. Use some of the ideas discussed above to establish your position as a summarizer.

(a)   In "Sickness as a resource," Mary Douglas demonstrates an "anthropological approach" to the study of cultural difference in the medical disciplines. From the evidence of this passage we might say that an anthropological approach would not focus on testing different practices for their success in "curing" sick people (and such tests in themselves might be regarded as culture-specific — what counts as a cure for one group may not count as a cure for another group). Instead, the anthropological approach would focus on *social norms* and *community*.

<table>
<tr><td>social norms</td><td>community</td></tr>
<tr><td>norms for being sick</td><td>therapeutic community</td></tr>
</table>

At the lowest levels, you will find a congregation of types, including "the sick Londoner," "the African patient," "friends [asking] if the doctor has been called in yet." At the end of the first paragraph, you will find a fairly high-level statement which does not descend directly to particulars: Douglas refers to situations where there may be "political pressure not to convert to the other side" — not to go over to alternative medical practices, whether those be "exotic" or "traditional." Can you think of examples of what such situations might be?

In the first sentence, Douglas mentions "complementary medicine": from a Western point of view, complementary medicine might include acupuncture, herbal therapies, and homeopathic healing.

**Sickness as a resource**

[…] the sick Londoner who is choosing complementary medicine [is] equivalent to the African villager who is confronted by the reverse option. The choice is not between science or mumbo-jumbo, but choosing the traditional versus the exotic system, and in effect it means choosing between therapeutic communities. The African patient faced with the choice between the Christian missionary doctor with an exotic pharmacopoeia and the traditional diviner with his familiar repertoire is under the same sort of pressures as a Westerner choosing between traditional and exotic medicine. For minor ailments he can pick and choose separate remedial items without incurring censure, but if it is his own life or the life of his child that is at risk, his therapeutic community will take a strong line. He may have friends on either side of the divide, or choosing may involve him in a complete switch of loyalties. It is rather like religious conversion: if there is a strong political alignment dividing the two therapies, there will be political pressure not to convert to the other side. That is a good beginning for the anthropological approach.

The next step is to follow the monitoring that is going on in any community. Wherever there is illness, warnings are being issued, and informal penalties being threatened. Talcott Parsons founded medical sociology when he identified and named the "sick role." When a person defines himself as sick, he can escape censure for doing his work badly, being late, being bad-tempered, and so on, but the community which indulges the sick role also exacts a price: the sick person is excused his remiss behaviour on condition of accepting the role, eating the gruel or whatever is classified as invalid food, taking the medicine, and keeping to the sick room, out of other people's way.

Having adopted the sick role, a person cannot play his or her normally influential part. The patient is reproved for trying to go on working; if the patient complains of pain, the answer is that complaining is aggravating the condition and a more severely restricted diet may have to be prescribed; every complaint is met with potential criticism so that the patient ends by lying back and accepting the way others have defined the sick role. Dragging around looking tired, his friends ask if the doctor has been called in yet, and if so, they want to know who, and are free with advice as to who can be trusted. It is a matter of pride for them if their favourite doctor is called, and a threat of withdrawn sympathy if it is one they disapprove. These friends interacting with the patient, listening to symptoms and offering advice, form what the anthropologist John Janzen (1978) calls the "therapeutic community."

At the early stages of illness, there is some choice: either behave as if you are well or admit to being sick and bear the consequences. If the illness worsens and the invalid refuses the advice of friends and family, it is going to be difficult to ask for the neighbourly services or the loans of money on which lying in bed depends. The rival merits of traditional and alternative medicines are put to the test, not according to the patient's recovery but according to the negotiating of the sick role. The outcome will depend on the therapeutic community. For the sick person, the power of the medical theory counts for less than issues of loyalty and mutual dependability, unless he or she is completely isolated.

The background assumption is that any society imposes normative standards on its members. That is what being in society involves. Living in a community means accepting its standards, which means either playing the roles that are approved, or negotiating the acceptability of new ones, or suffering from public disapproval. The option for spirituality is a form of negotiation. But of course communities differ in the amount of control they exert: some are quite lax and standardization is weak; others exert ferocious control. In this perspective it would be interesting to know whether the persons who have chosen alternative therapy have also chosen a therapeutic community to support them with friendship and counsel.

Mary Douglas 1996 "The choice between gross and spiritual: Some medical preferences." In *Thought Styles*. London: Sage, 33–35.

(b)   At the lowest level in this excerpt from James Clifford's book about "people going places" (1997:2) — about people's place being the product not only of their location but also of their journeys and others' journeys — we find the example of Matthew Henson and Robert Peary, and their trip to the North Pole. At the highest level, we find the abstractions *racism* and *class* — but you may also be able to construct other high-level terms with which to understand the episodes Clifford refers to.

### Traveling cultures

What about all the travel that largely avoids the hotel, or motel, circuits? The travel encounters of someone moving from rural Guatemala or Mexico across the United States border are of a quite different order; and a West African can get to a Paris *banlieu* without ever staying in a hotel. What are the settings that could realistically configure the cultural relations of these "travelers"? As I abandon the bourgeois hotel setting for travel encounters, sites of intercultural knowledge, I struggle, never quite successfully, to free the related term "travel" from a history of European, literary, male, bourgeois, scientific, heroic, recreational meanings and practices (Wolff, 1993).

Victorian travelers, men and women, were usually accompanied by servants, many of whom were people of color. These individuals have never achieved the status of "travelers." Their experiences, the cross-cultural links they made, their different access to the societies visited — such encounters seldom find serious representation in the literature of travel. Racism certainly has a great deal to do with this. For in the dominant discourses of travel, a nonwhite person cannot figure as a heroic explorer, aesthetic interpreter, or scientific authority. A good example is provided by the long struggle to bring Matthew Henson, the black American explorer who reached the North Pole with Robert Peary, equally into the story of this famous feat of discovery — as it was constructed by Peary, a host of historians, newspaper writers, statesmen, bureaucrats, and interested institutions such as *National Geographic* magazine (Counter, 1988). And this is still to say nothing of the

> Eskimo travelers who made the trip possible![1] A host of serv-
> ants, helpers, companions, guides, and bearers have been ex-
> cluded from the role of proper travelers because of their race
> and class, and because theirs seemed to be a dependent status
> in relation to the supposed independence of the individualist,
> bourgeois voyager. The independence was, in varying degrees,
> a myth. As Europeans moved through unfamiliar places, their
> relative comfort and safety were ensured by a well-developed
> infrastructure of guides, assistants, suppliers, translators, and
> carriers (Fabian, 1986).
>
> *Note*
> 1   Lisa Bloom (1993) has written insightfully on Peary, Henson, Eskimos,
>     and the various efforts by *National Geographic* to retell a deeply con-
>     tested story of discovery.
>
> James Clifford 1997 *Routes: Travel and Translation in the Late Twentieth Century.* Cam-
> bridge, MA: Harvard UP, 33–34.

## 3E Reporting Reporting

Since scholarly writers so often cite the words of others, summarizers of
scholarly writing can find themselves citing others' citations — reporting
reporting.

Writing about the experience of undocumented immigrants in the
southwestern US, and analyzing that experience for evidence of "community," Leo R. Chavez cites another's ideas:

> Suffice it to say that despite all the work that has been carried out
> on communities, the question still remains: What underlies a sense
> of community? Anderson (1983) examined this question and sug-
> gested that communities are "imagined." Members of modern na-
> tions cannot possibly know all their fellow-members, and yet "in
> the minds of each lives the image of their communion[....] It is
> imagined as a *community* because, regardless of the actual inequal-
> ity and exploitation that may prevail in each, the nation is always
> conceived as a deep, horizontal comradeship" (Anderson 1983:15–
> 16). In this view, members of a community internalize an image of
> the community not as a group of anomic individuals but as inter-

connected members who share equally in their fundamental membership in the community.

Leo R. Chavez 1994 "The power of the imagined community: The settlement of undocumented Mexicans and Central Americans in the United States." *American Anthropologist* 96
(1): 52–73, 54.

A careful summary of this passage would account for Chavez's own summarizing activity:

> In his study of the settlement patterns of undocumented immigrants
> in the US southwest, Chavez (1994) cites Anderson's notion of com-
> munity as "imagined": a subjective sensation of being connected
> with others, despite inequality and the absence of face-to-face con-
> tact, an "image of [...] communion with others" (Anderson cited
> in Chavez, p. 54).

This sort of "double reporting" defines the summarizer's position. The
summary is not saying that people imagine communities, nor is it saying
that Chavez says people imagine communities. What it *is* saying is that
Chavez says that Anderson says that people imagine communities.

Here part of the contribution to the scholarly conversation lies in tracing the statement. In the summarized version, "imagined community"
starts with Anderson, then steps over to Chavez, and then steps again —
into the summary. This summary records the idea's journey: its point of
departure, its use in another location, its arrival into a new piece of writing, trailing behind it mementos of its journey.

## 3F Experts and Non-experts

In the case above, Chavez is citing other scholars. But sometimes, in some
kinds of scholarly writing, the cited voice belongs not to a scholar but to
a research subject: someone who has been interviewed, or whose voice
has been otherwise captured for study. In this next passage, researchers
have studied racist and anti-racist attitudes in an inner-city neighbourhood in Rotterdam.

> The existence of discrimination is not denied by the participants who
> hold more racist views. Dutch people 'haven't always been angels
> themselves, that's for sure, because they've completely discriminated
> against people', and 'foreigners are certainly discriminated against, if

only because their skin's a different colour' (participants 'K' and 'L' respectively). Several times during the discussions, however, it is pointed out that it is not so much ethnic minorities who are discriminated against, but Dutch local residents (K: 'I feel now like I'm discriminated against instead of them'). Community and social workers, housing corporations, schools, and also municipality officials were accused of favouring ethnic minorities and of only standing up for minority groups. It was held, for instance, that Dutch children would receive less attention in schools and might even be left behind.

Maykel Verkuyten, Wiebe de Jong, and Kees Masson 1994 "Similarities in anti-racist and racist discourse: Dutch local residents talking about ethnic minorities." *New Community* 20 (2): 253–67, 257.

Whereas Chavez appears to agree with Anderson's notion of "imagined community" — or at least to take a position very near Anderson's — the writers of the passage above probably do not agree with some of what they cite from their research subjects. But, in a way, whether they agree or disagree is not the point. They are not arguing for or against the idea that ethnic minorities are favoured by official policy, and their study provides no evidence to support either position. Instead, Verkuyten et al. cite the words of others as indications of social phenomena. If we summarize the passage above as —

> In their research into attitudes towards ethnic minorities in an inner-city neighbourhood in Rotterdam, Verkuyten et al. (1994) discovered not only a generally shared acknowledgement of racism but also a perception of a kind of reverse discrimination: some informants expressed the view that ethnic minorities were favoured by official policy and institutional practice.

— we are not saying that racism exists or that ethnic minorities are officially favoured; nor are we saying that Verkuyten et al. say that racism exists or that ethnic minorities are favoured. Rather we are saying that Verkuyten et al. say that *some people say* that racism exists and that minorities are favoured. If we were to summarize the passage as —

> Verkuyten et al. report that, in the inner-city neighbourhood of Rotterdam which they studied, ethnic minorities were favoured by official policy and institutional practice.

— we would be misrepresenting the original.

We could say that when Chavez cites Anderson, he is citing fellow experts, and joining them in conversation. And when Verkuyten et al. cite "K," they are reporting the words of a person who is a non-specialist, not involved in the research conversation. But the categories **expert** and **non-expert** are not airtight, and the boundary between them can be contested. Below is an example where experts — "scientific circles" — and non-experts are cited, both groups providing examples of attitudes toward creole languages.

> Today, even in scientific circles, a persistent stigma is attached to creole languages.[1] Because their formative period was relatively recent, the 17th and 18th centuries, they are often seen as not yet fully formed complex languages. The descriptions of creole languages in some linguistic circles are similar to the attitudes of many creole speakers toward their languages. These languages are described as "reduced," simple, and easy to learn; lacking in abstract terms, they are inadequate for scientific, philosophical, and logical operations. For most of their histories, creole languages have not been considered adequate for government, schooling or Western religious services.
>
> The effect of pseudoscientific arguments or preconceived emotional ideas are evident in the negative attitudes lay persons generally hold toward creole languages and their speakers, and are revealed by the many pejorative terms used by both native and non-native speakers alike. Folk terminologies describe the French lexicon creoles as "broken French," "patois," "dialects," or "jargons," and many assume that creole languages are "diminished," "reduced," "deformed," "impoverished," "vitiated," "bastard" forms of the European standard languages that contributed to their birth.[2] Many educated and middle-class Haitians, members of the petite-bourgeoisie, as well as Haitian élites, view kreyòl [creole] as a simplified form of French at best. Many claim it is not a real language at all, but a mixture of languages without a grammar. The different varieties of kreyòl are viewed by Haitians of these social categories with a great deal of ambivalence. *Kreyòl rèk* [rough creole] and *gwo kreyòl* [vulgar creole] are often associated with pejorative connotations regarding the sounds (harsh, not harmonious, guttural, deformed), the grammatical features (debased, corrupted, elementary, lacking complexity), the social origin of speakers (rural, lower class), and defects usually

attributed to the speakers themselves (coarse, clumsy, stupid, illiterate, uneducated). On the positive side, the same varieties have been associated with national identity, authenticity, independence, sincerity, and trustworthiness. Much of this is connected to romantic notions abut rural people — rough, coarse, but also authentic, real.

*Notes*
1  Diamond's (1991) article in *Natural History* titled "Reinventions of Human Language: Children Forced to Reevolve Grammar Thereby Reveal Our Brain's Blueprint for Language" includes the following:
    Between human languages and the vocalizations of any animal lies a seemingly unbridgeable gulf [....] One approach to bridging this gulf is to ask whether some people, deprived of the opportunity to hear any of our fully evolved modern languages, ever spontaneously invented a primitive language [....] Children placed in a situation comparable to that of the wolf-boy [...] hearing adults around them speaking a grossly simplified and variable form of language somewhat similar to what children themselves usually speak around the age of two [...] proceeded unconsciously to evolve their own language, far advanced over vervet communication but simpler than *normal* languages. These new languages were the ones commonly known as creoles. [p. 23, emphasis added]
2  August Brun, a French scholar writing in the early part of the 20th century, claimed that "une langue est un dialecte qui a réussi. Un patois est une langue qui s'est dégradée" (quoted in Pressoir 1958:27). (A language is a dialect that has been successful. A patois is a language that has deteriorated.) Such a view is still held by some educated Haitians today.

Bambi B. Shieffelin and Rachelle Charlier Doucet 1994 "The 'real' Haitian creole: ideology, metalinguistics, and orthographic choice." *American Ethnologist* 21 (1): 176–200, 181–82.

An account of what people say can be analyzed for levels, with the lowest levels (in the analysis below) being named speakers quoted directly (Figure 3.2). (Notice that only the specialist speakers, in this passage, are specifically identified. What do you make of that?) The analysis incorporates a higher level than appears in the original, naming the larger phenomenon to which this situation belongs. (Higher still could be *social distinction, ranking.*) The analysis also diagrams a *conflict,* a *complication* or *ambivalence* the passage presents: the co-occurrence of negative and positive attitudes toward Haitian Creole.

The following summary assigns statements to this company of speakers:

Shieffelin and Doucet's (1994) survey of attitudes toward creoles reminds us of the persistent social habit of evaluating and ranking speech and speakers. In their descriptions of creoles, even linguists

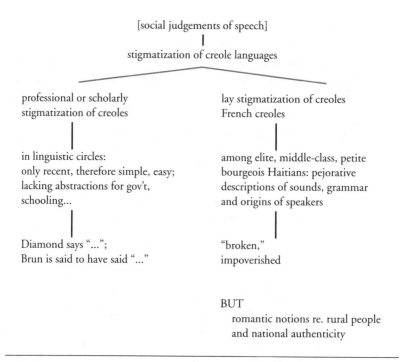

[social judgements of speech]
|
stigmatization of creole languages

professional or scholarly
stigmatization of creoles

in linguistic circles:
only recent, therefore simple, easy;
lacking abstractions for gov't,
schooling...

Diamond says "...";
Brun is said to have said "..."

lay stigmatization of creoles
French creoles

among elite, middle-class, petite
bourgeois Haitians: pejorative
descriptions of sounds, grammar
and origins of speakers

"broken,"
impoverished

BUT
romantic notions re. rural people
and national authenticity

Figure 3.2. Levels of generality for Shieffelin and Doucet (1994).

have tended to stigmatize these languages, referring to them as in-complete, and insufficient for use in government or schooling. Lay people also stigmatize creoles, characterizing these languages as ille-gitimate, "deformed," "impoverished": middle-class Haitians, for example, according to Shieffelin and Doucet, judge the sounds of Haitian Creole and the origins of its speakers pejoratively, yet, at the same time, celebrate an ideal notion of the rural classes.

Think of what the summary would be like without reporting expressions — something like "Haitian Creole is a reduced, simple language unfit for use in government or education; its sounds are coarse…" This would be a radical misrepresentation of the original.

While the distinction between experts and non-experts may seem pretty clear when when one considers professional ethnographers and their re-search subjects, it's not so clear in the next passage, which comes from an article analyzing the historical circumstances of "open admissions" in the US in the 1970s, when large numbers of "non-traditional" students entered university: members of minority and marginalized groups joined members of the groups which had traditionally comprised university populations. Here Lu cites Geoffrey Wagner (Professor of English at City College, New York) and author of *The End of Education*. Wagner is one of the "gatekeepers" whose reaction to open admissions Lu analyzes. Notice also the scholarly technique for indicating added emphasis: "(emphasis mine)." Sometimes you will see "(emphasis added)" or "(italics added)." In your own writing make sure you distinguish between emphasis you've added and emphasis that appears in the sources you quote.

> To Wagner, open admissions students are the inhabitants of the "world" outside the sort of scholarly "community" which he claims existed at Oxford and City College. They are dunces (43), misfits (129), hostile mental children (247), and the most sluggish of animals (163). He describes a group of Panamanian "girls" taking a Basic Writing course as "abusive, stupid, and hostile" (128). [...] Wagner predicts "the end of education" because of the "*arrival* in urban academe of *large*, indeed *overwhelming, numbers* of *hostile* mental children" (247; emphasis mine).
>
> Min-Zhan Lu 1992 "Conflict and struggle: The enemies or preconditions of basic writing?" *College English* December, 891–913, 893–94.

Originally, Wagner might have considered himself an "expert," but Lu's citation seems to have the effect of undermining that status, of transforming his words into indications of social attitudes, or earmarks of a political phenomenon. Just as Verkuyten et al. do not enter into scholarly conversation with the Rotterdam residents whom they cite, Lu captures Wagner as a social type rather than a fellow scholar. In this passage, for example, Lu cites isolated patches ("dunces (43), misfits (129)"); commandeers verbatim wordings ("'girls,'" "'abusive, stupid, and hostile'") to exemplify the original; adds emphasis by using italics where none appear in the original — in all, forcefully *re-accents* the original.

Let's take one more look at this process of contextualizing reported statements. The next passage comes from an elderly woman's memoir (recorded as oral history) of her childhood experiences 60 years before in a Catholic boarding school for aboriginal children in Canada.

... oh my was I ever homesick. You know home wasn't much, in fact the nuns didn't call it home, they called it our *camp*. And that used to hurt me. It still does when I think about it. When we'd talk about going home, they'd say, "You're not going home you're going back to your camp." That was their impression of the reserve. Well in a way they were right because the homes we had in those days were made out of great big log houses.

Mary Englund 1981 "An Indian remembers." In *Now You Are My Brother*, ed. Margaret Whitehead. Victoria, BC: Provincial Archives, 59.

An accurate summary would *not* be:

The children's homes were only camps.

At the very least, quotation marks would show that the writer is *not* vouching for this word:

The children's homes were only "camps."

More explicitly, the word can be attributed to its original speakers:

The nuns at the school referred to the children's homes as "camps."

But still we are missing aspects of context, which we can retrieve by adding another layer of citation —

Mary Englund remembers that the nuns at the school referred to the children's homes as "camps."

— and another layer of context:

Sixty years later, Mary Englund remembers that the nuns at the school referred to the children's homes as "camps."

Now the citation process includes a record of the survival of that word "camp" — enduring a lifetime in Englund's recollection, uttered once more on the occasion of the oral historian's research.

---

**Exercise 3**

The following passage comes from an essay by Raymond A. Anselment on seventeenth-century responses to smallpox. Write a two- or three-sentence summary of this excerpt, making sure you maintain the distinction between the positions occupied by the writer, the expert historians, and the seventeenth-century writers Anselment discusses.

> Seventeenth-century letters, memoirs, and diaries personalize the mounting figures in the Mortality Bills [weekly records of deaths occurring in London]. Not all families were as fortunate as that of Ralph Josselin, four of whose children survived the smallpox. John Chamberlain's letter to Sir Dudley Carlton informed him that viscount Lisle "hath lost his eldest sonne [i.e. son] Sir William Sidney of the small pockes, which were well come out and yet he went away on the sodain [i.e. suddenly]; he that now but one sonne left."... In his autobiography, William Stout described the sorrow that overwhelmed his mother when her two youngest sons died of smallpox soon after their father:
>
> > The loss of these two children, so near together and so soon after their father, was so [great an] affliction to my mother that she continued in much sorrow for a long time; as was also my sister, which added to her other bodily infirmities, reduced her very low.[1]
>
> ... Neither these reactions nor the moving responses of Mary, Countess of Warwick and Ann, Lady Fanshawe support the widely accepted modern belief that the high mortality rate among infants and children in the seventeenth century inured parents to their children's deaths. When "it pleased God to take" her only son just before he came of age and despite her efforts to save him, the Countess of Warwick wrote that her "sad and afflicted husband...cried out so terribly that his cry was heard a great way; and he was the saddest afflicted person could possibly be." Her own actions left her sorrow unstated yet obvious: she "instantly" left her house in Lincoln's Inn Field "and never more did I enter that house; but prevailed with my Lord to sell it."[2] ....

None of these poignant expressions of grief confirms Philippe Ariès's influential suggestion that parents sought refuge from pain and sorrow in a deliberate indifference to the danger of death so commonplace among their children.[3] The grief of both mothers and fathers, on the contrary, suggests an emotion only partly accountable by Lawrence Stone's controversial view of the period's gradual transition from the "Restricted Patriarchal Nuclear Family" to the "Closed Domesticated Nuclear Family."[4] In their understated eloquence, the sufferings of these parents are as heartfelt as any Stone found for the later years of allegedly growing family importance. Perhaps as he and others have suggested, the economic, humanistic, and religious forces of the Renaissance helped to shape the sensibilities that gave new importance to the value of the family as well as the individual. But perhaps the grief is instinctive.

*Notes*

1  William Stout, *The autobiography of William Stout of Lancaster, 1665–1752,* ed. J. D. Marshall, Manchester, Chetham Society, 1967, p. 76.
2  Warwick, op. cit. pp. 30–31.
3  Philippe Ariès contended in *Centuries of Childhood* that "People could not allow themselves to become too attached to something that was regarded as a possible loss" (p. 38). Dr. W. F. Bynum kindly called my attention to Michael MacDonald's criticism of Ariès's position: in *Mystical Bedlam,* Cambridge University Press, 1981, particularly 75–85, MacDonald questioned the prevalence in the seventeenth century of "emotional austerity and indifference to member of the immediate family."
4  Lawrence Stone, *The family, sex and marriage in England, 1500–1800,* New York, Harper & Row, 1977.

Raymond A. Anselment 1989 "Small Pox in Seventeenth-Century English Literature: Reality and the Metamorphosis of Wit." *Medical History* 33 (1): 81–83.

# 4

# Difficult situations for summarizers

So far, we've looked at passages from scholarly articles that contain the whole range of generality. The passage from Mary Englund's memoir in Chapter 3 is the exception; as you can see, it provides no abstractions, only low-level details. To summarize this account for use in a scholarly context, you need to provide significance to these details. Passages that offer only low-level details, or, at the opposite extreme, only high-level generalities are hard to capture in summary.

## 4A High Country

Some passages (and even whole articles and books) remain at high levels of generality. This passage, for example, presents no details, no specifics — only high-level abstractions.

> According to commemorative rhetoric, the past makes the present. Commemoration is a way of claiming that the past has something to offer the present, be it a warning or a model. In times of rampant change, the past provides a necessary point of reference for identity and action (Shils 1981). In contrast, the literature on social memory often emphasizes the importance of contextual factors in shaping commemorative practices and symbolism (Olick and Robbins 1998). Images of the past are malleable. Traditions are "in-

vented" and memories are altered for instrumental reasons in the present (Hobsbawm and Ranger 1983). Social memories are subject to, and are products of, production conflict and purposeful memory entrepreneurship (Wagner-Pacifici and Schwartz 1991). Producers, moreover, cannot control the ways in which images of the past are perceived (Savage 1994). Scholars therefore look at how people use memory to create identities and at how dominant narratives suppress alternative ones, and view the past as a terrain on which competing groups struggle for position (Bodnar 1992; Foucault 1977). These accounts emphasize that commemoration is explainable in terms of its contemporary circumstances: the present, from this perspective, makes the past.

Jeffrey K. Olick 1999 "Genre memories and memory genres: A dialogical analysis of May 8, 1945, commemorations in the Federal Republic of Germany." *American Sociological Review* 64: 381–402, 381.

An analysis of this passage for levels of generality produces something like Figure 4.1:

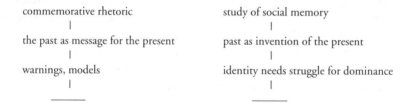

Figure 4.1. Diagram of high levels of generality in the Olick passage.

The lower levels are empty — and if, in summarizing this passage, you wanted to put your reader in closer touch with these ideas, you would have to come up with supporting details or specific examples. In the example below, the details supplied by the summarizer are emphasized.

> Public commemorations of the past include **monuments, ceremonies, speeches, and anthems**. Describing scholarly approaches to such commemorations, Olick (1999) points to contrasting schools of thought. One of these schools studies "commemorative rhetoric," and treats commemoration as a message from the past for the present (p.381). So, the public ways of commemorating **a war or a social movement, for example**, would be seen as a message from

the past to the present: an example to avoid or to follow. On the other hand, theories of "social memory" analyze commemoration as a story about the past invented in the present to advance some present interests over others (p.381). **We could think of memorials of the Vietnam War as an example: these memorials might be seen as promoting ideas which benefit some groups rather than others thirty years after the war has ended. We could apply Olick's distinction to the ways, in Canada, that accounts of the "birth" of national health care in the 1960s are repeated 40 years later. We can speculate** that commemorative rhetoricians would analyze these accounts as a "warning or a model" (p.381); while sociologists of public memory would analyze them as strategies in the current struggle to control the culture and economy of health care.

It's hard work summarizing a passage that is composed at a very high level of abstraction. And risky — perhaps these specific mentions are not the best illustrations of the phenomenon under examination. But, by coming up with examples, summarizers can measure their understanding of the passage, and also offer readers handholds as they make their way across these high-level ideas. The specific mentions provided by the summarizer show the **summarizer's position** — his or her perspective on the material summarized — without attributing that position to Olick. Notice, however, that this summary is nearly as long as the original. This may be a tendency of summary that attempts to represent a passage that remains at the higher "levels."

---

### Exercise 1

Here again is Leo R. Chavez summarizing the ideas of a much-cited theory of nation and national community. The summary stays at high levels. Can you think of specifics which would illustrate these ideas, and build a lower level?

What underlies a sense of community? Anderson (1983) examined this question and suggested that communities are "imagined." Members of modern nations cannot possibly know all their fellow-members, and yet "in the minds of each lives the image of their communion [....] It is imagined as a *community* because, regardless of the actual inequality and exploitation that may prevail in each, the nation is always conceived as a deep, horizontal comradeship" (Anderson 1983:15–16). In this view, members of a community internalize an image of the community not as a group of anomic individuals but as interconnected members who share equally in their fundamental membership in the community. The internalizations of the image and a sense of connectedness to the community is as important as actual physical presence in the community.

Chavez 1994: 54.

## 4B Low Country

The next passage presents information at a much lower level than the readings above about "commemorative rhetoric" and "imagined community."

### BRIAN

Brian is 14; his behaviour at school troubles staff and other students; he has become aggressive at home and at school; he sniffs glue. He is referred to a counselling clinic, and a schedule is arranged for him.

Brian is escorted each day to and from school either by family or by social services personnel. At school he is given "jobs" in the classroom during breaks. Two evenings weekly he is taken to a voluntary youth club run by some police officers in their spare time, and at weekends he joins a church youth centre for youngsters like himself, for outings and organized games. Once a week he also goes to an intermediate treatment centre, and one morning weekly he attends the clinic for group counselling and activities like painting and building models.

Adapted from Denis O'Connor 1987 "Glue sniffers with special needs." *British Journal of Education* 14 (3): 94–97.

The preference for low-level detail in the O'Connor passage is represented by Figure 4.2:

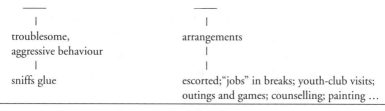

Figure 4.2. Diagram of low levels of generality in the O'Connor passage.

If you were to summarize this passage, you might find it hard to get free of the details or to make the summary any shorter than the original. But to summarize this low, "flat" passage for a scholarly context, you need to construct the higher levels — find words that name and condense these details. That is, you need to interpret the details as *meaning* something. So, for example, the high-level abstractions *deviance* and *surveillance* might be used to construct a higher level. The summarizer interprets details as meaning "deviance" and "surveillance." From this, an even higher level can be constructed: *social control* (Figure 4.3).

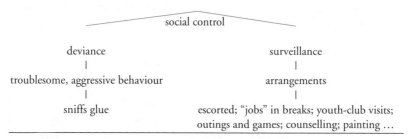

Figure 4.3. Diagram of reconstructed levels of generality for the O'Connor passage.

It's hard work summarizing a passage that is composed at extremely low levels. And risky — perhaps these abstractions are not right. Maybe *deviance* is a rather negative interpretation of Brian's behaviour. A summarizer might take a more positive view, and might interpret Brian's behaviour as *resistance*, to school and family impositions, for example. Or *surveillance* might fail to capture the arrangements for Brian as *good* for him. A summarizer might interpret the details as evidence of *therapy*, and *healing*. Or his troublesomeness might be interpreted as *dysfunction*. Each of these high-level abstractions is an interpretation of the details, and the summary which uses them will express the summarizer's point of view. One person might summarize the passage this way:

> The case of Brian, reported in O'Connor (1987), illustrates institutional practices of therapeutic surveillance. The 14-year-old's deviant behaviour is identified, and then managed through a series of monitoring activities, mechanisms of social control executed at the level of daily life.

Another person might summarize the passage as illustrating means of attending humanely to dysfunction and incorporating the troubled boy into supportive social networks. As interpretations, such high-level abstractions show the summarizer's position: his or her perspective on the material summarized.

---

### Exercise 2

Find abstract words to construct higher levels of meaning in this passage, a report from sociological research on attitudes toward crime. In a two- or three-sentence summary, report Mae's situation, using the abstract terms you have come up with. (It's possible that not all the terms you propose will come into play in your summary.)

**Interview with Mae**

Mae is 68 years old, Australian-born of British ancestry; she lives alone in a small country town in New South Wales. She lives in her home behind multiply-deadlocked front and back doors and windows, afraid of "home invasion." The only time Mae has had to contact the police was when a neighbour threw a firework on her roof. Mae is not poor — living in her own home in retirement — and is reasonably fit and well. Eighteen months ago, her husband died of natural causes. Since then, Mae has stopped watching any crime series on television — even series she had watched comfortably with her husband before he died. Indeed, the same shows seem to have changed for her since then: "That's the trouble, they're getting too much like what's happening out on the streets ... like what you read in the paper."

While she avoids all crime on television because "You see these things happening and I think you imagine that it's going to happen to you," Mae has taken to reading the local and national newspapers far more since her husband died. Her knowledge of crime comes almost entirely from this media source, since she does not go out much and has never experienced a criminal incident. It is in these newspapers that Mae has "become far more aware of the drug problem now." In the local paper she scrupulously reads the court cases, finding here the accounts of "home invasions" which she fears so much. Her reading of the paper tells her that nine out of ten cases are "about drugs"; and Mae is thus quite able to construct a causal narrative of crime, where youth unemployment leads to drug-taking and thus to "home invasions." As a result, she has "only recently" begun worrying about her grandchildren and drugs. This is also something she "sees so much of on TV, where people are dying from taking drugs. Peer pressure and all those sorts of things. It doesn't matter how good a child is — they can be turned around, can't they?"

Adapted from Deborah Lupton and John Tulloch 1999 "Theorizing fear of crime: Beyond the rational/irrational oppositions." *British Journal of Sociology* 50 (3): 507–23, 516–17.

## 4C Narrative: A Special Kind of Difficult Situation

Narratives are organized chronologically: things, people, places are mentioned according to the order in which events occurred. Scholarly writers meet narratives in many sectors of the disciplines, but they are probably most likely to encounter them in literary studies and history. When we look at narrative from a summarizer's point of view, we find conditions something like those we have just been investigating, in anecdotal reports and research interviews. Narratives typically remain at a low level: particular people and things, particular actions and events. Consider, for example, the narrative passage below. It is the beginning of the well-known fairy tale "Little Thumb."

There was once upon a time a man and his wife, fagot-makers by trade, who had seven children, all boys. The eldest was but ten years old and the youngest only seven.

*many children, close in age → fertility*
*8 males → masculine dominance?*

They were very poor, and their seven children incommoded them greatly, because not one of them was able to earn his bread. That which gave them yet more uneasiness was that the youngest was of a very puny constitution, and scarce ever spoke a word, which made them take that for stupidity which was a sign of good sense. He was very little, and when born no bigger than one's thumb, which made him be called Little Thumb.

*poor → poverty*
*needy children → dependency*
*very small → diminutiveness*
*LT stays quiet → reticence*

*people are wrong about him → misjudgement*

The poor child bore the blame of whatsoever was done amiss in that house, and, guilty or not, was always in the wrong; he was, notwithstanding, more cunning and had far greater share of wisdom than all his brothers put together; and if he spake little he heard and thought the more.

*always blamed → injustice*

*wiser, alert → intelligence, attentiveness*

There happened now to come a very bad year, and the famine was so great that these poor people resolved to rid themselves of their children. One evening, when they were all in bed and the fagot-maker was sitting with his wife at the fire, he said to her, with all his heart ready to burst with grief:

*they get even poorer → hardship, scarcity*

*decide to get rid of children*

*father is sad → sentiment, love*

"Thou seest plainly that we are not able to keep our children, and I cannot face to see them starve to death before my face; I am resolved to lose them in the wood tomorrow, which will be very easily done; for while they are tying up fagots, we may run away and leave them without their taking any notice."

*but he plans to leave them → trickery, conspiracy, ambivalence*

"Ah!" cried the wife, "and cans't thou thyself have the heart to take thy children out along with thee on purpose to lose them?"

*mother loves the boys, protests → love, sentiment, conflict*

In vain did her husband represent to her their extreme poverty: she would not consent to it; she was indeed poor, but she was their mother. However having considered what a grief it would be to her to see them perish with hunger, she at last consented, and went to bed all in tears.

*mother resists, father persuades* → **dispute, conflict, persuasion**

*mother agrees but weeps* → **grief, regret**

Little Thumb heard every word that had been spoken; for observing, as he lay in his bed, that they were talking very busily, he got up softly and hid himself under his father's stool that he might hear what they said without being seen.

*LT notices the talk* → **attentiveness**

*hides & listens* → **concealment, cunning**

Charles Perrault 1969 "Little Thumb." In *The Blue Fairy Book,* ed. Andrew Lang. New York: Airmont, 266–67.

Figure 4.4 illustrates how readers of this narrative may pay attention to the following details, actions, and conditions:

| man and wife | 7 children, ages 7-10, | | | a decision |
|---|---|---|---|---|
| | puny youngest | blaming of youngest, who is silent | no food | "… to lose them in the wood tomorrow" |

Figure 4.4. Analysis of low-level information in the "Little Thumb" passage.

A summary could be written from this analysis:

> Having seven sons between the ages of seven and ten, and no food, a man and wife decide to abandon their offspring in the forest. The youngest child is puny, and gets unfairly blamed for everything.

However, such an analysis might raise questions as to the significance of these events and conditions — the connections between blame and abandonment, for example. And some aspects of the story which are evident in the original — the father's ambivalent sentiments, the smallest boy's intelligent silence — are lost in condensation. Telling details vanish. By using the techniques suggested in Chapter 3 and the last section (4B), you can write a more conceptual summary — one suitable for scholarly purposes — which supplies the higher-level concepts that the original text doesn't provide *and* preserves the effect of these details. You can also give names to the story's episodes and build the higher levels by reading for abstractions which interpret the lower-level details.

This reading for abstraction provides materials for a more conceptual, interpretive summary:

> In a situation of great **scarcity**, Little Thumb's parents resolve to abandon their seven hungry sons in the forest. But **scarcity** and **abandonment** are complicated by **injustice** in the family — Little Thumb is unfairly blamed for everything — and by **misjudgement** — he is reckoned as dull, when in fact his **intelligence** of the world is sharper than others': he overhears the parents' **conspiracy**. This is a story not only of **hardship** and **scarcity** but also of **concealments** lurking in **abandonment**, hidden **virtue**, and secret **intentions**.

Other summarizers might come up with different abstractions to interpret the story's details, and still others might have different focuses, for example, *fertility* — the abundance of children amidst this scarcity, or *grief* and *ambivalence* — the complexity of the father's sentiments, or *masculine dominance* — the mother is outnumbered by males, and the father overcomes the mother's objections. (If you know the rest of the story, you may remember that Little Thumb and his brothers come to an ogre's house in the forest. The ogre's wife is genuinely concerned for the little boys, while her husband plans to eat them. But Little Thumb outsmarts everybody.)

Some narratives do provide general statements that contain higher-level concepts. Fables, unlike most fairy tales, include the 'lesson' or moral at the end of the story — an authoritative feature of the genre. Aesop's "The Fox and the Grapes" is a well-known example:

> One hot summer's day a Fox was strolling through an orchard till he came to a bunch of Grapes just ripening on a vine which had been trained over a lofty branch. "Just the thing to quench my thirst," quoth he. Drawing back a few paces, he took a run and a jump, and just missed the bunch. Turning round again with a One, Two, Three, he jumped up, but with no greater success. Again and again he tried after the tempting morsel, but at last had to give it up, and walked away with his nose in the air, saying: "I am sure they are sour."
>
> It is easy to despise what you cannot get.
>
> Translated by Joseph Jacobs.

Although Aesop's brief narrative presents characters who are animals, the moral indicates that the fable isn't *about* animals. One can come up with higher abstractions — for instance, *self-deception* — to name the central moral concern of the fable.

In literature courses, students are often warned not to retell the story; their papers may be penalized for what their readers call "plot summary," that is, a list-like account of events in the original work. Yet professional scholars often summarize plot. Here, a literary scholar, publishing in a major journal in the field, summarizes the plot of a novel his readers may or may not know about, although the opening phrase — "**A** novel by **a** Maori writer from New Zealand" — suggests that he estimates that many of his readers do not know about this book:

> A novel by a Maori writer from New Zealand, Witi Ihimaera's *Tangi*, shows how a strategic refusal to accommodate the reader can stand at the very core of a work's meaning.
>
> The story of a young man's coming to terms with the death of his father, *Tangi* revolves around the Maori extended funeral service that gives the book its title. Tama has left the small Maori community in which he was born, gone to the "big city" (Wellington), and found a *pakeha* (white) girlfriend, but by the end of the novel he has decided to come home to take care of the family farm. Though the point is not spelled out, this return, a return to the Maori values represented by Tama's father, entails leaving his *pakeha* girlfriend and, in a larger sense, the *pakeha* world that he has entered in Wellington.
>
> The novel thus is about arrivals and departures and the greetings and partings that accompany them.

> Reed Way Dasenbrock 1987 "Intelligibility and meaningfulness in multicultural literature in English." *PMLA* 102: 10–19, 16.

What makes "plot summary" like this acceptable? Its generalizing, interpretive abstractions seem to be the features which distinguish it from the kind of "plot summary" that literature teachers object to. For example, Dasenbrock begins with "a strategic refusal to accommodate the reader." This interpretive abstraction brings the story within the range of the research question Dasenbrock is asking: how to understand misunderstanding; how to understand "multicultural literature" without resorting to either the idea that "good" literature is "universal" and should be comprehensible to everybody (we are all the same) or the idea that authentic literature will be understandable only to the particular, local culture which produces it (we are all different).

---

### Exercise 3

James Thurber's modern beast fable fails to comply with the authoritative conventions of the genre: the 'lesson' or meaning is not given. Thurber's fable leaves it to readers to come up with conceptual interpretations. Write an Aesop-type lesson (a general statement) at the end of "The Rabbits Who Caused All the Trouble." Then see if you can name the central concern, using a generalizing abstraction (a single word or a phrase).

Within the memory of the youngest child there was a family of rabbits who lived near a pack of wolves. The wolves announced that they did not like the way the rabbits were living. (The wolves were crazy about the way they themselves were living, because it was the only way to live.) One night several wolves were killed in an earthquake and this was blamed on the rabbits, for it is well known that rabbits pound on the ground with their hind legs and cause earthquakes. On another night one of the wolves was killed by a bolt of lightning and this was also blamed on the rabbits, for it is well known that lettuce-eaters cause lightning. The wolves threatened to civilize the rabbits if they didn't behave, and the rabbits decided to run away to a desert island. But the other animals, who lived at a great distance, shamed them, saying, "You must stay where you are and be brave. This is no world for escapists. If the wolves attack you, we will come to your aid, in all probability." So the rabbits continued to live near the wolves and one day there was a terrible flood which drowned a great many wolves. This was blamed on the rabbits, for it is well known that carrot-nibblers with long ears cause floods. The wolves descended on the rabbits, for their own good, and imprisoned them in a dark cave, for their own protection. When nothing was heard about the rabbits for some weeks, the other animals demanded to know what had happened to them. The wolves replied that the rabbits had been eaten and since they had been eaten the affair was a purely internal matter. But the other animals warned that they might possibly unite against the wolves unless some reason was given for the destruction of the rabbits. So the wolves gave them one. "They were trying to escape," said the wolves, "and, as you know, this is no world for escapists."

From Fables for Our Time (1940), rept. *The Norton Reader*, shorter 8th ed., p. 530.

## Exercise 4

Using the reading-and-noting techniques introduced in this chapter and in Chapter 3, including note-taking for abstraction, write three- to four-sentence interpretive summaries of the two narrative fragments below. Both narratives tell about the era of residential schools in British Columbia, but they are different kinds of narrative: the way information is presented is different. In (a), the speaker who describes personal experiences is not the one who writes; this is an oral narrative which has been shaped and edited by a transcriber for a written context. In (b), the writer's description of a particular place and time incorporates and interprets transcribed oral histories. Passage (b) is written for a scholarly context, and it proceeds at a much higher level of generality than passage (a).

(a)   "School" is from the memoir of Mary Englund, a transcribed oral history collected in 1980, late in Englund's life (we encountered another passage from her memoir in Chapter 3). Englund is answering an historian's questions about her experience in a residential school in the second decade of the twentieth century. As Englund reports at the beginning of this memoir, children of school age were gathered from First Nations villages and settlements by priests, and transported to boarding schools.

### School

We weren't allowed to speak our language in school. We had to speak English right from day one. [...] It was a difficult situation. See they had different Indian dialects. Along the

Fraser Valley they had the Stalo and the Thompson and us here was the Chelhalis. We talked very differently than they did. So if we talked to them it was all English. Even if we could talk with one another, the nuns wouldn't allow it. Of course, there was a lot of us that could talk the same language; you take from Fountain to Pavillion down to Mount Currie we all talked the same language. When we were alone in some corner we did talk our own language and if the Sisters caught us it was, "You talk English!" That's where a lot of girls kind of forgot their language. If you're there, stayed there a certain length of time, you forget certain words in Indian. You couldn't explain yourself too much in Indian as you would in English. They said it was better for us to speak English because we could learn English and read and write better if we kept our English, if we spoke English instead of talking Indian.

When the principal came over — Father Rohr, he was French — they'd sit and talk French and we knew very well they were talking about us, all of us, they could talk French. We used to tell them that, "How come you can talk French in front of us, and you wouldn't allow us to talk Indian in front of you?" And of course they got after us for that. You weren't allowed to question. Oh yes, they weren't very nice in that respect.

Of course all the parents thought that was great you see, that we should talk English and be able to write so that we'd be able to write letters when we got home, to do things for the Indian people. You were something great when you come home, "Oh she can write now." They were kind of proud of us in a way once you were able to write your name, your mother's name, your father's name and whoever was in the family. We were doing all right. They were proud of you then. I remember my grandmother — I don't know how old she was but she was partly blind and she was all crippled with arthritis — she'd pat us on the head because we can write.

We were not to tell our parents what went on in the school. That was another rule. We were not allowed to discuss what goes on in school when we go home. We never got sugar at school, no sugar in our porridge or in our tea so when we went home I guess this one girl was telling her parents how she never got sugar at school. When she got back to school she was really reprimanded by the principal Father Rohr. And he didn't go about it in a nice way. He went about it in a way very insulting, telling you what you did in your *camp* and what you told your father and mother and the tattletales. And your parents never had anything to say of what you were doing in the school because they didn't know. [...]

Englund 1981: 63–64.

(b)   "Alert Bay," excerpted from *An Error in Judgement*, provides an account of conditions in a small, isolated community on Vancouver Island. In this section of her book, Culhane Speck focuses on the effect of the residential schools which Englund remembers.

### Alert Bay

An Anglican-administered industrial residential school, St. Michael's, which housed upwards of 200 students, was established in Alert Bay in 1929. Attendance was compulsory, and the Indian Act provided for a variety of punishments which could be levied against unco-operative parents, including fines and jail sentences. Students were prohibited from speaking their own language, and along with training in Christian scriptures and a basic academic program up to a grade 8 level, boys were taught carpentry, mechanics, farming, and animal husbandry, while girls received instruction in cooking, sewing and homemaking.

The explicit goal of the residential school system was to break the bonds between generations, thus "freeing" the young from the shackles of tradition and the influence of their families. Native parents, of course, made every effort to thwart this estrangement from their children and more and more people migrated from the smaller, more isolated Kwakwaka'wakw villages to Alert Bay in order to be able, at least, to visit with their children regularly. For the most part graduates of the residential schools did not assimilate into Canadian society. Many had no desire to, and others who tried found the doors closed to them. At the same time, when they returned to their home villages they often found they had lost both the ability to communicate fluently with parents and grandparents, and the practical, as well as social, skills necessary to fit into village life.[1]

While rank and social status determined by the potlatch system continued to function within Kwakwaka'wakw society, new divisions rooted in colonial relations arose and either overlapped with the aboriginal hierarchy or co-existed beside it. The terms and conditions for survival and opportunities for upward mobility — often synonymous terms in this context — were now defined by the dominant non-Native society and were therefore most available to Native people who possessed one or more of the following attributes: conversion to Christianity, mission or residential school education, at least formal denunciation of potlatching and other elements of aboriginal culture, mixed blood, and residence in Alert Bay rather than in one of the outlying villages. Some Indians did become successful skippers or boat owners in the commercial fishing industry and a few found steady work in logging. Others owned and ran small stores on the reserves. The majority, however, worked when work was available and/or received government relief. (…)

By the end of the 1930s, most of the Kwakwaka'wakw living in Alert Bay had converted to Christianity, and education, rather than being resisted, began to be encouraged for the young.

"We had to think about what will be best for the kids," a Kwakwaka'wakw elder would later explain."[2]

*Notes*

1   Ernest Willie, presentation to *The Goldthorpe Inquiry*, (1980), Transcript. Vol. 1, pp. 94–113.
2   Jack Peters, presentation to *The Goldthorpe Inquiry*, (1980), Transcript. Vol. 1, p. 48.

Dara Culhane Speck 1987 *An Error in Judgement: The Politics of Medical Care in an Indian/White Community*. Vancouver, BC: Talonbooks, 84–85.

# 5

# Definition

Until now we have found writers taking a position in relation to other speakers, and this chapter continues to explore writers' opportunities to take a position.

However, it is not only the writers who occupy positions in the research community: readers themselves also occupy positions in it — sometimes near the writer, sometimes further away. In this chapter we look at **definition** and **apposition** as means of negotiating the space between writer and reader.

Like summary, definition has a classroom history as a form of expression called for by teachers to see if students have committed something to memory. In research genres, however, definition serves other functions, some of which may be unfamiliar to the student new to university.

Definitions bring important terms into focus. For readers who need some clarification, definition sharpens the picture. As we shall see in a moment, it helps a writer address readers who may be unfamiliar with the terms employed by researchers who are being cited, or with the particular research tradition in which they work.

But definition is by no means only for the purpose of informing the uninformed. For readers already familiar with a term, definition confirms common ground: the writer encourages readers to identify with the spirit of the definition. In this case, definition has the goal of corroborating and engaging what the informed reader already knows, involving this established knowledge in developing a discussion.

Before we examine these functions of definition, let's look at a traditional source of definitions — the dictionary.

## 5A Dictionaries

People rely on dictionaries — either practically, by looking words up, or theoretically, by comforting themselves that, should any problem of meaning arise, a dictionary could settle it. Often associated with this reliance is an idea that dictionaries are responsible for meaning: they make meaning, or they make words mean what they do.

Actually, this idea is backwards. Writers of dictionaries describe what the meaning of the word already is. Or, better said, they describe how people use a word. Some language specialists don't talk about definition at all. Rather, they say that the "meaning" of a word is the set of circumstances under which it can be efficiently used. So, it would be inefficient for a person to use the word "chair" when he wanted someone else to hand in an essay:

> Your chairs are due next week.

This seems to be one of the circumstances where it is not efficient to use the word "chair."

If we adjust our view of dictionaries, and see them as following rather than preceding use, we see that the community of speakers who use the word is the source of its meaning. These speakers (and writers), through their interactions and routine activities, develop and negotiate word meanings: the conditions under which a word can be efficiently used. If we go further, along lines established by current reasoning about the social order, we must acknowledge that "community" should be "communities": within the larger society, people get together in different groups, following different routines. These shared routines are sustained by shared interpretations of the world — and shared habits in the use of certain words, including the shared habits of specialist communities. No dictionary can report all these possible communities of speakers and the tacit agreements they have amongst themselves as to the appropriate use of certain words. So, while no dictionary would provide a definition of "chair" that justifies "Your chairs are due next week," a community of language users made up of woodwork teachers and their students could very well find the use of the word "chair" in this sentence appropriate and efficient under that circumstance.

Once we accept, first, that dictionaries only describe uses of words rather than establish definitions, and, second, that those recorded uses are only the most general kind, we can see that there is still work to be done — terms to be captured and refined in the account of their possible uses.

## 5B Appositions

In Chapter 4, we found that sometimes — mainly in narrative — we have to make interpretive abstractions to build higher levels from some fairly concrete, lower-level foundations.

Most passages you summarize, however, will already be built up to higher levels, and will present you with ready-made abstractions (which is not to say that you cannot then build a little higher still, or cantilever the higher levels with your own interpretive abstractions). Since these abstractions in themselves condense and interpret lower-level specifics, you will probably transfer them from the original to your summary. Consider this passage (which follows from a passage we looked at in Chapter 3):

> Since it is imagined, a sense of community is not limited to a specific geographic locale (Gupta and Ferguson 1992). Immigrants are said to live in "binational communities" (Baca and Bryan 1980), "extended communities" (Whiteford 1979), "transnational communities" in "hyperspace" (Rouse 1991), and "transnational families" (Chavez 1992). These concepts highlight the connections migrants maintain with life in their home communities; living dislocated on the other side of a political border does not necessarily mean withdrawing from community or membership.
>
> Chavez 1994: 54.

A summary might keep the abstraction *transnational communities*:

> Chavez's work (1994) on undocumented immigrants offers new perspectives on transnational communities.

But it's possible — likely, even — that not all readers are familiar with Chavez's work, or familiar enough with the term "transnational communities" to be exactly sure of what the writer of the summary means to say that Chavez has said. So the summary can *define* the term, using a grammatical structure called an **appositive:**

> Chavez's work (1994) on undocumented immigrants offers new perspectives on transnational communities: communities, that is, whose members leave their homes and settle in another country but nevertheless maintain important connections with those original homes.

In effect, the summary says "transnational communities" *again* — in other words. By doing so, the summarizer recognizes the position of the readers, and their possible unfamiliarity with or uncertainty about the term. The summary implicitly acknowledges that the term is somewhat specialized and limited in its distribution — at least for the time being — to certain research genres. It also demonstrates a respect for the complexity of the term: its capacity to capture the cumulative reasoning of people researching issues in human migration. At the same time, by using new words, the summary develops a new position on the concept — a new emphasis, a new version.

As instruments of definition, appositives can help the writer to develop a position by narrowing the application of an abstraction. Here's a passage that defines through apposition:

> Academic knowledge is now generally recognized to be a social accomplishment, the outcome of a cultural activity shaped by ideology and constituted by agreement between a writer and a potentially sceptical discourse community.
>
> Ken Hyland 1999 "Academic attribution: Citation and the construction of disciplinary knowledge." *Applied Linguistics* 20 (3): 341–67, 341.

If we stop reading at the comma, we realize that "social accomplishment" could mean a lot of things. What does it mean for knowledge to be *social*? What is it about knowledge that makes it an *accomplishment*? Using an appositive, the writer specifies what "social" will mean in this case, and also unpacks terms hidden in "social accomplishment": *cultural activity, ideology, community.* Appositives are a relatively unobtrusive way of activating an abstraction or specialized term. While a more extensive definition might inappropriately suggest that the reader is ignorant, the appositive quickly enriches established understandings or improves uncertain ones. By doubling a mention, appositives intensify the atmosphere around an abstraction.

In formal terms, we can say that an appositive creates a structure with equivalent material on each side of it, for example:

They left a mess: empty soft-drink cans, styrofoam cups, fast-food wrappers.

a mess          empty soft-drink cans, Styrofoam cups, fast-food wrappers

This example uses a colon; the example above used a comma. Other structures can also open a sentence for an appositive definition. Parentheses can do this, and so can "or." Explanatory footnotes can elaborate a term. Or nearly synonymous terms can accumulate to confirm the sense in which a term in being used. The next passage shows some of these techniques. Here, an historian reports his study of the controversy in the 1920s surrounding the unsolved murder of a young Scottish nanny working for a well-to-do family on the west coast of Canada, a case in which the racist press and political figures accused the family's Asian butler. Kerwin interprets these events through a series of accumulating abstractions, which have been emphasized in bold.

> **Contemporary knowledge (or "discourses") about racial biology**, the effects of race-mixing, and the ability of two races to live within the same nation limited the vocabulary of the major players in this story, setting the ground rules for the debate. **Scientific knowledge of the day**, which concluded that miscegenation between Europeans and Asians was biologically disastrous, was **common sense** to people like Victor Odlum and Mary Ellen Smith. **Dominant understandings of British Columbia's history**, constructed through various narratives, further shaped interpretations of the Janet Smith case and the **"problem" of miscegenation**.
>
> Scott Kerwin 1999 "The Janet Smith Bill of 1924 and the language of race and nation in British Columbia." *BC Studies* 121: 83–114, 104.

Notice that Kerwin places the more specialist abstraction "discourses" in parentheses, to elaborate on "contemporary knowledge." Doubling the two terms like this both (1) improves our sense of what "discourses" are, reminding us that a discourse is a form of knowledge and that it carries the signs of its historical period, and (2) attaches "contemporary knowledge ... about racial biology" to other research that inquires into the themes and preoccupations of public discussion — into "discourses," that is. The doubling also selects the sense in which the term "discourses" is being used in this passage.

### Exercise 1

Complete these sentences with appositives — that is, by saying the italicized term again, in other words.

Despite their nomadic lifestyle, RVers studied by Counts and Counts (1994), exhibit *territoriality*:

Little Thumb experiences *injustice*:

Referring to social practices such as dating, sex education, and provision of spousal benefits, Calhoun (1994) describes their outcome as the *heterosexualization of desire*:

Mary Englund's memoir of life in a residential school suggests a regime of *surveillance*:

### Exercise 2

This passage introduces an article on methods of decision-making in the management of fisheries: ways of deciding, for example, when and for how long to permit fishing, what size of catch to allow, and how to control ecological factors affecting fish habitat. It acknowledges the competing interests and contexts in which such decisions are made: while marine biologists count fish stocks, proponents of ecological concerns advocate certain measures, and those whose livelihoods depend on catching fish may advocate other measures. The authors of this article recommend "fisheries management science" as an approach to this situation, and focus on *risk* as a term of this "science." In a two- or three-sentence summary of this passage, include a definition of *risk*. What does *risk* mean in this context? (And why is it an important concept in this context?)

> Recent and spectacular resource crises have brought pressure on fisheries management agencies to change the way they do business. Shortcomings of current fisheries management systems include the inability to account for the inherent uncertainty of fisheries systems, and the inability to meet a multiplicity of fisheries objectives such as socio-economic and operational management considerations in decision-making (Hannesson, 1996). Future management must focus on management of integrated fisheries, rather than solely on fish populations (Larkin, 1988). This integrated emphasis will require a change in approach and development of modified

methodologies to allow evaluation of options against a suite of diverse management objectives including conservation, economics, and social and operational considerations within a stochastically varying system. This requires conceptual change towards analysis of fisheries management decisions characterized by an integration of traditional biological science methods with operational management considerations and a scientific approach to decision-making. In previous papers we coined the term "fisheries management science" to describe this approach (Stephenson and Lane, 1995).

Making decisions in fisheries management, as with all practical management decision problems, involves what in common parlance is termed "risk." Specifically, the outcomes of decisions depend on occurrences beyond our control that may have undesirable consequences. Since most decision problems cannot be avoided, it is incumbent on decision makers to deal with all potential consequences of proposed actions — undesirable and otherwise — and to include their possibilities of occurrence in developing and evaluating decision alternatives. The extent to which decision alternatives must be considered, and undesirable outcomes may occur, provide a measure of the riskiness of the decision problem. The absence of this notion of "risk analysis" in decision-making is a major weakness in fisheries management systems.

From the decision analysis literature, it is generally accepted that "risk analysis" is comprised of two components: (i) risk assessment and (ii) risk management (Balson et al., 1992). Risk assessment is the process that evaluates possible outcomes or consequences and estimates their likelihood of occurrence as a function of a decision taken and the probabilistic realization of the uncontrollable state dynamics of the system. Hilborn et al. (1993), for example, describe the results of this risk analysis component through a simple two-dimensional decision table model. Risk management is a process whereby decision makers use information from risk assessment to compare and evaluate decision alternatives.

D.E. Lane and R.L. Stephenson 1998 "A framework for risk analysis in fisheries decision-making." *ICES Journal of Marine Science* 55: 1–13, 1–2.

## 5C Sustained Definitions

Definition can be as short as a gesture — a brief delay in the discussion as an abstraction is glossed and readers make contact with its complexity — or it can command more sustained attention. In this section we approach sustained definition, beginning with techniques for formal definition first developed in classical rhetoric.

The techniques for formal definition focus first on the thing-to-be-defined, using the structure of a particular kind of sentence to accomplish this focus. Taking the thing-to-be-defined as its subject, the **formal sentence definition** isolates the phenomenon for scrutiny. We could say that the focus of the formal sentence definition is *ideal*.

Consider the following:

> Daycare is the institutional provision of caretaking services to young children, including feeding, supervision, shelter, and instruction.

This passage ignores cases where it is hard to distinguish between babysitting and daycare, where children are not exactly fed but feed themselves (or refuse to eat, or bring their own snacks), where care is provided on so informal a basis it might not be called "institutional" at all. It provides an ideal, formal definition of *daycare*, offering a statement of equivalence: on one side is the phenomenon, *daycare*, and on the other side is the definition:

> *... the institutional provision of caretaking services to young children, including feeding, supervision, shelter, and instruction.*

The defining side of the statement first enlarges our view by identifying the larger class to which *daycare* belongs —

> *... the institutional provision of caretaking services ...*

— and then narrows our view again by identifying the features which differentiate *daycare* from other members of its class (from, for example, *health care* and *education*):

> *... to young children, including feeding, supervision, shelter, and instruction.*

The next definition shows the same pattern of enlarging to classify and reducing to differentiate. This is the classical pattern of formal sentence definition. The passage shows this pattern again and also shows one of the development options open to the writer: following formal definition, the writer can "double" the definition by saying what the phenomenon *does*.

> Broadcasting is a system of social control which, through the transmission of electronic signals, normalizes the diverse experiences of individuals. Broadcasting interprets events and life conditions in ways which confirm society's ideological centre.

Here the definition first expands our focus by identifying the class to which broadcasting belongs (systems of social control), and then differentiates it from other members of the class (laws or customs, for example). Moreover, this passage shows that formal definition can be in itself a step in an argument. Someone else could have defined *broadcasting* differently — as a result of having interpreted data differently, or having different data to interpret, or having a different disciplinary perspective.

> Broadcasting is a system of communication which, through the transmission of electronic signals, illuminates public and private life alike. By linking widespread communities through a shared network of information, broadcasting ensures that citizens in democratic societies recognize common and crucial features of their experience, and enables them to respond to those features as issues.

The two definitions of *broadcasting* would serve different arguments. This disparity won't surprise you if you think of definition as the presentation of a high-level, interpretive abstraction which the writer assigns to lower-level observations or data. So the definition is bound to be an expression of the reasoning and insight which have led the writer to assign the name in the first place.

Whereas formal definition isolates the phenomenon for scrutiny, **sustained definition** expands by locating the phenomenon amongst other, related phenomena in the world. In the next passage, an economist leads up to and defines *revolution*. The definition presents this event not in the usual political or historical terms but in new, economic or market ones: entrepreneurship, clients, employees, property transfer.

The potential revolutionary leader is an entrepreneur who recruits, deploys, and compensates insurgents. The potential revolutionary leader maximizes the expected wealth of his clientele, which is an alternative set of property owners and/or an alternative parasitic ruling class. A revolution in this theory is an attempt to depose the incumbent ruler and his clientele in favor of the revolutionary leader and his clientele. **In other words**, a revolution attempts either to establish new property rights, or to enthrone a new ruling class, or both.

Herschel I. Grossman 1999 "Kleptocracy and revolutions." *Oxford Economic Papers* 51: 267–83, 268 (emphasis added).

It is quite challenging and (to many readers) unusual to think about revolution in this way instead of in terms of oppression and liberation, or disorder and violence. Happily, Grossman doesn't rest with just one statement of the definition. He *doubles the definition*, and says it again — "[i]n other words."

In the next passage, a philosopher conducts one stage of his inquiry into ways to understand the debate over gun control.

Most defenders of private gun ownership claim we do have a moral right [to bear arms] — as well as a constitutional one — and this right is not an ordinary right but a fundamental one [....]

If they are correct, they would have the justificatory upper hand. Were this a fundamental right, it would not be enough to show that society would benefit from controlling access to guns.[1] The arguments for gun control would have to be overwhelming. Yet there is also a hefty cost in claiming that this is a fundamental right: the evidence for the right must meet especially rigorous standards.

What makes a right fundamental? A fundamental right is a nonderivative right protecting a *fundamental* interest. Not every interest we individually cherish is fundamental. Since most interests are prized by someone, such a notion of "fundamental interest" would be anemic, serving no special justificatory role. Fundamental interests are special; they are integrally related to a person's chance of living a good life, *whatever her particular interests, desires, and beliefs happen to be.* For example, living in a society that protects speech creates an environment within which each of us can pursue our particular interests, goals, needs, and development, whatever our interests happen to be. Is the purported right to bear arms like this paradigmatic fundamental right?

*Note*

1   Todd C. Hughes and Lester H. Hunt, "The Liberal Basis of the Right to Bear Arms," *Public Affairs Quarterly* (in press).

Hugh LaFollette 2000 "Gun control." *Ethics* 110: 263–81, 264.

Here the definition advances the inquiry. Rather than activate readers' established knowledge of the abstraction *fundamental right* or improve or clarify their understanding of the term, LaFollette stipulates the exact conditions that must be met for a right to be "fundamental." This contribution advances the inquiry by bringing the focus of the discussion to a particularly elusive and potentially controversial abstraction.

Sometimes definition works on *how words are used*, rather than committing the writer (and reader) to a particular use of the term. Here researchers on the processes that turn occurrences into public events analyze how the terms *parade* and *march* are used by both lay people and researchers.

> Insiders may accept these forms [of public action] as natural categories of action, while detached observers can observe the ways in which the categories themselves are constructed and evolve over time. The "protest" is one such ritualized form that conveys roughly the same meaning to activists, police, news reporters, the general public, and social scientists alike. This shared meaning has blinded researchers to the constructed nature of "protest" and led them to assume an unproblematic isomorphism between form and content in their definitions of protest events. But, as Tilly (1978) first told us 20 years ago, the forms or repertoires of protest shift across time and space and new forms of protest are often created by adapting nonprotest forms to new purposes. Identical forms may carry very different content. "Parade" and "march" are two names for exactly the same form (McPhail and Wohlstein 1986), and the words can be used interchangeably even though in the United States in the 1990s the popular connotations of *parade* involve entertainment, while the word *march* popularly applies only to message events. Likewise, there are many kinds of rallies, from pep rallies to protest rallies: they share the form of a stationary gathering with speeches containing informational and emotional content, but vary greatly in the issue they may address. As protest repertoires evolve, message

content is often added to event types created for other purposes. In the United States in the 1990s, ceremonies, musical performances, literature distribution, and amateur street theater are all event types that are typically "apolitical," but all have carried protest content in past times and places and can and do sometimes carry protest content in the 1990s.

Pamela E. Oliver and Daniel J. Myers 1999 "How events enter the public sphere." *American Journal of Sociology* 105 (1): 38–67, 40–41.

---

### Exercise 3

Reread the passage on gun control (pp. 81–82). Write a two- or three-sentence definition of *fundamental right*: "In LaFollette's discussion (2000) of the elements of debate over gun control, a **fundamental right** is…." You may want to include in your definition what is *not* a *fundamental right*. You might also try to come up with an example of a fundamental right other than the one LaFollette uses (freedom of speech). And you might find that his definition still leaves some things unclear, or uncertain. If so, you can include this uncertainty in your definition: "It is unclear from this part of LaFollette's discussion whether…."

### Exercise 4

In *Verbal Hygiene* (1995), from which the next passage is excerpted, Deborah Cameron, a linguist, investigates attitudes towards language: people's tendency to associate certain features of speech and writing with decency and orderliness, and other features with slovenliness and defiance. Her analysis of a particular historical expression of such attitudes makes use of an abstraction — *moral panic* — which has been at work in other disciplines: social theory, criminology, and, as she says, "cultural [history]." In the passage below, she provides a long definition of *moral panic*.

Summarize this passage by note-taking for gist, and then assemble these gists to compose your own definition of *moral panic*. Elaborate this definition by (1) finding, from your experience, other examples of moral panic; (2) explaining why moral panic is an important focus for inquiry; and/or (3) reflecting on the role of the media in producing moral panic.

### Moral panic

I am going to suggest that the grammar furore [controversy over school curriculum in Britain in the 1980s and early 1990s, accompanied by many claims in the press and from political figures that young people didn't know grammar, and were illiterate] bears more than a passing resemblance to the sort of periodic hysteria cultural historians have labelled "moral panic" (Cohen 1987). Although there are differences as well as similarities, I believe the parallel is an illuminating one if we wish to understand why, in Simon Jenkins's words, "the nation's grammar stir[red] the political juices". Before we consider the grammar debate itself, it is therefore worth looking more generally at the phenomenon of moral panic.

A moral panic can be said to occur when some social phenomenon or problem is suddenly foregrounded in public discourse and discussed in an obsessive, moralistic and alarmist manner, as if it betokened some imminent catastrophe. In the past hundred years in Europe and America we have had outbreaks of this kind centring on prostitution and "white slavery", drugs, the "Jewish problem", juvenile delinquency, venereal disease, immigration, communism, overpopulation, pornography, rock music and pit bull terriers.

These are not claimed as cases of moral panic simply because they inspired public anxiety: some degree of concern about many of them would be perfectly reasonable. But there are times when concern goes far beyond what is reasonable. In the words of the criminologist Jock Young, "moral panic" describes 'cases where public reaction [is] completely disproportionate to the actual problem faced' (*Guardian*, Letters, 9 July 1994). In a moral panic the scale of the problem is exaggerated, its causes are analysed in simplistic terms, anxiety about it climbs to intolerable levels, and the measures proposed to alleviate it are usually extreme and punitive. Analysts have suggested there are underlying sociological reasons why public concern gets "out of hand" in this way; and that vested interests are often at work encouraging it to do so.

Moral panic works by channelling, at least temporarily, the diffuse anxieties and hostilities that exist in any society towards a single, simple problem, such as "drugs", "Jews" or "communism". The discovery of the "problem" entails the creation of a scapegoat — the junkie, the fifth columnist, the Zionist conspirator. This generic "folk devil" is usually identified with a real social group, whose members then bear the brunt of hostility and blame. Moral panic thus has the potential to lead to such extreme forms of repression as witch-hunts and pogroms, and in some cases may even be orchestrated for that purpose.

Scholars have suggested that moral panic in the form we know it is a product of the modern mass media [....] The most commonplace incident or pedestrian report can be turned into an issue by media attention, whereas without that attention the same incident would go unnoticed and the report would gather dust. Having thus established something as an issue, the media can return to it under the guise of "responding to public concern" — even though that concern is of their own making.

Deborah Cameron 1995 *Verbal Hygiene*. London: Routledge, 82–83.

## 5D The Social Profile of Abstractions and Their Different Roles in Different Disciplines

As we have seen, summarizing often entails using abstractions to marshal low-level details. Moreover, these abstractions — revolution, transnational communities, gun control — seem particularly likely to attract definitions. When we found abstractions in Chapter 4 to interpret the details of "Little Thumb," the sky was the limit: do you notice that the father's attitude is odd? Let's call that *ambivalence*! Do you notice Little Thumb hiding under the stool? Let's call that circumstance *concealment*!

But it is not quite right to say that the sky is the limit, for as we move from discipline to academic discipline we notice that some abstractions are more likely than others to participate in the scholarly conversation,

and that different abstractions prevail in different disciplines. To put it another way, in each scholarly community — among sociologists, historians, chemists — some abstractions are more likely to engage current scholarly concerns and issues, and more likely to enter into exchange with other abstractions which are currently highly valued. For example, amongst the excerpts we have read so far, we have encountered the abstraction *community* at work on a number of research sites. Similarly, reflecting on the positions and representations of "boondockers" in Counts and Counts' work, or of the ethnic minorities discussed by subjects of Verkuyten et al.'s research, we might interpret these conditions as related to *marginality*, an abstraction current in many disciplines in the humanities and social sciences. If in reading "Alert Bay" or the passages from Mary Englund's memoirs in Chapter 4 you came up with an abstraction like *colonial domination*, you would have begun to participate in discussion which circulates amongst those engaged in post-colonial reasoning. Some abstractions enjoy more prestige than others: they attract scholarly interest.

This phenomenon should come as no surprise. Genre theory predicts that language will reflect the shared attitudes and interests of the community that produces it. The circumstances of prestige and interest are described by a scholar cited earlier in this chapter. Hyland observes that knowledge in research communities is a "social accomplishment" — the outcome of people listening to one another, addressing one another, being in the same neighbourhood, sharing topics and questions, developing some issues and neglecting others, negotiating common understandings and priorities.

Yet, while this kind of exchange is common to all disciplines, the **sociality** of knowledge — the ways in which knowledge is the product of social activities — differs somewhat in different disciplines, and the roles of communal abstractions differ accordingly. Roughly speaking, the differences arrange themselves along the continuum from the so-called hard sciences at one end to the humanities at the other, with the social sciences in between. In her detailed and valuable study of writing in the humanities and social sciences, focusing on literary studies, social history, and psychology, Susan Peck MacDonald (1994) observes that abstraction in literary study is much less constrained than it is in psychology. In literary study, interpretations of particulars can compete, and rival one another. Somebody might say, for example, that "Little Thumb" is *not* about *ambivalence* at all; rather, it is about *rivalry* — and there wouldn't be any way of settling this contest, except perhaps to wait and see whose interpretations got cited and used elsewhere, whose abstractions entered the conversation and got voiced by others. In psychology, however, terms are used in ways that are methodical enough to "adjudicate" claims communally. MacDonald focuses especially on the abstraction *attachment*, which is in use in research in developmental psychology. *Attachment* is the relationship infants or small children form with their caregivers. It has many complexities and many (measurable) aspects and dimensions, and researchers ask many questions about it. But they (more or less) agree on which behaviours and attitudes to call "attachment" and which ones not to call "attachment." So, for example, if a literary scholar interpreted Little Thumb's father's conflicted attitude or his mother's tearful protests as *attachment*, these researchers would not likely regard the statement as contributing to *their* conversation about children and families. On the contrary, as MacDonald contends, the consensus among researchers in developmental psychology on what constitutes *attachment* emerges from a "conceptual frame," a means of "dismiss[ing] some kinds of interpretations and ask[ing] questions about others" (73).

Not surprisingly, researchers in the sciences handle abstraction differently from their colleagues in the humanities. In *Writing Science: Literacy and Discursive Power* (1993), M.A.K. Halliday and J.R. Martin offer means of discriminating amongst the roles of abstraction in different disciplines. They distinguish between abstraction in the sciences — which, they say, is "technical," and dedicated to the project of "classifying" the world — and abstraction in the humanities — which, they say, is not technical. For example, and borrowing the example from Martin, a physical geographer uses the abstract term *abrasion* as an element of a system that classifies forms of erosion (which is itself a technical abstraction). This system distinguishes *abrasion* from other types of erosion. If an historian, on the

other hand, uses a term like *solemnity* to develop an interpretation of a memorial parade, *solemnity* does not classify the parade technically.

Similarly, the historian writing on the unsolved murder of a Scottish nanny used "contemporary knowledge," "scientific knowledge of the day," "common sense," "dominant understandings," and, especially, "discourses" to summarize and interpret a series of events in Western Canada in the 1920s. While his interpretation could invite correction and refinement or revision, or a suggestion of a better way to look at this case, it is unlikely that someone would say, "No, that cannot be classified as a discourse because a discourse is always and in every case *x*. What you refer to is not in fact *x*." But a geographer identifying a formation in the landscape as the result of abrasion might be contradicted: it is not abrasion, it is another (possibly as yet unnamed) type of erosion. What the geographer has pointed to is properly situated at some other place in the system of classification.

We can observe some of the classificatory work that abstractions do in the passage below, which is from an article that seeks to improve means of recognizing personality types. Among the terms that are in bold, which ones might you hear or utter in everyday, non-specialist talk? Of these, which would you estimate has a *technical* dimension in this context? Which terms seem to belong to the discipline of personality psychology, and seem unlikely to make an everyday appearance? If we referred to Little Thumb's father as prone to "hypervigilance and ruminative rationalization," would personality researchers recognize our statement?

Although members of each of the three high-distress groups are prone to **anxiety** and **depression**, they manifest very different **personality structures**. Although sensitized individuals (i.e., those with high distress and moderate restraint) report experiencing **excessive negative affect**, they do not seem to be especially predisposed to particular **personality disorders** (Weinberger and Schwartz, 1990). They are hypothesized to have moderate levels of **ego development** (conformist/conscientious) in which "neurotic" concerns about the inherent conflicts between the **id** (i.e., wishes, desires) and the **superego** (i.e., internalized prohibitions) are salient (cf. Fenichel, 1945). Consistent with traditional repression-sensitization literature (Byrne, 1961), the sensitized group is likely to cope with **stress** by employing **hypervigilance and ruminative rationalization**. Paradoxically, sensitizers tend to stew about nonessential aspects of their **affects**, often camouflaging the defensive nature of behavior that may often involve **displacement**. Their attachment model is hypothesized to vary within the preoccupied or fearful spectrum, where what is salient is a concern about their own **worthiness** in **relationships** (Griffin and Bartholomew, 1994; Mikulincer and Orbach, 1995).

Finally, oversocialized individuals also experience high levels of **subjective distress**; however, they are highly restrained and very concerned about imposing their needs on others. Hence, they are often shy, unassertive, and guilt-prone (Weinberger and Schwartz, 1990). Although there has been little direct empirical investigation to date, oversocialized individuals are likely to compensate for any signs of antisocial affects through such mechanisms as reaction formation and undoing, where they feel that they can never do enough to make up for any **affective outbursts** or **egoistic behavior**. In the literature using the Marlowe-Crowne, they are often labeled "**defensive high anxious**" (Weinberger et al., 1979); in a sense, they can be conceptualized as unsuccessful repressors.

Daniel A. Weinberger 1998 "Defenses, personality structure and development: Integrating psychodynamic theory into a typological approach to personality." *Journal of Personality* 66 (6): 1061–77, 1074 (emphasis added).

Terms are working hard in this passage to classify behaviour, and being called on to improve and refine their technicality. But even in this highly classificatory atmosphere, we still see the signs that these terms are a "social accomplishment." For one thing, we see the reporting expressions which trace these claims and terms to their origins in the research community:

- … (Weinberger and Schwartz, 1990) …
- They are hypothesized to have …
- Consistent with traditional repression-sensitization literature (Byrne, 1961) …
- … is hypothesized to vary …
- Although there has been little direct empirical investigation to date …
- … they can be conceptualized as …

We also see appositives:

- moderate levels of ego development (conformist/conscientious)
- the superego (i.e., internalized prohibitions)

These appositive structures show the writer/researcher estimating the extent and stability of the terms (their social distribution), confirming their application for this purpose, and activating their components for this occasion. Even technical abstractions call for the cooperation and participation of readers.

We further extend this social dimension of abstraction on another plane when we observe the role of definition in perfecting research instruments. Here physical anthropologists concentrate on the technical definition of *blade* to question longstanding assumptions of a connection between human evolution and the development of techniques for producing these blades.

### What are blades and what have people said about them?
The standard morphological definition of a blade is any flake more than twice as long as it is wide, although some investigators prefer ratios of 2.5 or even 4 to 1. The technical definition is somewhat narrower, limiting use of the term to elongated blanks with parallel or slightly curving edges. Normally ….

Ofer Bar-Yosef and Steven L. Kuhn 1999 "The big deal about blades: Laminar technologies and human evolution." *American Anthropologist* 101 (2): 322–38, 323.

Here economists gather abstractions which have been used to analyze the economic behaviour *charity* or *philanthropy*: specifically, in this case, the action of making donations to colleges or universities.

### A. A theory of giving

In the charitable giving literature, social scientists have distinguished several possible motivations for donations: 1) altruism, 2) reciprocity, and 3) direct benefits. Each of these will now be discussed in a college giving context.

Thomas H. Bruggink and Kamran Siddiqui 1995 "An econometric model of alumni giving: A case study for a liberal arts college." *The American Economist* 39 (2): 53–60, 53.

These two instances of technical definition reveal different motivations for using the definitions as research instruments. In the first case, the record of the discipline's work on identifying blades will organize the researchers' critical review of traditional classifications of eras of human development and progress. (Are these people Stone Age?) In order to do this, there has to be some social consensus amongst researchers on what counts as a *blade*. In the second case, efforts to technicalize abstract names for giving money away could have practical applications in planning fund-raising drives.

Researchers get so accustomed to the particular operations of abstractions in their field that these operations can seem "natural" to them — natural, that is, rather than social, and the outcome of exchange, cooperation, and negotiation. The way they use abstractions will seem to them "logical," "accurate," "clear," "precise," whereas other uses of abstraction will seem "illogical," "inaccurate," "vague," or "fuzzy." Students, however, can have a different view. Taking courses in a variety of disciplines, they are not so likely to see the different uses of abstractions as "natural." In fact, in experiencing a range of sometimes contradictory reactions to their work, they would be justified in thinking that the acceptability or unacceptability of uses of abstraction is arbitrary, rather than natural. Sometimes what they write is logical, sometimes it's called illogical; sometimes what they write is clear, sometimes it is considered vague. Better than "natural" *or* "arbitrary," let's say "social." Different groups engaged in different kinds of research-and-writing activities (or different **discourse communities**) develop, through their association and communal purposes, different techniques for making and representing knowledge.

These differences can also affect the material conditions of learning in different courses. In disciplines that depend on technical abstractions, students spend a lot of time acquiring command of these terms and preparing to have their command of these terms tested. This can be hard work. But it might be even harder work, for some, to acquire facility with the prestige abstractions of the humanities, where the operation of terms is more covert and tacit, and less openly recognized as a matter of consensus and collaboration.

---

### Exercise 5

Compare the presentation of definitions in two or three of your textbooks from different courses (if possible, choose textbooks from at least two different disciplines — the sciences, social sciences, and humanities). Try to generalize about the approaches to definition preferred in each disciplines. Consider some of the following questions.

- Where do the definitions tend to occur? In a glossary? In the body of the textbook?

- In general, do the definitions strike you as *technical* (i.e., stable and designed for classifying phenomena) or *non-technical* (provisional and open to reformulation by other writers)?

- What kinds of definitions tend to be presented as brief appositions?

- What kinds are presented as sustained definitions?

- Are definitions ever attributed to specific researchers?

- Do any terms receive more than one definition (proposed, perhaps, by different researchers in the field)?

### Exercise 6

Analyze the use of definition in a scholarly article, perhaps one that you are using for a research essay in one of your courses. Consider some of the following questions.

- Where do the definitions tend to occur? What sorts of words or terms tend to be defined?

- How does the writer present definitions (i.e., apposition versus sustained)?

---

- Are definitions attributed to other researchers?

- What role does definition serve in the article? Does the writer seem to assume that the reader doesn't know the meaning? Does definition establish common ground? Does definition establish a precise or technical meaning?

- Are the meanings of words or terms contested or seen as having different possible meanings?

Compare your findings with those of other students.

# 6

# Orchestrating voices, making arrangements for speakers

Up to this point, each of your summaries has brought one writer (or one partnership of writers, in the case of co-authored articles) to the page. You have concentrated on making arrangements for this speaker, those arrangements also signifying the **position** you are taking.

But, as we observed in Chapter 3 in the section on "Reporting reporting," many of these writers have themselves incorporated other voices: not only the voices of research subjects when these have been the site of inquiry, but also the voices of other scholars, and often several other scholars. In fact, it is probably rather rare for scholarly writers to enter into dialogue with only one other writer. As a rule, they convene the scholarly conversation by bringing several or many other voices to the page, and arrange for these speakers to talk to one another. Sometimes, as is the case in the article by South and Crowder at the beginning of Chapter 2, these guest speakers talk all at once, the common themes of their writings amounting to a chorus:

> Initial skepticism over the impact of neighborhood conditions and neighborhood contexts on the behavior of adolescents and young adults (Jencks and Mayer 1990) has spurred considerable research purportedly documenting such effects (Aneshensel and Sucoff 1996; Billy, Brewster, and Grady 1994; Corcoran et al. 1992; Duncan 1994; Duncan, Connel, and Klebanov 1997; Elliott et al. 1996; Entwisle, Alexander, and Olson 1994; cf. Evans, Oates, and Schwab 1992).

Other times, two or three voices are heard in exchange with one another. Here an archaeologist first cites three writers (or two pairs and a single) on the connection between the status and position of producers of goods and the nature of social complexity in the surrounding community. Then two of the cited voices (Costin 1991 and Clark and Parry 1990) engage in conversation with each other:

> Recent studies of links between the organization of production and sociopolitical complexity have explored the importance of different kinds of craft specialization, particularly the difference between independent and attached specialization (Brumfiel and Earle 1987; Clark and Parry 1990; Costin 1991). Independent specialists "produce for a general market of potential customers" while "attached production is sponsored and managed by élite or governmental institutions or patrons" (Costin 1991). Thus independent specialists generally produce utilitarian goods in response to a social "demand", while attached specialists typically make luxury goods, wealth items, or weaponry at the behest of powerful patrons (Costin 1991, 11-13).
>
> There is some diversity of opinion about how broadly the general notion of craft specialization and attendant concepts such as attached and independent specialization should be defined. Costin (1991) favours fairly narrow definitions appropriate to the analysis of the productive regimes of quite complex societies. Clark and Parry (1990) use the same terms much more broadly, identifying elements of specialization even in situations of minimal sociopolitical complexity. In this respect, my discussion follows Clark and Parry more closely than Costin, but I am not particularly interested in insisting that the makers of Paso de la Amada figurines were "specialists" or "non-specialists". What I find useful in craft specialization theory is the perspective it provides on producer/consumer dynamics with respect to alienable goods — in particular, the idea that independent artisans producing goods specifically for alienation emerge as a response to consumer demand.
>
> Richard Lesure 1999 "Figurines as representations and products at Paso de la Amada, Mexico." *Cambridge Archaeological Journal* 9 (2): 209–20, 210.

The writer gives the other speakers room to demonstrate their differences, positioning himself closer to one than to the other. But he then disengages himself from the conflict to select the overall consensus of their ideas as applicable to his inquiry into small ceramic figurines and their capacity to tell us about social organization.

The circumstances of this exchange belong to the summarizer who has called on these speakers in particular, found a point of shared or interestingly divergent interest, and set the terms of the conversation. It takes some skill to make hospitable arrangements for speakers — to introduce strangers to one another, to renew acquaintances. The sections which follow offer you a chance to develop this know-how by focusing on different types of speakers.

## 6A Orchestrating Scholarly Voices

Summary of more than one speaker can sometimes reproduce a discussion that has taken place face-to-face — or, that is, "page-to-page": *A* wrote something, and *B* responded to what *A* wrote. *A* and *B* know each other — or, at least, *B* has read what *A* wrote — and the summarizer reproduces this part of the conversation. For example, in the first exercise in Chapter 3, Counts and Counts introduce Bellah et al. in order to distinguish between "communities" and "lifestyle enclaves." A summary of Counts and Counts might include this distinction — but how does the summarizer show that the idea of "lifestyle enclaves" originates in Bellah et al.? A reporting expression can do this: "Counts and Counts draw on a definition of 'lifestyle enclaves' from Bellah et al. to explain differences between resort park residents and boondockers (Bellah et al. cited in Counts & Counts, 1992, p. 169)." In this case, parenthetical citation emphasizes that Counts and Counts are orchestrating other writers who speak in their article. Or, in the case of quotation, a writer might emphasize that a writer is quoting another speaker: (Bellah et al. *quoted* in Counts and Counts, 1992, p. 169).

The obvious limitation with recreating "page-to-page" dialogue is that the **orchestration** of speakers is largely set by *B*: Counts and Counts have only allowed Bellah et al. to speak briefly, and it is difficult to start a new conversation. Just as scholars rarely create a dialogue with just one speaker, they infrequently orchestrate a discussion of writers they haven't read directly. Such is apparently the case for South and Crowder, who recreate a series of responses to a single study: Jencks and Mayer (1990) expressed skepticism about neighbourhoods having much effect on young people's behaviour, and then over the next six years a number of researchers —

Aneshensel and Sucoff (1996); Billy, Brewster, and Grady (1994); Corcoran et al. (1992); Duncan (1994); Duncan, Connel, and Klebanov (1997); Elliott et al. (1996); Entwisle, Alexander, and Olson (1994); cf. Evans, Oates, and Schwab (1992) — reacted to Jencks and Mayer's claim, publishing findings that are "purportedly" to the contrary.

In other cases, the "face-to-face" quality of the speakers' relationship is not so immediate. It's not so much that one wrote in reaction to another, but that they are in earshot of one another. They research similar objects, address similar questions. So here a researcher (Ken Hyland 1999) who is investigating citation itself cites two writers (or a single and a pair) in the same paragraph, weaving their findings together, representing them in shared sentences (and also providing direct contact with each of the sources).

> Myers (1990) and Berkenkotter and Huckin (1995) have traced the passage of research articles through the review procedure and see the process as one of essentially locating the writer's claims within a wider disciplinary framework. This is achieved partly by modifying claims and providing propositional warrants, but mainly by establishing a narrative context for the work through citation. One of Myers's case study subjects, for example, increased the number of references from 57 to 195 in a resubmission to *Science* (Myers 1990:91). Both Myers and Berkenkotter and Huckin see academic writing as a tension between originality and humility in the community, rhetorically accommodating laboratory activity to the discipline. So while Berkenkotter and Huckin's scientist subject sought to gain acceptance for original, and therefore significant, work, the reviewers insisted "that to be science her report had to include an intertextual framework for her local knowledge" (Berkenkotter and Huckin 1995:59).
>
> Hyland 1999: 342–43.

While Berkenkotter and Huckin do not directly mention Myers — and so, the relationship is not exactly "face-to-face" — the similarity of their studies (how researchers revise their work to get it published) is similar enough for Hyland to let them speak one after the other on the same topic. Differences between the cited writers are set aside, in the interests of establishing common ground: a finding confirmed by at least two studies. This common ground is mapped by the summarizer. (For another occasion, though, the *differences* might be the theme of the summary.)

The examples above involve writers who directly summarize other writers or who share a common research situation with them. The similarity of the research situation, or of the fact that their publications directly responded to one another, makes orchestrating the different writers relatively straightforward. Sometimes, however, writers seem to have something in common because they use the same terms or **abstractions**; but because they research different things, orchestrating them is more difficult.

Passages 1 and 2 below both involve a technical term and its acronym — "traditional ecological knowledge" (TEK) — but the use of the term issues from different research situations. In Passage 1, Henry P. Huntington et al. briefly define TEK in the context of their study of beluga whales.

### PASSAGE 1

Beluga whales (*Delphinapterus leucas*) are circumpolar in distribution and are hunted by indigenous peoples throughout the Arctic (Kleinberg et al., 1964). While some previous biological research on belugas has used the expertise of local hunters to plan the research and to add to data gathered from scientific observations (e.g., Frost and Lowry, 1990), a practice which continues through the work of the Alaska Beluga Whale Committee (Adams et al., 1993), little has been done to document systematically such local expertise, also known as traditional ecological knowledge (TEK). The primary purpose of this research was to capture TEK data in order to (1) describe beluga ecology as seen by indigenous hunters and elders and (2) identify specific contributions such data can make to scientific understanding of beluga ecology.

Henry Huntington and the Communities of Buckland, Elim, Koyuk, Point Lay, and Shaktoolik 1999 "Traditional knowledge of the ecology of beluga whales (*Delphinapterus leucas*) in the Eastern Chukchi and Northern Bering Seas, Alaska." *Arctic* 52 (1): 49–61, 69.

In Passage 2, which is taken from the beginning of another article, George W. Wenzel focuses on different definitions of TEK.

### PASSAGE 2

[TEK is] knowledge and values which have been acquired through experience, observation, from the land or from spiritual teachings, and handed down from one generation to another. (Definition of TEK in GNWT policy statement, as quoted in Abele, 1997:iii)
    TEK is *knowledge*. (Hunn, 1988:14, italics in original)

In recent years, scientists have come to Nunavut in search of Inuit traditional ecological knowledge …. when Inuit knowledge is collected … it is almost always taken out of context, misinterpreted or given meaning different than it had in the first place (Stevenson, 1996a:3).

The first of the above statements constitutes the formal definitions of traditional knowledge as defined by the Government of the Northwest Territories. The second and third, both by anthropologists, encapsulated two important contemporary, if not necessarily harmonious, views of traditional ecological knowledge that together intimate not only why TEK has become an important intellectual issue, but also an increasingly political topic in the contemporary North.

George W. Wenzel 1999 "Traditional ecological knowledge and Inuit: Reflections on TEK research and ethics." *Arctic* 52 (2): 113–24, 113–16.

These writers obviously have something in common: TEK. They work in the same scholarly area, and there is good reason for them to get to know one another. But their claims about TEK issue from different kinds of research situations. Whereas Huntington et al. *use* TEK in their research on the migrations and movements and other behaviours of beluga whales in Alaska, Wenzel *reflects on* TEK itself. Arranging for these two researchers to speak to each other, we would need to explain the different circumstances from which their statements issue — an important occasion for putting to use your practice in characterizing the discussion you are citing. Huntington et al. (1999) is an instance of research in marine biology; Wenzel (1999) is an instance of review of and reflection on research methodology.

It is also possible for a writer to orchestrate a scholarly discussion between speakers who are already in dialogue with each other and others who are not. The specific circumstances of these types of conversations require careful negotiation. A reader needs to be able to see that the new speakers did not directly address this research situation. The next passage comes from a report by researchers who are studying South Africans' accounts of beaches as *places* following the elimination of apartheid and the end of segregated beaches. Here they first provide an historical account of, as they say, the "concept of place-identity in environmental psychology." You will see that, at this stage, the cited speakers "know" each other: the Proshansky et al. paper is a response to "earlier calls"; that paper in turn is criticized and appreciated, and its proposed concept is narrowed in **definition** (we can see the social process by which somewhat technical definitions are arrived at).

### The concept of place-identity in environmental psychology

A key moment in environmental psychology's critique of a disembodied notion of identity was the publication of Proshansky, Fabian, and Kaminoff's (1983) paper on place-identity (cf. Groat, 1995). Although it has been subjected to various criticisms, the paper was invaluable in establishing place-identity as a sensitizing construct, bringing to fruition earlier calls for an "ecological conception" of self and personality (cf. Craik and McKechnie, 1977). Adopting a general and inclusive definition, Proshansky et al. described place-identity as a "pot-pourri of memories, conceptions, interpretations, ideas and related feelings about specific physical settings as well as type setting" (1983, p. 60). As a distinctive substructure of the self, they reasoned, place-identity might function to underwrite some personal identities, render actions or activities intelligible, express tastes and preferences and mediate efforts to change environments.

Later researchers have found this formulation suggestive, if a little nebulous. Though using Proshansky as a theoretical resource, Korpela (1989) prefers a narrower definition of place-identity: as a psychological structure that arises out of individuals' attempts to regulate their environments. Through practices of environmental usage, he argues, we are able to create and sustain a coherent sense of self and to reveal our selves to others. At the heart of this psychological structure is a sense of belonging, for "place-belongingness is not only one aspect of place-identity, but a necessary *basis* for it. Around this core the social, cultural and biological definitions and cognitions of place which become part of the person's place-identity are built" (Korpela, 1989, p. 246, emphasis in original). In this conception, human actors are cast as imaginative users of their environments, agents who are able to appropriate physical contexts in order to create, here, a space of attachment and rootedness, a space of being. The personalization of dwellings is an oft-cited example. By this practice, "home" places are organized and represented in ways that help individuals to maintain self-coherence and self-esteem, to realize self-regulation principles.

John Dixon and Kevin Durrheim 2000 "Displacing place-identity: A discursive approach to locating self and other." *British Journal of Social Psychology* 39: 27–44.

Continuing, Dixon and Durrheim then introduce a stranger (Rowles 1983) to the conversation. To make it quite clear that this speaker is not responding directly (or even indirectly) to the previous contributions, the writers point to another group — "scholars working in other research traditions" — and we take the speaker who gets the floor next as belonging to this group working in an ethnographic, rather than psychological, tradition.

> The importance of belonging to processes of self-definition has been noted by scholars working in other research traditions, confirming Korpela's claim that it is a central feature of place-identity (see e.g., Cuba and Hummon, 1993; Tuan, 1980). Rowles' (1983) research with the elderly residents of an Appalachian community provides an eloquent empirical demonstration of the idea. Rowles distinguished between three senses of "insidedness", expressing different aspects of his respondents' affinity with their surroundings. "Physical insidedness" designated their "body awareness" of their environment, expressed as a kind of tacit knowledge of the physical details of place (e.g., knowing how to find one's way). "Social insidedness" designated their sense of connection to a local community, a recognition of their "integration within the social fabric" (p. 302) (e.g., of knowing others and being known). Finally, "autobiographic insidedness" designated their idiosyncratic sense of rootedness. Often unspoken and taken for granted, autobiographical insidedness seemed to arise out of individuals' transactions within a place over time. It was this mode of place identification, Rowles suggested, that was especially important to his elderly respondents. Although they had witnessed considerable changes in their home town of Colton and had found their mobility increasingly restricted, they were able to maintain a sense of belonging by remembering incidents, places, contributions and relations in their personal lives there.

> Dixon and Durrheim 2000: 28–29.

Other scholars writing in environmental psychology might have produced an account similar to the first two paragraphs. But after that point, Dixon and Durrheim present a voice that would be a less predictable contributor: their introduction to the conversation of Rowles' study of Appalachian elders is a novel arrangement. They have introduced someone (relatively) unknown to the others in the field, and they make him welcome by telling where he comes from (an "empirical" project), giving him lots of time to speak, and especially recommending his "eloquent" contribution.

---

### Exercise 1

Write a summary of Passage 1 from Huntington et al. (above, p. 97) that focuses on the term "traditional ecological knowledge" (TEK). Then develop it by bringing Huntingdon et al. into conversation with Wenzel (Passage 2, pp. 97–98). In doing so, you might consider Huntington et al. as an example of how TEK is used, rather than putting Huntington et al. up against Wenzel all by themselves (for this could somewhat misrepresent the case: Huntington et al. and Wenzel are not in direct dialogue with one another).

### Exercise 2

Passages 3 and 4 below are both concerned with Norbert Elias's theory of the civilizing process. Orchestrate a discussion between John McGuire and John Pratt that is careful to note each of their research contexts.

In Passage 3, John McGuire, a social historian, is talking about capital punishment and analyzing episodes in the history of capital punishment in Australia. Everyday experience might lead us to expect that he will focus on the debate over whether there should be capital punishment at all, but, actually, his focus is on the staging of the act itself. He refers to Michel Foucault's famous and compelling account (*Discipline and Punish: The Birth of the Prison* 1979 [1975]) of the transformation of public execution — grisly and fatal tortures performed before large audiences of citizens — into the much less public techniques of punishment carried on in modern prisons. But McGuire also says that Foucault's interpretation of the history of state-sponsored punishment is now competing with another interpretation: Norbert Elias's theory of the "civilizing process."

### PASSAGE 3

The decision to conceal the execution ritual from public scrutiny has attracted little scholarly attention from historians of capital punishment in Australia [....] The body of English-speaking work that has been produced on the subject has mainly concentrated upon the end of the spectacle in America and England.[1] Among this work, there is evidence of a trend to de-emphasize what David Garland has described as Foucault's "power perspective",[2] in which the symbolic act of execution is interpreted as having fulfilled a decisive political function in reasserting the power of sovereign over subject until its dramatic replacement in the late eighteenth and early nineteenth centuries by a new disciplinary technology of power — the prison. In its place has emerged a greater attention to the role of cultural factors in determining the movement away from public punishments.[3] Louis Masur's work in particular has emphasized that transforming sensibilities towards violence in American society provided the impetus for the concealment of the offensive and brutalising spectacle of the public execution.[4] The motivation for this culturalist approach has stemmed from the work of the sociologist, Norbert Elias, whose attention to the influence of psychological sensibilities on the process of historical change has inspired scholars in a variety of fields, including the study of punishment.[5] While Elias's work has provoked a number of criticisms,[6] the concept of the "civilizing process" is a useful explanatory tool when applied to the history of capital punishment. In explaining the course of European history from the Middle Ages to the early twentieth century, Elias emphasized the interaction between processes of state formation, on the one hand, and psychological and behavioral transformations in the individual, on the other. As the state gradually began to monopolise the use of physical force and its administrative apparatus became increasingly centralised, there was an accompanying transformation in the individual towards self-restraint or self-discipline — in short, a "civilizing process" was apparent ("civilizing" being understood here not to refer to a society being civilised in an absolute sense but, rather, to the process by which a society gradually becomes more civilised over time).

One must be cautious in applying a theory that was developed to explain a specific historical circumstance to another quite distinct situation, yet it remains to be seen how applicable Elias's theory is to areas other than western Europe. Indeed, for any analysis of the European "civilizing process" to be complete, the colonial settler states that comprised its margins should be taken into account.

*Notes*

1   See especially: Randall McGowen, 'Civilizing Punishment: The End of the Public Execution in England', *Journal of British Studies*, vol. 33, no. 3, 1994, pp. 257–82; David D. Cooper, *The Lesson of the Scaffold: The Public Execution Controversy in Victorian England*, Ohio University Press, Athens, Ohio, 1974, and in his article 'Public Executions in Victorian England: A Reform Adrift', in William B. Thesing [….]

2   David Garland, *Punishment and Modern Society: A Study in Social Theory*, Oxford University Press, Oxford, 1990, p. 131.

3   See especially: Masur, *op. cit.*; Pieter Spierenburg, *The Spectacle of Suffering: Executions and the Evolution of Repression: From a Preindustrial Metropolis to the European Experience*, Cambridge University Press, Cambridge, 1984; and Garland, *op. cit.*, especially chaps 9 and 10.

4   Masur, *op. cit.*, especially pp. 103–10.

5   Elias's theoretical contribution is best outlined in *The Civilizing Process*, vol. 1: *The History of Manners* (1939), Blackwell, Oxford, 1983 [….]

6   See for example [….]

John McGuire 1998 "Judicial violence and the 'civilizing process': Race and transition from public to private executions in Colonial Australia." *Australian Historical Studies* 111: 187–209, 188–90.

In the next passage, John Pratt offers further commentary on Elias's theory of the *civilizing process* — in another research context, which is referred to at the end of the passage.

## PASSAGE 4

### The civilizing process

What is it, though, that is meant by the term civilized? It carries with it common-sensical notions about values and practices which, in general, differentiate Western societies which are thought to make up the civilized world, from those other social formations which do not. Here, though, I am using it as a theoretical construct in the manner of Elias ([1939] (1994)). For him, "civilizing" was one element in a triad of controls whereby individuals exercised self-control (the other two being control of natural events and control of social forces). The intensity of this self-control at any given time in a particular society could thus be seen as an indicator of its stage of development (Elias 1970). Importantly, then, "civilizing" in the Elisian sense did not mean "progress" nor did it invoke value judgment. Instead, it was the contingent outcome of long-term socio-cultural and psychic change from the Middle Ages onwards, that brought with it two major consequences. First, the modern state itself gradually began to assume much more centralized authority and control over the lives of its citizens, to the point where it came to have a monopoly regarding the use of force and the imposition of legal sanctions to address disputes. Second, citizens in modern societies came to internalize restraints, controls and inhibitions on their conduct, as their values and actions came to be framed around increased sensibility to the suffering of others and the privatization of disturbing events (Garland 1990). In these respects, while Elias himself used changing attitudes to bodily functions and to violence to demonstrate these claims, it also seems clear that the development of punishment in modern society follows this route and provides a helpful demonstration of the Elias thesis. One of the most important consequences of the gradual spread of these sentiments was, as Pieter Spierenburg (1984) has illustrated, a decline and tempering of corporal and capital punishments over this period — to the point where, at the onset of modernity, the public performance of such punishments had all but disappeared and their administration in private was increasingly subject to regulations and "scientific" scrutiny. As I want to show in relation to English prison development, these trends have since continued. In the course of the development of much of modern society punishment became "a rather shameful societal activity, undertaken by specialists and professionals in enclaves (such as prison and reformatories) which are, by and large, removed from the sight of the public" (Garland 1990:224).

John Pratt 1999 "Norbert Elias and the civilized prison." *British Journal of Sociology* 50 (2): 271–96, 272–73.

## 6B Identifying Different Genres and Orchestrating Non-Scholarly Voices

Section 6A involves writers who have things in common: they are relatively contemporaneous and they are scholars. However, there are occasions when older scholarship or non-scholarly writings need to be introduced. These writers may hold different, problematic views on certain subjects, or they may not be researchers at all — they may represent genres or situations not primarily focused on research.

The next passage appears in an archaeologist's study of the role of alcohol in legitimating authority in Celtic societies: chief-sponsored drinking and feasting in the Iron Age. Some of her data are archaeological: material artefacts recovered in physical investigation. Some of her evidence, however, is documentary: written accounts of feasting in Iron Age societies. So you will see her bringing together speakers whose statements issue from radically different contexts: she cites "Classical authors" on Celtic societies and a modern author describing Tlingit (North American West Coast) society.

You will see that to bring these two types of speakers together she makes special arrangements like those of Dixon and Durrheim above (see p. 99): research in "*many ethnographic contexts* ... [provides] *additional* information" (emphasis added) on preindustrial societies. You will also see that the Classical authors are introduced with great care, and with attention to their peculiarities. It's almost as if difficult writers wait in an anteroom while the summarizer explains and anticipates their odd behaviour: in this case, they fail to take account of what modern scholars would be interested in, and have a tendency to obsess over the "bizarre" and to "romanticize or demonize 'exotic' peoples" (which the Celts would have been to these Classical authors). Moreover, they can be rather unreliable reporters, from a modern point of view: when they lack data on one group of exotic people, they just repeat what has been said about some other group. In effect, the summarizer says, "Now, I've got some people I want you to meet. You can't believe everything they say, and I've heard them dwell on some things that might not interest you. But, even though they're kind of strange, I think they've got some valuable information. Here they are. Let's all be polite."

> The general formula followed by most Classical authors describing the alien cultures on their peripheries was modelled on Herodotus and consisted of several categories of information: 1) population; 2) antiquity and ancient history; 3) way of life; 4) customs (Tierney 1960, 190). Unfortunately for modern scholars the unusual and bizarre aspects of the last two categories were generally recounted in some detail, while information considered mundane, common knowledge or uninteresting was less frequently recorded. Two pitfalls facing the modern scholar attempting to derive "facts" from these accounts are "Randvölkeridealisierung" (Tierney 1960, 214) and "ethnographische Wandermotive" (Tierney 1960, 201). The first is the tendency of Classical ethnographers to romanticize or demonize "exotic" peoples. The second refers to the borrowing of descriptions of customs from accounts of one culture and transposing them wholesale or only slightly modified to a completely different group of people, whenever hard facts were lacking or could benefit from being fleshed out in a more dramatic way [....]
>
> Despite these potential difficulties, several significant themes related to Celtic drinking and feasting behaviour (both insular and continental) recur in Classical sources. Some of these themes, particularly those also found in the later insular Celtic texts, may result from similarities between geographically and temporally different groups of the Celts (Nash 1976, 116). One such theme is that of the king's or hero's portion at a banquet, described as early as Phylarchus (Tierney 1960, 197). Another is the concept of guest-friendship, mentioned by Diodorus Siculus (Tierney 1960, 250) and again by

Caesar (Tierney 1960, 274); both accounts stress the Celtic emphasis on open-handedness and generosity as important virtues.

Generosity as the defining characteristic of a good chieftain or king is a common theme in both Classical and insular texts, but also in many ethnographically recorded societies at a chiefdom level of organization. Athenaeus' account of Lavernius' banquet is a good example (Tierney, 1960, 248). The Celtic chieftain Lavernius, pleased by the praise of a poet at his feast, scatters gold along the plain behind his chariot, and "the poet picked it up and sang another song saying that the very tracks made by his chariot on the earth gave gold and largesse to mankind" (Tierney 1960, 248).

Athenaeus' verbatim transcription of four of the nine surviving extracts of Book 23 of Poseidonius' *History*, the recognized "Bible" on the Celts, describes food, drink, and heroic feasting and combat, and bardic display at great length. In fact, the passage on food and drink is the longest surviving portion of Poseidonius' Celtic ethnography. This may reflect the special emphasis on food and drink in the Celtic world observed by Poseidonius.

The symbolic as well as functional significance of feasting is documented in many ethnographic contexts (Chapman 1980, 66); such sources provide additional preindustrial configurations for modelling prehistoric social organization. The Tlingit potlatch is a good example of a society in which feasting acts as an institutionalized form of social regulation. As described by Kan, "the unity and solidarity of clan relatives were emphasized by the obligatory sharing of property and food that characterized their relationships" (1989, 65–6). The status of a Tlingit aristocrat depended on the rank and wealth of his parents (especially his mother), marriage to a person of equal or greater rank, the number and scale of potlatches sponsored by his parents in his honour, and accomplishments in activities which generated wealth and enabled him to give his own potlatch(es) or actively participate in those given by his matrikin (Kan 1989, 82).[1]

*Note*
1   Note the key role played by feasting in establishing and maintaining status in this society.

Bettina Arnold 1999 "'Drinking the feast': Alcohol and the legitimation of power in Celtic Europe." *Cambridge Archaeological Review* 9 (1): 71–93, 72–73.

We don't have to go so far afield to find difficult speakers. In many undergraduate courses, reading assignments include (or sometimes focus exclusively on) textbooks: academic genres composed by specialists for non-specialists. Rather than make new knowledge, or take another step along a line of inquiry, or interrogate the accumulation of knowledge in a field, textbooks synthesize what is known so far.

Of course, many textbooks provide an historical view of knowledge in a discipline, or sub-field of a discipline, and bring to light the social dimension of knowledge as a product of interaction amongst researchers. In this respect, they resemble the research genres. And many textbooks offer a critical overview of knowledge in a field, implying directions for further inquiry. In this respect too they resemble the research genres.

But their position vis-à-vis their readers differs from that of the research genres. First, they construct readers as "not knowing": if anyone has a question, it's the student/reader; if anyone has the answer, it's the textbook. (In the research genres, as we have seen, writers represent themselves as sharing questions with their readers.) Second, they construct readers as listeners rather than co-conversationalists (although many textbooks will provide exercises and assignments which direct their readers to a limited role as participants in scholarly discussion).

The academic textbook genres and the research genres each have their place, and the authors of the latter often become authors of the former. Writers in the research genres can hear the difference between research article and textbook. When reading the following passage from a textbook, try to identify what features of the research genres are missing.

> One of the direct benefits of the end of the 45-year cold war between the United States and the Soviet Union has been a substantial decline in foreign military and political presence in the Third World. An indirect cost of this withdrawal, however, has been the acceleration of ethnic, tribal, and religious conflict. Although ethnic and religious tensions and occasional violence have always existed in LDCs [Less Developed Countries], the waning of superpower influence triggered a revival of these internal conflicts and may even have accelerated the incidence of political and economic discrimination. Ethnicity and religion often play a major role in the success or failure of development efforts. Clearly, the greater the ethnic and religious diversity in a country, the more likely it is that there will be internal strife and political instability. It is not

surprising, therefore, that some of the most successful recent development experiences — South Korea, Taiwan, Singapore, and Hong Kong — have occurred in culturally homogeneous societies.

Michael P. Todaro 1997 *Economic Development.* New York: Longman, 34.

Students may learn to recognize the different styles which indicate the circumstances under which statements are produced in textbooks and research articles: the first acting to inform, the second acting to inquire. However, the differing purposes of the textbook and research genres can put students in a difficult position when gathering materials for a paper in an undergraduate course: they consult research articles, chapters, and books — but they also still hear the informative voice of the textbook on similar topics. If they repeat the statements of the textbook without attributing them, taking them as common knowledge and public truth, they fail to observe the scholarly requirement of providing the traces of statements, the footprints that statements leave in their history of use. Yet even if they do attribute the statements to their authors, they can still interrupt a scholarly conversation by bringing in a speaker who had prepared for a different kind of discussion. How can this speaker be accommodated?

Just as Bettina Arnold made special arrangements for "Classical authors" (pp. 106–107), you can introduce the textbook speakers with an account of their origins and intentions. For example, consider this passage:

> *Prejudice* is defined as a positive or negative attitude based on information or knowledge which is either illogical, unrelated to reality, or is a distortion of fact, and which is unjustifiably generalized to all members of a group. Although prejudice can be either favourable or unfavourable, psychologists use the term most frequently in the negative sense.

> J.E. Alcock, D.W. Carment, and S.W. Sadava 1994 *A Textbook of Social Psychology* 3rd ed. Scarborough, ON: Prentice Hall, 222.

Alcock et al. might be introduced to a research conversation by contextualizing their discussion:

> In their introductory book on social psychology, Alcock et al. (1994) offer a general definition of *prejudice*: [....] This definition suggests that prejudice could be corrected by referring to external reality or logic.

In this case, the special arrangement identifies the writing situation: an introductory course in social psychology. A reader might expect that researchers in the field of social psychology would likely test this definition. As the passages on TEK and the civilizing process in Section 6A indicate, different researchers often develop specific definitions that are applicable to what they are studying (e.g., Huntington et al. use the term TEK with specific reference to beluga whales) or they may even make the term itself part of what they are studying (e.g., Wenzel reflects directly on how TEK has been defined). With these passages, we emphasized the importance of characterizing the cited discussion. Non-research genres like textbooks, which primarily serve to educate, need similar attention. In these cases, the fact that the authors may also be researchers does not mean that they are addressing other researchers.

Another case, popular writing, may initially seem to present an obvious non-research situation. Consider consumer publications like newspapers or magazines that are funded by advertisement or subscription through mass distribution to a general audience or specific non-research interests (e.g., hobbies, sports, fashion). Some of these special interests may be extremely useful to researchers. For example, in their ethnographic study of RVers, Counts and Counts cite popular magazines, such as *Trailer Life* and *Highways*, that cater to RVers. Similarly, research in education might benefit from professional publications read by teachers. Or a study of political rhetoric might take recourse to opinion-editorials published in newspapers or political magazines. In all of these cases, the writing situation will be relatively easy to identify, and the speaker can be introduced accordingly.

However, there are situations that are more difficult to identify. The writers of books written for a popular audience may be researchers, but they are not addressing other scholars or even students. Whereas the situation of an article can be identified by looking at the publication (e.g., is it a consumer magazine or an academic journal?), a book can be harder to place, because books are published by all sorts of publishers. Here is a passage from a book on demographic trends, written by experts but addressed to a broad audience distributed beyond the scholarly community.

> A country filled with young people is one whose retailers compete predominantly on price. In such a country, anything that can lower the average cost of production and reduce the price to the consumer is important. A young Canada during the 1960s and 1970s enabled the big retail mall to be born and thrive, making it possible for stores

to lower costs and pass the savings on to customers. The malls won't disappear but their glory days are over. In the 20 years to come, the demographic shift will favour a revival of neighbourhood specialty stores supported by local customers for whom price is no longer the most important factor in a purchase decision.

Stores that can deliver good products and good service will dominate this new marketplace, while stores that waste consumers' time and treat them rudely will disappear. The art of customer service is something at which Canadian retailers are notoriously incompetent because, until the late 1980s, they were operating in a marketplace that didn't require it. It's no accident that countries such as Japan and Germany discovered quality and service before we did. Their populations are much older than ours, and their retailers had to respond to the demands of a changing marketplace a decade or more earlier than ours did. The Canadian retailers that prosper in the changing market place of the coming years will be those that succeed in adopting customer service as a way of life.

David K. Foot and Daniel Stoffman 1996 *Boom, Bust and Echo: How to Profit from the Coming Demographic Shift.* Toronto: Macfarlane Walter & Ross.

Here is a linguist well known in scholarly circles but on this occasion writing for an audience as broad as that addressed by Foot and Stoffman above.

A similar conflict exists between [a couple I will call] Louise and Howie, about spending money. Louise would never buy anything costing more than a hundred dollars without discussing it with Howie, but he goes out and buys whatever he wants and feels they can afford, like a table saw or a new power mower. Louise is disturbed, not because she disapproves of the purchases, but because she feels he is acting as if she were not in the picture.

Many women feel it is natural to consult with their partners at every turn, while many men automatically make more decisions without consulting their partners. This may reflect a broad difference in conceptions of decision making. Women expect decisions to be discussed first and made by consensus. They appreciate the discussion itself as evidence of involvement and communication. But many men feel oppressed by lengthy discussions about what they see as minor decisions, and they feel hemmed in if they can just act without talking first. When women try to initiate a freewheeling discussion by asking, "What do you think?" men often think they are being asked to decide.

Communication is a continual balancing act, juggling the conflicting needs for intimacy and independence. To survive in the world, we have to act in concert with others, but to survive as ourselves, rather than simply as cogs in a wheel, we have to act alone.

Deborah Tannen 1990 *You Just Don't Understand: Women and Men in Conversation.* New York: Ballantine Books, 27–28.

What features of scholarly style are missing from these two passages? If these were research publications, what would be different about them? By analyzing the style of the writing, you can make guesses at the situation. Foot and Stoffman, for example, make bold assertions and prognostications: e.g., "In the 20 years to come, the demographic shift *will* favour a revival of neighbourhood specialty stores ..." (emphasis added). Tannen expresses similar certainty and makes unqualified generalizations: e.g., "*Women expect* decisions to be discussed first and made by consensus" (emphasis added). Neither writer seems concerned with what others have to say or with research on their topics. At least they don't summon other voices: there is no citation and little in the way of reporting expressions in these passages. Both writers are experts, but here they do not seem to be speaking to other experts. Will these outgoing, friendly speakers fit into the scholarly conversation you have arranged? Will they pay attention to the qualifications, abstractions, and uncertainties of the other guests? Or will they try to dominate? Chances are, these popular speakers won't fit in. Their statements will not interact with others' — and the conversation will be difficult to continue.

If you feel committed to including the popular speaker, you can take some measures, though, to introduce the new arrival to the other guests: "Writing for a general audience and addressing such-and-such, x simplifies..."; "While x's claims overlook the uncertainty of evidence in this area, they do represent/speak to widely held interest in/concerns about...."

Watch out for books whose covers list "PhD" after the author's name. This doesn't mean that the PhD is a hoax or not a good one, but that the authority of the book is being recommended to a non-scholarly audience. In the scholarly community, advertising that one has a PhD is not likely to impress, since most writers participating in scholarly discussions have one.

Finally, let's consider the Internet, a special case that can make it difficult to identify the writing situation. The Internet is a benefit to researchers. At the very least, it offers efficient access to library catalogues and easy access to indexes that allow discipline-specific searches for publications on a topic. Increasingly, articles and whole scholarly journals are now available in electronic form, either directly through index searches or on their own servers. In these cases, you should be especially careful to note the address or Uniform Resource Locator (URL) of the index or article (some indexes offer permanent URLs for articles, while others generate temporary URLs). Because libraries subscribe to index licenses, a research librarian can help you understand the appropriate citation protocol for your library.

There are some complications, though, mainly arising from the operation of browsers and search engines. These technologies can lead you to domains where research publications mingle with popular publications, and both of these find themselves in the company of organizations sponsoring more or less viable points of view, and individuals promoting their own interests or ambitions for publicity. Recent amalgamations of online periodical indexes have, as well, tended to blur the distinction between peer-reviewed research publications and general-audience journalism.

How can you tell if you are finding speakers suitable for introduction into scholarly conversation? Online research journals will include the circumstances of publication: names and affiliations of members of the editorial board; procedures for submission and review of articles. Look for these indications. Stand-alone publications may be harder to evaluate. But your experience in identifying the characteristic sounds of scholarly voices should be a reliable guide for you by now.

Making arrangements for scholarly conversation is a challenge for undergraduates: as newcomers to research communities, they can find it hard to prepare an appropriate list of guest speakers. But it's also a challenge for graduate students, and sometimes for professional scholars, too.

---

**Exercise 3**

In the exercises at the end of Chapter 4, you summarized passages from Mary Englund's "An Indian Remembers" and Dara Culhane Speck on Alert Bay. Using the techniques in Chapter 4 for generating high-level names or abstractions, orchestrate the passages from Englund and Speck. In doing so, keep in mind that the passage from Englund is a transcript of a recorded interview with Mary Englund in which she recalls aspects of her life at a residential school in Mission, BC, in the early twentieth century.

**Exercise 4**

The following passage comes from an undergraduate textbook. What features of style distinguish it from a research publication? (This time the question is harder to answer, for the writer carefully accounts for the first appearance, later refinements, and eventual acceptance of current knowledge about "tribal" diets.) If you wanted to use this information in an inquiry into Western conceptions of *health*, how would you represent your source?

Smith correctly concluded that the lack of dental decay and tooth loss observed in the tribal peoples was due to increased tooth wear, which kept the teeth clean and polished. He attributed the increased wear to the consumption of less cooked and less refined food and the absence of knives and forks, which meant that more chewing was required, as well as the presence of grit or "dirt" in the food. It was later learned that the absence of refined carbohydrates also contributed to healthy tribal teeth. The reduced tooth wear of contemporary peoples who eat industrially processed foods is likely related to the common problem of impacted molars, as Grover Krantz (1978) has observed. People eating coarse foods wear down the grinding surfaces of their teeth, which creates enough jaw space to accommodate the third molars when they erupt. When there is no significant wear, these "wisdom teeth" often must be extracted.

The association between traditional dietary patterns and healthy teeth was documented more systematically in a series of field studies conducted by American dentist Weston Price (1945), between 1931 and 1936. Price visited some of the most traditional peoples in Amazonia, East Africa, Australia, and throughout the Pacific and found that tooth decay and periodontal disease were virtually absent among self-sufficient peoples but steadily increased as they adopted the food patterns of industrial societies.

In 1956, shortly after Price's dental research, T.I.. Cleave, a doctor in the British Royal Navy, used medical data on tribal peoples to isolate a single feature in the diets of industrialized people that caused what he called the "saccharine disease," a wide-ranging complex of conditions including tooth decay, ulcers, appendicitis, obesity, diabetes, constipation, and varicose veins. Like both Smith and Price before him, Cleave (1974) was impressed by the fact that tribal peoples did not suffer from many of the common ailments of civilization, and he attempted to find the special conditions that made the tribal peoples healthier. His primary finding was that the traditional foods of tribal groups were consistently much higher in dietary fiber than the highly refined complex carbohydrates consumed by industrialized peoples. Higher-fiber diets speed the transit time of food through the digestive system, thereby reducing many common diseases of civilization. It took many years for his findings to be incorporated into popular nutritional wisdom in the industrialized world, but now high fiber, along with low fat and low salt, is widely accepted as an important component of a healthy diet.

John H. Bodley 1997 *Cultural Anthropology: Tribes, States, and the Global System* 2nd ed. Mountain View, CA: Mayfield, 147–48.

## Exercise 5

Sometimes course books are not textbooks designed to introduce newcomers to a discipline but comprehensive and informative representations of a point of view. The next passage comes from such a book. What features distinguish it from a research publication? How might you introduce this writer to a scholarly conversation?

It may seem incredible that anyone in the Americas should perceive the continents' impoverished, largely marginalized indigenous peoples as a threat, but individuals and states are products of their history, even if they deny it. In countries where indigenous people form the majority or a substantial minority, the white, Western elite and the governments they dominate show the classic psychology of rich exploiters who have grown paranoid through fear or greed. "They know only too well what they have done to the Indian, and are paranoid that the Indian might one day do the same to them," says one Bolivian aid worker.

A complex racism was part of the institutionalization of the conquest, providing the historic rationale for human rights abuse. Medieval Hispanic concepts of "purity of blood" (*limpieza de sangre*) were transferred to the Indies, and American Spaniards became obsessed with classifying the various permutations of race. Racism, including cultural discrimination, became the ideological framework that justified the domination of the invaders and the subordination of the conquered.

Phillip Wearne 1996 *Return of the Indian: Conquest and Revival in the Americas.* London: Cassell, 64.

# Readers reading: Part one

Handbooks for writing recommend knowing your audience. This seems like sound advice. But who is your audience? How do you get to know your readers? What causes markers to react negatively rather than positively to a student's writing? To answer the latter question, we need to learn more about academic readers — their reading practices, values and expectations. The next two chapters will help us gain valuable information about our readers. But before we begin our examination of readers, let's look at the ways in which *social context* or *circumstance* affect how we use language and how people respond to us.

## 7A Who Do You Think You're Talking To?

In everyday conversation, we have a good idea of who our listener is: it's the person in front of us. Sometimes the person is a family member or a friend, and conversation is easy. Sometimes the person is a stranger, and this can make conversation more difficult. But usually we have some legitimate, acknowledged reason for addressing the stranger: they're a receptionist in a doctor's office; a sales clerk; a person enrolled in the same fitness class — we have information that enables us to address them usefully in the situation. In any case, once we get going, we check the listener's response; we make inferences, and adjust our emphases, themes, ways to address people.

Still, even face-to-face, we can sometimes struggle with inferences about our audience. Language and cognitive specialists study these efforts:

Herbert Clark's work on "audience design" (1992), for example, investigates people's habits of inference in addressing others, finding that conversation keeps us busy at various levels of consciousness as we estimate the frame of mind of our co-conversationalists and others who might overhear us. We estimate others' knowledge of the world, calculating the extent of **mutual knowledge** — what can be safely assumed and what needs to be explained. Some of Wallace Chafe's studies discover, in addition to these calculations, our ongoing estimates of **listeners' centre of attention**: what is in the spotlight for them, what has slipped into the shadows.

When we are writing, we can't see our audience in front of us, to watch their reactions, but often we know so much about them that we don't need to see them. For example, working in genres like the postcard or the personal letter, we normally have a reliable picture of our reader. Also, we have received postcards and letters ourselves, so we have experience of our own responses to certain forms, and also of the social occasions and expectations which call for postcards and letters.

On the other hand, when we are working in genres like the letter of complaint (e.g., to request compensation for a defective product) or the letter of application, we have, generally, much less information about our audience — except, probably, as a social type: a corporate employee handling public relations or a human resources director. If we have not ourselves received many or any complaints or applications, we can't rely on our own response to such documents when we make decisions about what to include, what to leave out, how to word things, and what order they should take. If, however, we are dedicated complainers or job applicants, we may be familiar with typical outcomes of our writing — redress or silence, offers or brush-offs. From these responses, we infer aspects of the situation and alter our approach for the next time.

How do student writers of university essays learn to position themselves in relation to their readers? How do student writers infer aspects of this situation? The exercise which follows can help you and your instructor talk about how you interpret your situation as a student writer.

---

### Exercise 1
In groups of three or four, discuss your answers to the questions below. Make notes of the answers and your discussion. You will need them for Exercise 2.

- What do you do and how do you feel when you get marked essays returned? For example, do you look at the grade, read the instructor's comments, throw the assignment out, re-read it, tear it to bits, show it to your friends?
- What do you consider typical marking commentary on essays? What kinds of things do markers say about your essays in particular?

Collaborate with other members of your group to compose a 300- to 400-word summary of your findings, accounting for differences and similarities in your habits and perceptions. Try to make a connection between your habits and attitudes upon having a marked essay returned to you and your ideas of professors' typical remarks. For example, if you celebrate the return of the essay, this may be directly related to professors typically expressing delight at particular aspects of your essays.

### Exercise 2

Using the information you have gathered in Exercise 1, and sharing your findings with other members of the class, locate the student writer's distance from or proximity to their markers: in what sense do student writers "know" those who read and mark their work — as friends, acquaintances, strangers, social types? Is the student writer's experience of the *academic* genres like that of the writer of the postcard or like that of the writer of the job application? From the information you have collected in Exercise 1, what inferences would you make about the situation, and about academic readers? How do you picture readers of your essays? How do these readers read? What do you know about them, so far?

## 7B Attitudes Toward Language

Student writers can have negative opinions about readers' sincerity and open-mindedness. Sometimes they attribute a disappointing grade to insincere efforts and closed-mindedness on the part of their reader/marker. There are occasions when this assessment might be justified: in any writing context, we can find readers with agendas of their own, a bone to pick, or a chip on their shoulder.

But to dwell on the idiosyncrasy and resistance of markers is to lose sight of more productive characterizations of readers. As a first step in building a more helpful characterization of readers, we will consider academic readers' responses in a very broad context: that of *attitudes toward language* itself.

From several excerpts we read in earlier chapters, we have learned that people tend to have rather pejorative — and moralistic — attitudes toward unfamiliar ways of using language. Shieffelin and Doucet (excerpt from "The 'real' Haitian creole," 1994; see Chapter 3, pp. 48–49) report severe judgements about creole languages and their speakers: according to popular views, creole expression is not only incorrect and corrupt but also ugly and coarse. It's worth noticing that linguists themselves can be involved in perpetrating these views, and worth reminding ourselves of the political possibilities of scholarly activity and "expertise." But it's perhaps even more noteworthy that laypeople — non-experts — are confident and ready in their judgements of the status of other people's speech. It seems that when we learn language, we also acquire instruments for ranking other users of language. Deborah Cameron ("Moral Panic," 1995; see Chapter 5, pp. 83–84) considers these evaluative behaviours as part of the nature of language itself.

Just as we learn to rank others, we can also learn to rank ourselves. Pierre Bourdieu (1991) analyzes people's attitudes toward language as evidence of "**symbolic domination**": domination, that is, which operates not through physical coercion but through psychological/social processes. Undergoing these processes, people internalize the values that subordinate some members of society to the advantage of others. In effect, symbolic domination recruits people to the service of their own domination. Through their experience of schooling especially, but also from other social experience, people learn to disparage their own speech and writing, to suspect it of errors, and to feel intimidated by the speech of those whom they have been taught to regard as exemplary — usually the members of the privileged classes, or those who have spent a long time studying in institutions of higher learning. (So we could predict that many creole speakers will not only know how to speak creole but will also know how to rate their own speech as *low* in relation to that of speakers of Standard English or French.)

Outlining and reflecting on the origins and history of Standard English, James Milroy and Lesley Milroy (1991 [1985]) identify the "**complaint tradition": the cultural practice of publicly deploring the state of the language, announcing its decline from an earlier perfection (this ideal time usually coinciding with the complainer's own schooldays). Young people's speech and writing in particular are often the target of complaint. Milroy and Milroy trace the complaint tradition back several centuries, and other scholars have traced North American traditions of complaint about student writing to the 1880s at least, when changes in the social order in late nineteenth-century America resulted in new, middle-class populations seeking higher education — and meeting the disapproval of élite classes.

Instances of the complaint tradition are not hard to find. For example, in a recent opinion piece in a newspaper, a "[j]ournalist and biographer ... of William Shakespeare" condemns the Harry Potter books as simple and publicity-seeking only, as not deserving the excitement which attends them. The Harry Potter books, he says, are not like the Alice books, or the Simpsons, or other contemporary and excellent books and programs for children. Thrown into this severe evaluation of a popular series are some claims from the complaint tradition: (1) "Britain is a country with dramatically *declining standards of literacy*, increasingly dragged down to the lowest common denominator by the purveyors of all forms of mindless entertainment"; and (2) the object of the writer's disdain and the public's delight has "a pedestrian, *ungrammatical* prose style which has left [him] with a headache and a sense of a wasted opportunity" (emphasis added).

The complaint tradition has a long history and promises to persist into the future, despite scholarly efforts to discredit complainers. Either language is always and perpetually in decline, or complainers are always and perpetually complaining, no matter what. Referring to complaints and panics about standards of literacy, Milroy and Milroy also point out that there is no evidence to suggest that levels of literacy today are in decline.

Nevertheless, language remains the site of stigma, social ranking, and evaluation. We could think of speakers who disparage their own or others' speech and writing as participating in the political life of the language. Most commentators on this situation mention the role of education (as an institutional practice) in providing the experience and criteria for evaluating speech and writing. Without mass education, modern complainers would have fewer reasons and occasions for complaint, and speakers and writers would be less intimidated, and less susceptible to symbolic domination.

From this broad perspective on attitudes toward language, we can narrow our focus to the practices of academic readers. Like anyone else, academic readers and markers participate in the political life of the language. And because they work in highly specialized areas of research, they can be even more likely to participate in symbolic domination. Scholars rely on specialized terminology, abstractions, and other particular ways of speaking and writing in order to create knowledge, to debate it, and to maintain their own status as researchers and experts.

It's possible that some elements of the typical commentary that students get on their work (e.g., their writing is "sloppy," "careless," or "awkward") are motivated by ideas about standardized usage, including the complaint tradition. These aspects of commentary tend to be more informative about attitudes toward speech and writing, and about social ranking (teaching people to know their place), than about the writer's success as a participant in the scholarly conversation. We can regard this as useful information: in the long run, it is probably good to come into realistic contact with evaluative attitudes toward language. As Bourdieu points out, "linguistic relativism" (any usage is as good as any other) can be "naïve" (1991:52–53). But continuous contact with evaluative attitudes can also overshadow more practical information about readers' expectations of scholarly writing.

## 7C Traditions of Commentary on Student Writing

Genre theory — the idea, that is, that typical ways of speaking and writing enable typical social activities — suggests that different writing situations will call for different forms of expression. By now, we are well aware that the research genres display features which are not necessarily unique to them but which are arranged in ways that distinguish research writing from other kinds of writing. And we are noticing that the research genres differ amongst themselves: marine biology has things in common with archaeology but has ways of speaking that it doesn't share with archaeology; anthropology resembles psychology in some ways but not in others. Diverse ways of doing research tend toward diverse ways of using language.

The complaint tradition, on the other hand, presupposes that where variety exists, there is only *one* correct form (Milroy and Milroy (1991 [1985]). These **unitary views** of language produce their own genres: handbooks of usage, for example ("Improve your English with this handy and authoritative reference text!"). We could also call the marker commentary on student essays a "genre," one traditionally supported by unitary views of language. Composition textbooks often provide their users (students and teachers alike) with marking symbol guides: *run-on, gr, awk, logic, vague, ww* (= "wrong word"), *org* (= organization), *evidence*. Designed to operate universally across genres, the symbols can suggest that "[lack of] logic" or "vagueness" is identifiable regardless of reader or situation. Traditional advice given to students on their essays often mention "argument" (you need one), "evidence" (you need this for your argument), and "details" (you need these to support your argument). But these all-purpose terms can be misleading. In her study of writing in history, Sharon Stockton (1995) found that

> "[a]ll faculty agreed ... that *argument* is the key word for good writing and that the absence of argument constitutes the central problem in students' written work" (50), but that expectations differed depending on students' level, and "[i]n fact, faculty assignments, grades, and comments on student papers seem to imply that explicit argument as such was not the central issue of concern" (51). Despite professors' calls for *argument*, "[u]ltimately, assignments and evaluations show that written sophistication in student writing was in this department a function of *narrative* complexity" — "a certain specialized form of narrative" (52). When professors said "argument," they had a variety of other things in mind.

Janet Giltrow 2000 "'Argument' as a term in talk about student writing." In *Learning to Argue in Higher Education*, ed. S. Mitchell and R. Andrews. Portsmouth, NH: Boynton Cook/ Heinemann, 132–33.

In this case, traditional advice on (or complaint about) student writing was misleading. In other situations, traditional commentary can usefully represent a reader's uneasiness, and yet fail to point to the particular conditions which would satisfy the reader's expectations. For example, a literature professor, reading a student's essay for a Shakespeare class, wrote "evidence?" in the margin next to the writer's claim: "In the absence of the romantic bond, Othello's life would lose much of its meaning, and he would revert to his role as a 'soldier for pay'." When asked to explain his comment, he elaborated:

> "There are a number of problems there; I asked for evidence. I am asking for evidence as to whether [Othello] was ever spoken of in those terms by anyone including himself as a 'soldier for pay' because that has certain connotations to it and he is a general after all. Is 'soldier for pay' a formulation which matches someone's view of Othello in the play? Is there any evidence that he loses the romantic bond? That this would happen? That he would go back to being a general?"
>
> Giltrow 2000: 134.

Here the traditional comment "evidence?" unfortunately obscures a particular marker's more complete and informative response: a reader of a literature essay needed to hear some voice from the play corroborating the student writer's prediction about Othello. Using general terms like "evidence," marginal commentary can fail to express the reader's **genre-specific expectations** — in this case, the literary-critical expectation that the student writer's statements will be woven with wordings from the original text. In a different research genre, "evidence" would mean something else.

Sometimes traditional notations can appear contradictory. For example, an academic reader sometimes asks for "specifics" in the presence of specifics: a student writes in a paper for a course in the sociology of the environment, "our water comes from a metal tap and flows down a metal drain … we drive over concrete roads and highways"; and the professor responds, "This is the point at which I wonder when it's going to get more specific" (reported in Giltrow 2000:136). In this case, the "specifics" the student has offered failed to impress the reader of a sociology paper. But if used in another genre — for example, in an "essay" question on a language-proficiency examination — these "specifics" could inspire a positive response.

It is possible that traditional marking commentary can go on at *too high a level of abstraction* to be entirely informative to writers; as the above examples show, traditional notations can transmit misleading, incomplete, or contradictory information. This high level of abstraction and generality no doubt has its own social function: it suggests a unanimity, a consensus about what "good" writing is (it is "clear," "coherent," "logical"; it has an "argument"), a solidarity amongst authoritative readers. The idea that "good" writing can be identified and characterized in these ways is no doubt comforting to markers. Yet student writers remain puzzled by these responses in the margins of their papers.

We can see that traditional commentary has its shortcomings. For one thing, it can be influenced by the ideologies of language which produce the **complaint tradition** — deeply held views about correctness and commitments to protecting the language from the (perceived) mess its users make of it. Taking traditional commentary to heart, writers might come to think of writing mainly as a struggle to reach an inaccessible ideal: their sentences will never be good enough. But more important perhaps is the generality of commentary, suggesting a timeless and universal standard for expression, when, in fact, even in the research disciplines, diversity and change prevail.

Rather than give up on feedback altogether, we can work on developing techniques for giving and getting useful response to writing. The techniques we concentrate on in the following sections focus on *the reader's experience of using the text*: how the reader understands, anticipates, makes meaning. We find out about how readers behave when they meet words, sentences, paragraphs. From this information, we draw a portrait of the reader.

## 7D Alternative to Traditional Commentary: The Think-Aloud Protocol

People studying readers' behaviour try to find out about reading comprehension: how do readers get messages from texts? What kind of writing makes the message obscure? What kind makes it clear? You can probably imagine that this kind of research is not easy. If we want to find out about how people obey traffic signals, we can put ourselves at an intersection and watch cars speeding up, slowing down, stopping, and then going again. But how can we watch people read?

To catch readers in the act, researchers have devised ways of measuring small physical signs of reading, like eye movement. And other measures try to get at comprehension itself by asking readers questions about what they have read, or asking them to do other tasks connected with their reading.

Another technique for researching the reading process is the **think-aloud protocol**. The think-aloud method (Warren 1988) asks subjects to report the ideas that are going through their heads as they perform a task, like writing an essay or reading one. Think-aloud reports are like eyewitness testimony of events that researchers can't witness themselves. Rather than using typical marking expressions, such as "wrong word" or "faulty diction," readers simply report what is going through their heads as they come to an understanding of what they are reading. With this kind of report available, writers can decide what revisions might benefit readers.

The think-aloud protocol resembles forms of usability testing of documents. In the process of composing manuals, instructions, information bulletins, and other genres, technical writers sometimes test their documents' efficiency by having them read out loud — by people who might purchase software, for example, or citizens who might seek information about a government program, or car owners who might need to know about a vehicle recall. As they read aloud, the subjects report their understanding, and their difficulties. In light of these reports, and informed about where other readers are likely to have trouble, writers then revise (or not — there have been some studies on when and whether technical writers actually *do* revise after usability testing). The think-aloud protocol is thus both an instrument of research and a tool for professional writers.

It can also contribute to students' conceptions of their readers, as research conducted by Karen Schriver (1994 [1992]) has shown. Gathering her subjects from senior writing classes and dividing them into experimental and control groups, Schriver provided the experimental group with ten transcripts, over a six-week period, of readers using written instructions for aspects of operating a computing system. In the meantime, the control group was taught audience analysis and text design by more traditional methods.

In the following excerpt from a transcript (bold type), a reader reports his thoughts (italics) while reading:

> *OK, now I'm going to try* ... **Commands for English Text. EMACS enables you to manipulate words, sentences, or paragraphs of text.** *These commands sound like the ones I'd use all the time — good.* **In**

addition, there are commands to fill text, and convert case. *I don't know what it means to fill text. I guess it means putting data from one text into another ... that is, filling the text with what you want in it. Well, I guess I'll soon find out.*

Editing files of text in a human language *human language? Boy that sounds strange, what could they be distinguishing here? Maybe computer language or machine language from human language?* ought to be done using Text mode rather than Fundamental mode. *Well, I don't know what text mode or fundamental mode is, so how will I know which I'm in? Let's see ...* Invoke M-X Text Mode to enter Text mode. *I won't do that because I do not have time to see the other section. That's terrible to tell me to ...* See section 20.1 [Major Modes], p. 85

Karen Schriver 1994 (1992) "What document designers can learn from usability testing." *Technostyle* 19 (3/4): 22 (emphasis added).

Testing at the beginning of the study showed that the two groups were equivalent in their ability to predict when readers would have trouble with what they were reading. Testing after six weeks of instruction found that, while the control group had not changed in their ability to predict readers' difficulties, the experimental group's ability to identify where actual readers had in fact had trouble understanding what they were reading improved by 62 per cent. Improving dramatically in the accuracy of their analyses, these students also changed in the way they talked about problems: their remarks became more reader-centred or "I"-centred ("readers might not see the connection here," "I don't understand this word") and less text-centred ("this paragraph is too long"). The control group changed much less in this dimension of analysis.

## 7E Adapting the Think-Aloud Protocol in the Writing Classroom

Think-aloud can be practiced on any piece of writing, for any piece of writing is a document to be used, in some way, and readers can report their experience of making use of it. This method can be adapted for use in the academic writing classroom.

Like technical writers observing a person working with a draft of a software manual, we observe a reader working with an instance of schol-

arly writing — a summary, a proposal, a research paper. From these observations, we learn where potential readers may have problems with a
particular piece of writing. But we also learn about more than just particular sentences in particular writings. As Schriver's research shows, writers
can also learn from think-alouds when the read-aloud text is not their
own: overhearing a reader working on someone else's writing, they gain
experience which they can use to sketch their portrait of the reader.
Schriver's research suggests that this kind of close-up experience of readers' behaviours can be generalized — to anticipate readers' responses to
our own work-in-progress, to explain responses to previous work, to help
us plan future work.

Thinking out loud while reading doesn't necessarily come naturally.
For one thing, most thinkers-aloud have long experience of traditional
marking commentary and, in their first attempts, are liable to reproduce
its sounds ("this is well organized," "there should be a thesis statement,"
"this flows"). And, face-to-face with the writer, thinkers-aloud may be
tempted to praise, contracting perhaps for praise in return. It's also tempting to just read, and not comment.

Recognizing that readers may not be sure of how to break the silence, we
have developed models and guidelines for thinking aloud. The model below has been used in research studies. Here an instructor is thinking aloud
as she reads (original text, in bold; reader thinking aloud, in italics):

> **The purpose of this paper will be to show how the representation
> of Africans can be extended to the representation of women in
> *Heart of Darkness* written by Joseph Conrad.** *This sounds like the
> essay question to me. That's not terrible, but I find I don't really pay
> attention when I hear the sound of an essay question.* "The Heart of
> Darkness *written by Joseph Conrad"* — *that sounds as if I don't know
> Conrad wrote* Heart of Darkness. *I'd prefer something like "Conrad's*
> Heart of Darkness." **This will be accomplished by the analysis of
> the inhuman role of women in the story,** *"the inhuman role of
> women"* — *I stop there* — *the women behave in a non-human way?
> that doesn't seem to be right* — *oh, maybe. I'm thinking of Kurtz's "In-
> tended" … "inhuman"? oh well …* **the supremacy imposed upon
> them, and their physical attributes which emit a darker figure of
> the human woman.** *"supremacy"? in what sense? I think I see what
> he's getting at, but it's hard work getting through this sentence: what*

*does "supremacy" have to do with "inhuman" and then "darker figure"?*
*"human woman"? Maybe the body ... there could be something here in*
*the disparity between dark interpretations of the body and interpreta-*
*tions of woman as supreme ideal, but this whole first paragraph re-*
*minds me of the introduction to a five-paragraph essay: thesis statement,*
*three points.*

We also provide explicit guidelines for those who will be responding in
instructional situations — students, teaching assistants, professors.

### Guidelines for readers

You are not a marker/evaluator; you are a person *using* a document.
You make *no judgements*; you only report what's going on in your
mind.

As you read, report moments when you're working inefficiently —
not understanding.

| But rather than saying ... | aim for ... |
|---|---|
| this is ungrammatical | *I'm having trouble with this sentence. There's something about it that makes me stop. I've read this sentence twice. Now I'm going on but I'm still not sure ....* |
| this is the wrong word | *This word makes me stop. Why do you say "social" agenda? That's a positive term to me, but you seem to be using it in a negative way.* |
| | *I don't really know what "peer review" means.* |
| | *I have no idea.* |
| there's no thesis statement | *OK, I'm through the first paragraph, but I can't really say what you're going to focus on. Is it the public perception, or the corporate model? I hope I find out in the next paragraph.* |

> *I'm through the first paragraph, and*
> *I figure you see a connection between the*
> *"back-to-basics" idea and the*
> *"standardization" Zieber mentions.*
> *I think you're going to talk about that.*

repetition

> *I think you already said this — or*
> *did I get it wrong? Is there some-*
> *thing different here and I missed it?*

no transition

> *I'm having a hard time making*
> *a connection between this paragraph*
> *and this one — this is about the*
> *university's "service agenda" and this*
> *one is about "depersonalization." Is*
> *the connection that they're both*
> *individualistic? That's my guess but I*
> *don't know if that's what you intend.*
> *It's hard work here.*

the main point should
be at the start

> *Oh now I see what you're saying.*
> *I'm going to go back and re-read*
> *to see if I missed something.*

As you read, report moments when you're working efficiently — understanding, getting new ideas of your own:

> **who learns and why** *yes I see that — the "who" is about access, and*
> *that's a question of social class and the distribution of wealth, and the*
> *"why" is about the role of knowledge in the society, or in the economy.*
> *I'm thinking it's also "what" — if you put the who and the why to-*
> *gether you start to go towards the answer to the "what" — what should*
> *be taught?*

Offer frequent reports of the **gist** of what you're reading:

> *OK so far I have this main idea in mind: the Zieber article might seem*
> *more radical but it's actually more traditional. That's what I'm getting*
> *from this.*

Our earlier discussion of the complaint tradition and symbolic domination might lead you to suppress all notice of what appear to you to be

"errors" in spelling or grammar. But if you *do* notice something, say so! It's part of your experience of using the piece of writing, and useful information for the writer. If spelling and grammar turn out to be tremendous obstacles to your appreciation of the writer's intentions, then you need to report this circumstance. But you might also try to report the degree to which missing apostrophes or odd spellings are confounding your efforts to find meaning:

> *I notice that "is" comes after "institution and government" — that should be "are," I think, but it's not stopping me ...*

> *I've lost this sentence, I thought it was ending. Now I see a comma, so I'm going back to re-read ...*

By giving the writer the measure of difficulty — "it's minor, so fixing this isn't going to make much difference over all"; or, "it's a big block, so it had better be attended to" — you make "grammar" a matter of the *reader's experience* of the text, rather than a matter of living up to the rules for correctness.

And to these suggestions for readers, we add guidelines for writers, encouraging them to take advantage of this opportunity to see what happens when their writing is out in the world, on its own, without their recommendation or apology.

### Guidelines for writers

> You don't need to explain or justify what you've done. Instead, value the chance to watch someone making meaning from what you've written. Listen carefully to your reader's comments. Take notes. Your reader's response will guide your revision strategies.

Earlier in this chapter, we said that think-aloud can be practiced on any piece of writing. Here is an example of an experienced academic reader thinking-aloud as she reads a passage from Ian Hunter's 1988 book, *Culture and Government*:

> **Unlike classical education** *I guess I have a general idea of what this is, although I'm not sure how he sees it in this context,* **Romantic aesthetic education** *I'm stopping here, "Romantic aesthetic education", does that mean that "Romantic education" was aesthetic? or that "aes-*

*thetics" was one branch of Romantic education? I think it's the latter* was directed at the individual's aesthetico-ethical organisation *"aesthetico-ethical," I don't like "o" suffixes, but lots of people use them; so this would be moral development going along with learning to appreciate beauty* — at producing *here is an explanation* a synthesis out of the divided "ethical substance" *I stop there, what is that? I'm just going back, maybe I missed something, no … ;* and this practice of ethical reconciliation has indeed passed into the modern teaching of English. *I don't understand the "divided substance" but I have a hunch about reconciliation — not that I could explain this to anyone, so far* Unlike the latter, however, *OK the romantic idea is different from the modern one* the Romantic aesthetics of self-cultivation was for most of the nineteenth century a more or less voluntary "practice of the self" *"practice of the self," not sure what that is but I like the sound of it, I guess it's equivalent to "self-cultivation," improving yourself, something you do on your own initiative,* confined to caste groupings at one remove from the emerging machinery of popular education *it was something the élite did, I think that's it, although "one remove" sounds not very far away and the élite would be very far away from the classes served by "popular education," maybe I don't use "at one remove" the proper way. OK it was élite practice, I think that's it, but I wish there were a specific — what groups of people did this, what did they do? Maybe it doesn't matter that I don't know what "divided substance" is; I'm not sure what it has to do with the élite being separate from the masses. But I get the general idea that …*

What should the writer do with the reader's commentary? Well, he doesn't have to do anything: his book is published, and he is well known. But when we overhear this commentary, we learn about the difficulties a reader can have when she encounters many complicated, high-level abstractions and no lower-level mentions.

---

**Exercise 3**

Passage 1 below is the opening section of a literary narrative, written in a fairly traditional "realist" style. Guided by the suggestions and models above, practice think-aloud: read Mistry's text aloud, stopping and reporting those moments when you experience an unusual effort to understand (after a word, phrase, sentence, end of paragraph), including places where you need to re-read, question and speculate, or want to offer ideas of your own. Do this exercise with a partner; remember to read and report aloud.

## PASSAGE 1

The morning express bloated with passengers slowed to a crawl, then lurched forward suddenly, as though to resume full speed. The train's brief deception jolted its riders. The bulge of humans hanging out of the doorway distended perilously, like a soap bubble at its limit.

Inside the compartment, Maneck Kohlah held on to the overhead railing, propped up securely within the crush. He felt someone's elbow knock his textbooks from his hand. In the seats nearby, a thin fellow was catapulted into the arms of the man opposite him. Maneck's textbooks fell upon them.

"Ow!" said the young fellow, as volume one slammed out of his lap and back onto the seat. "Everything all right, Om?"

"Apart from the dent in my back, everything is all right," said Omprakash Darji, picking up the two books covered in brown paper. He hefted them in his slender hands and looked around to find who had dropped them.

Maneck acknowledged ownership. The thought of his heavy textbooks thumping that frail spine made him shudder. He remembered the sparrow he had killed with a stone, years ago; afterwards, it had made him sick.

His apology was frantic. "Very sorry, the books slipped and —"

"Not to worry," said Ishvar. "Wasn't your fault." To his nephew he added, "Good thing it didn't happen in reverse, hahn? If I fell in your lap, my weight would crack your bones." They laughed again, Maneck too, to supplement his apology.

Ishvar Darji was not a stout man; it was the contrast with Omprakash's skinny limbs that gave rise to their little jokes about his size. The wisecracks originated sometimes with one and sometimes the other. When they had their evening meal,

Ishvar would be sure to spoon out a larger portion onto his nephew's enamel plate; at a roadside dhaba, he would wait till Omprakash went for water, or to the latrine, then swiftly scoop some of his own food onto the other leaf.

If Omprakash protested, Ishvar would say, 'What will they think in our village when we return? That I starved my nephew in the city and ate all the food myself? Eat, eat! Only way to save my honour is by fattening you!'

Rohinton Mistry 1995 "Prologue: 1975." *A Fine Balance.* Toronto: McClelland & Stewart, 3–4.

Passage 2 below is the opening section of an article about Jamaican Creole, and attitudes toward that language. In contrast to Mistry's style in the passage above, this passage is written in a scholarly style. Guided by the suggestions and models above, practice think-aloud: read Wassink's text aloud, stopping and reporting those moments when you experience an unusual effort to understand (after a word, phrase, sentence, end of paragraph), including places where you need to re-read, question and speculate, or want to offer ideas of your own. Do this exercise with a partner; remember to read and report aloud.

## PASSAGE 2

Recent discussion among both Jamaican scholars and laypeople suggests that Jamaicans' attitudes toward Jamaican Creole (hereafter JC) are changing.[1] This change, some suggest, has accompanied the increased popularity of Dancehall culture and nationalistic "consciousness raising" efforts (Christie 1995, Shields-Brodber 1997).[2] Concurrent with these revisionist efforts, there came a call in 1989 by the (Jamaican) National Association of Teachers of English (NATE) to validate JC in the schools. This event reflected movement at an institutional, policy-making level, while the rise of Dancehall operated at the level of popular culture. Such a shift in attitudes toward "things Jamaican" marks a significant conceptual reorientation, in light of the high esteem that historically has been given to British culture, and more recently to American culture.

## A history of low prestige

It has been said that language is the theater for the enacting of the social, political, and cultural life of a people, as well as the embodiment of that drama (Alleyne 1993). After roughly 150 years of Spanish occupation, Jamaica came under British control in 1655. English became the language of prestige and power on the island, reflecting the social status of its users, while the emergent Creole was regarded as the fragmented language of a fragmented people.[3] One theory of creole genesis holds that, because slaves were transported to the West Indies from a number of different ethnic groups along the western coast of Africa, they shared no common language; thus, in the new colony, they acquired a simplified variety of English in order to communicate with their British rulers and one another, while retaining no West African forms (Turner 1949; Alleyne 1984, Chap 6; Holm 1989:471–2). Historically, then, the speech of the slaves has been regarded as infantile by laypeople and linguists alike (Turner 1949) — as language that was not fully formed. It was not "proper" English; but then, because many of its lexical items resembled English ones, there was no reason to think it might be anything other than English.[4]

Language-internal clues also corroborate the low-prestige of JC. The language-internal phenomenon of pejoration, which has accompanied the emergence of many creole languages, has also figured into the history of Jamaican Creole "Patois." Lexical items from West African sources have taken on negative connotations, particularly in communities with large acrolect- or standard English-speaking populations. An example of one such pejoratized word is *nyam* "to eat", which has come to suggest an animal's way of eating rather than eating in a general sense. When used to describe human eating, *nyam* connotes sloppy or uncultivated devouring of food, as in "Don't *nyam* your dinner" (Alleyne 1976), or, "He had to *nyam* and scram!"

In a socio-linguistic investigation of attitudes toward a language variety that arose out of contact among groups of people coexisting under conditions of unequal power, it must be recognized that such social conditions affected the context of development of the new language. Research has shown that attitudes toward language can be markedly polarized and tightly held — both institutionally and personally, openly and internally.

*Notes*

1   Linguists tend to refer to this language as "Jamaican Creole," but it is widely referred to as "Patois" by native speakers. The two terms will be used interchangeably in this paper, particularly because the term "Patois" was widely used by respondents in the interviews reported.

2   Briefly, "Dancehall" is a largely urban working-class phenomenon in vernacular Jamaican culture, associated with styles of dance, music, clothing — and (important in this context) lyrics that strongly favor Jamaican Creole (Cooper 1993).

3   Interested readers are directed to Lepage 1960 and Cassidy 1961 for introductions to the history of the island which discuss issues of linguistic development.

4   Taylor (1963:804) gives an example of how lexical correspondence and similar phonological form have mistakenly been taken as adequate grounds for assuming that the grammatical categories of one language (French) operate in another (Martinican Creole).

Alicia Beckford Wassink 1999 "Historic low prestige and seeds of change: Attitudes toward Jamaican Creole." *Language in Society* 28: 57–92, 57–58.

## Exercise 4

After reading and thinking-aloud about the passages in Exercise 3, answer the following questions:

- What have I learned about my own reading practices?
- What expectations do I have when reading literary narratives as opposed to reading scholarly work?
- What have I learned about the reading practices of others?

## 7F   Reading on Behalf of Others

Classroom situations bring to light some special conditions of think-aloud response. Readers who are fellow students or the instructor share with the writer certain knowledge of the immediate scholarly situation: readings, assignments, circumstances exclusive to that course. Consider the following first sentence of an essay, and two possible comments on the part of the marker:

> The four articles have in common a focus on the experience of marginalized identities in times of social change.

> Traditional commentary:      *What articles?*

> Think-aloud commentary:      *I know which articles you're referring to, but others wouldn't.*

For the student writer, the "traditional" remark "what articles?" can seem odd. After all, the marker *knows* about the articles.

A reader who is trying to avoid traditional commentary may choose to keep quiet at points like those exemplified above. After all, she *does* know which articles the writer is referring to. But readers are reading on behalf of other readers: people who have not been in this class and are unfamiliar with the reading list. So think-aloud includes one's own reactions and the reactions of readers whose difficulty in understanding is predictable. Similarly, in reading the following sentence, a marker encounters a specialist term which has been thoroughly discussed in class:

> Chavez's work (1994) on undocumented immigrants offers new perspectives on **transnational communities**.

The instructor marking the essay might respond with a traditional instruction: "Define." Since the marker was present during discussion, and has read the materials being discussed, this too can seem odd. Or it can be taken as a blanket directive to define everything in sight, no matter how apparently well known. A thinker-aloud might also stop and report at this point, not because they don't know the meaning of "transnational community" but because they sense the possibility of another reader — another participant in scholarly discussion — coming across this specialist term. They want the meaning of the specialist term to be established to accommodate readers who were not privy to the classroom discussion.

These are the conditions that trigger the **appositives** we discussed in Chapter 5. If, thinking aloud in response to a fellow student's writing, you find yourself concerned about others' understanding, report your estimate of a possible difficulty on behalf of other readers.

What does this say specifically about student writing in the university? It suggests an awareness of the way in which academic writing does not just respond to the immediate concerns of a given course, but bridges the gap between the classroom and a broader research situation: the instructor-reader needs to see the writing relating to the larger conversation that the course intersects with.

Above, we saw how traditional commentary taking the form of a question — "what articles?" — might confuse a student writer. In fact, markers often respond with questions. A study conducted with five writers responding online to one another's work showed the ambiguity of reader questions (Cowan et al. 1998). As the researchers worked on analyzing responses and measuring the revisions which resulted, they found that the meaning of the questions could be ambiguous.

> Text:     According to Kabeer, following Giddens, community
>           membership is made up of both rules *and* resources.
> Marker:   *What's the difference?*

In this example, does the question mean that the reader *doesn't know* what the difference is between "rules" and "resources"?

> *What's the difference?* meaning: I don't know what the difference is.

Or is the question really an instruction to do something?

> *What's the difference?* meaning: You should define these terms and explain the difference.

Or is the question a sign of the reader engaging with the point?

> *What's the difference?* meaning: I'm thinking that the *difference* is complicated. Maybe a "rule" can be a "resource" in some circumstances. I wonder if the "rule" about female seclusion could be a "resource" contributing to ethnic identity.

When reporting a question in think-aloud protocols, try to specify your intentions:

- I don't know what this is.

- I can imagine readers appreciating seeing this briefly discussed.

- You've made me think about this, and now I wonder …

## 7G   Reliability of Readers

How far can you count on your thinking-aloud reader? What if your reader is not particularly experienced in the genre in which you are writing? What if you are inexperienced and the reader is as inexperienced as you are? What if you are asked to think aloud on a paper for a social geography course, and you have never seen a paper or taken a course in social geography before?

> *If you are the reader*, declare your position: *"I don't even know what social geography is…. I don't know anything about social geography, but still I'd say that it's hard to see how this paragraph relates to what you say in your introduction … now this seems to repeat what you've said before … OK what you're saying is…."*

> *If you are the writer*, consider the source: this is a novice's effort to understand what you have written. The novice will have some experience of scholarly writing, and their responses will still be valuable.

All think-aloud responses to a piece of writing are inevitably formed by the reader's particular position in the world, a position that includes personal experiences, interests, disciplinary affiliation, political leanings, and many other factors.

We might wonder, then, how idiosyncratic responses are, overall. In the study mentioned above (Cowan et al. 1998), the researchers were particularly interested in the degree to which readers' independent responses agree. They found that, during the four-month period of the study, agreement amongst readers increased. It seems that being in earshot of readers reading, thinkers-aloud developed a sense of a larger audience and became spokespersons for that audience, which included them but also went beyond them. Without explicit coaching to do so, readers began to read on behalf of others, or their ways of expressing their responses made them more representative of others' reactions. This is a limited finding, but enough to encourage the practice of listening in on other writers getting feedback.

As Schriver's research on think-aloud protocols shows, writers can learn about readers by examining and considering transcripts of readers' responses to others' writing. With this benefit in mind, we've included an example of think-aloud responses by experienced readers of academic writing at the end of Chapter 8.

---

### Exercise 5

The excerpt below is the beginning section of a student paper. Practice thinking-aloud with a partner, using the suggestions and model above: read out loud, stop and report your thinking. When you experience difficulty in understanding, stop and report this difficulty; when you are reading efficiently, report this experience.

Everyone has their own definition of community. For some people it is the place they grew up. For others it is the place they live and work in. Anderson says community is "imagined" (quoted in Chavez 1994). But what is community? Webster's (1987) defines community as "a unified body of individuals; ... the people with common interests living in a particular area; ... an interacting population of various kinds of individuals ... in a common location." What happens to a community when its original basis, the idea people have of its founding and its reason for existing, is threatened? In this paper I will investigate one such case: coastal communities where fishing has been a way of life and now the salmon stocks are greatly reduced and, in some cases the fishery has been closed.

# 8

# Readers reading: Part two

Chapter 7 put us in touch with our readers. The **think-aloud protocol**, an alternative method of giving reader feedback, put us in hearing range of the reading process, and revealed that readers employ a variety of strategies for understanding while reading. We've seen that prevailing attitudes about language affect speakers' judgements about usage. And the particular context or circumstance for reading affects readers' expectations and reception of a written document. This chapter extends our study of readers by looking at various theories about reading and interpretation. Understanding readers' **cognitive** and **social responses** will help us draw a more accurate portrait of our readers; in turn, we'll become better predictors of their particular needs. To this end, we'll continue practicing think-aloud protocols, and, in this chapter, learn to analyze and convert reader feedback into strategies for revision.

## 8A Think-Aloud and Genre Theory

Writers know — or get to know — how to write in ways that will satisfy a situation, and readers read in ways that include their recognition of a situation. **Genre theory** begins with this tendency: the mutual recognition of and responses to recurring types of situations. It's not rules and enforcements that make writing acceptable but *contact* with recognizable instances. Genre theory finds the *regularities* (not rules) of writing in readers' and writers' *social experience*.

Think-aloud techniques coax out this readerly know-how. By focusing on readers' experience of reading — readers' efforts to understand — think-aloud articulates what would otherwise remain unspoken. The focus is on what works for readers, what they expect, rather than on what satisfies rules. If you, as writer, receive think-aloud protocols from several different readers, over time you will be able to identify occasions where readers typically have trouble, as well as those occasions where the trouble may be more or less idiosyncratic. Think-alouds also reveal both social and cognitive occasions for trouble. The following two examples of think-aloud illustrate the difference between a social response and a cognitive response.

The example below shows a reader stopping at an unqualified or unattributed claim.

| Text: | Reader thinking-aloud: |
|---|---|
| For centuries, women had no alternative but to marry or go into religious orders. | *Well that might have been true in some cases but there were alternatives, a woman could become the housekeeper of a widowed father or brother for example, and different areas of Europe…* |

The think-aloud response reveals a particular reader's position, which is conditioned by a particular experience in the world. This reader expects to find complexity, limitation, readiness for exceptions when she reads scholarly writing, expectations that typify writing in the research genres. Other readers — ones experienced in journalistic genres, for example — might not stop at all at this statement. Other social expectations would condition their response in reading.

How could the writer assist a reader with this sort of response? Perhaps simply acknowledging exceptions would help: e.g., "For centuries, women had *few* alternatives but to marry or go into religious orders." Or, perhaps, introducing reporting expressions (see Chapter 2) and identifying the generalization as coming from a given researcher would help the reader see that the claim is part of a conversation.

Sometimes, however, a reader might stop for reasons we could see as more cognitive than social — that is, a problem with understanding that would likely cause almost anybody to stop. The following example relates to a passage we encountered in Chapter 3. In the original study,

Counts and Counts distinguish between "boondockers," who park their recreational vehicles — usually for free and unofficially — on (US) federal lands and "private-park RVers," who stay in organized, commercial facilities. In the example below a reader looks for connections between statements: a reason for the second sentence to appear in the context of the first.

| Text: | Reader thinking-aloud: |
|---|---|
| RVers have pot-luck dinners, and they exchange addresses before they hit the road again. "Private-park" RVers object to the way "boondockers" live. | *oh…what's the connection between these statements? pot-luck and addresses, that sounds like friendliness, but then there are objections. Maybe the boondockers don't have pot-luck dinners? Is that why the private-park people object? Or maybe both types of RVers have rituals but they don't get together? Is that the contradiction here? I don't know. I need some help.* |

Having no guide from the writer, the reader struggles on her own. This could be seen as a cognitive response — a reaction which records efforts at reasoning.

How could the writer of the example on RVers assist a reader with this sort of cognitive response? Research done in the early 1980s suggests that readers take cues from higher-level content in interpreting details, and in storing the meaning of those details (see Section 3B on levels of generality). The think-aloud response above indicates that a difficulty arises when the reader tries to understand the relation between details: address exchanges and potlucks seem positive, but objecting to how boondockers live seems negative. This cognitive need can be addressed by introducing **abstractions** which instruct the reader in how to use or relate the details.

> RVers have pot-luck dinners, and they exchange addresses before they hit the road again. **Yet this reciprocity occurs alongside stigmatization**. "Private-park" RVers object to the way "boondockers" live.

Now pot-luck and address-exchange mean "reciprocity," and reciprocity is posed as at least partly conflicting with "stigmatization." The scholarly practices of abstraction we explored in earlier chapters are not just formalities: they have important cognitive functions as guides for readers, directives to understanding.

Understanding and anticipating reader's cognitive needs will be further explored in Section 8B ("The mental desktop") below. But first, the social needs of readers warrant further study. In the example of a social response involving the historical roles of women, the reader expresses concern based on the social expectation that academic writing will be careful about exceptions and qualifications. As we noted, this is not a response that all readers would have. Readers with different expectations may accept this sort of generalization. In this sense, the response is social and not exactly cognitive. But in the example involving the RVers, while the response is clearly cognitive — an attempt to understand how details relate to one another — the suggestion to use abstractions to help a reader seems to rely on social expectations. For example, a reader accustomed to journalistic rather than academic genres might pause over the abstractions "reciprocity" and "stigmatization."

As we have seen in Chapter 5 (Section 5D, "The social profile of abstractions and their roles in different disciplines"), **abstractions** have a social as well as a cognitive aspect. For instance, in the humanities and some social sciences, some abstractions enjoy more prestige than others; these abstractions seem to have a current career in the life of the discipline, as meanings are challenged and changed over time. By contrast, in the sciences and (again) in some social sciences, technical abstractions are often the product of collaborative effort amongst researchers; the circumstances in which they are used are widely agreed upon, and their meanings remain stable over time.

As useful as abstractions can be, not all genres call for them. We have seen that narrative may touch abstractions only intermittently, and in some cases not at all. Telephone books have high-level, generalizing titles — "Calgary," "San Diego" — and then plunge into details of names and addresses and phone numbers. How do people manage with genres like telephone books, when they seem to have trouble with mention of pot-luck dinners?

People using telephone books don't read, stop, and say "I'm having trouble with this. What's the connection here? What is this about?" They don't need high-level abstractions to guide their understanding of the details of names and addresses because they bring a question of their own to the page ("What's John's phone number?"). The question provides a context for interpretation. Conversely, readers of "RVers have pot-luck dinners" may not have a ready-made context of interpretation for this statement.

One way of understanding the contexts of interpretation and understanding is to apply **relevance theory**. The conditions which make a statement understandable are described by linguists Sperber and Wilson (1986) as having to do with relevance. The term "relevance," in its everyday sense, is easy to grasp: someone might say, regarding mention of pot-luck dinners, "How is this relevant?" But for Sperber and Wilson, the term also measures *degrees* of relevance: a statement is relevant in indirect relation to the effort it takes to find the context in which it is meaningful. The more processing effort it takes a reader to find a context for interpretation, the less relevant the statement is for that reader. For example, in the following —

> JANE: John, what's your phone number?
> JOHN: 888-9999

—"888-9999" is highly relevant to Jane because the context — Jane's question — is immediately accessible. It takes very little effort for Jane to find this context. On the other hand, the reader who encountered mention of private-parkers' criticisms of boondockers in the context of mention of pot-luck dinners and address-exchange has to make a much bigger effort to discover a larger context in which the criticism is meaningful.

We can apply relevance theory to **genre theory**. Some genres, serving contexts which both reader and writer recognize, can in part look like the pot-luck passage, where the connection between adjacent statements — the relevance of one to the other — is not clear on the surface. In reference genres, like encyclopaedias or computer manuals, sentences next to each other can seem to bear only a general relation to one another. Here is an entry from *The Encyclopaedia of Aquarium Fish* (Coffey 1977) for Brachygobius or "bumblebeefish":

> A native of Indian and south-east Asia. Has a yellow body with broad, vertical, dark brown or black bands. It is most at home and spends most of its time close to the bottom of the aquarium. (70)

This is generally about the bumblebeefish, but what is the connection between the fish's origin, its appearance, and its favourite spot? Does the author mean to say that, *because* of its dark-striped yellow body, the fish lurks at the bottom? What does the fish's colour have to do with the bottom of the aquarium? However, most readers would not ask such questions. The social use of encyclopaedia genres is such that readers bring information requirements with them ("What's a bumblebeefish? I have to do a report for school"), and these requirements contribute to the context for interpretation of details.

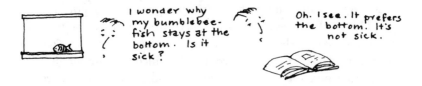

So the reader's *context of understanding* makes the sentence "It is most at home ... close to the bottom of the aquarium" relevant, and meaningful. (It has immediate contextual implications.)

Abstractions can also be analyzed for their relevance. Some abstractions are poised at the thresholds of many easily accessible contexts in certain disciplines. They can operate powerfully to make details meaningful, although all abstractions, in academic contexts at any rate, probably contribute to relevance. In this sense, the writer responding to the reader's cognitive need to understand the connection between pot-lucks and boondockers uses the abstractions "reciprocity" and "stigmatization" and builds a transition between two apparently contradictory details. At the same time, the abstractions also signal relevance by providing a context in which the details are potentially meaningful.

### Exercise 1

Working with a partner, read the following two passages aloud. As you read, stop and offer comments about what works for you, as reader, and what gives you difficulty. Offer also your expectations of the particular passage by drawing on your background experience, or lack thereof, with the genre. Now analyze the think-aloud commentary. Are particular difficulties or successes in reading and understanding connected to

- prevailing rules for "correctness"?
- relative experience with the genre?
- cognitive needs?
- social expectations?

How might the writers of the respective passages revise in order to address your responses?

### PASSAGE 1: THE BEGINNING OF A STUDENT ESSAY

Cameron's study of "verbal hygiene" (1995) shows that public concerns of grammar are related to political issues: controversy about grammar in school curriculum in Britain was furthered by political conflict. Milroy and Milroy (1991) show that concerns about grammar have a history and they are connected to the processes that "standardized" English. Both these sources show language in public debate. How do these concerns show up in private discussions? In this essay I will examine a study done by Verkuyten, De Jong and Masson (1994) to find cases where language is an issue for the inner-city residents talking about ethnic minorities. I will also look at ways that ideas about language are the same as or different from ideas people have about others' lifestyles. To do this I will look at Counts and Counts' ethnographic study of RVers and the way they perceive boundaries between "them" and "us."

### PASSAGE 2: AN ENCYCLOPEDIA ENTRY

KOSOVO, small south central republic in what was YUGO-SLAVIA between MACEDONIA, SERBIA, and ALBANIA. Its 10,000 ha/24,700 acres of vineyards in spectacular inland mountain and valley settings are largely devoted to the production of Amselfelder branded wine for sale in Germany. Train-loads of light red are sent in bulk to Belgrade for STABILIZA-TION, sweetening, and shipment. The light aromatic fruit of the PINOT NOIR was certainly the inspiration behind this brand. CABERNET FRANC, MERLOT, PROKUPAC, and GAMAY are also part of the region's production.

> Kosovo is a poor region and throughout the 1980s was heav-
> ily dependent on its exports of the Amselfelder range. This
> dependence became a serious liability when Yugoslav turmoil
> made the German importers realize how easily other eastern
> European vineyard areas could copy the style.
>
> A.H.M.
>
> Angela Muir 1994 "Kosovo." *The Oxford Companion to Wine.* ed. Jancis Robinson.
> Oxford: OUP.

## 8B The Mental Desktop

We will explore one more technique for composing our portrait of the
reader. Derived from cognitive studies, this technique pictures the reader
organizing a **mental desktop**: a space on which statements arrive, one
after the other, as the reader advances through a text.

If your actual desktop is like many people's, it gets covered with piles
of paper, and you end up paying attention only to what's on top — the
most recently arrived material — until these pages themselves get covered by new arrivals. Reading can be like this, too, if what we are reading
is very difficult for us: we concentrate on one sentence or a few sentences
at a time. In the meantime, previous sentences are sometimes forgotten.

The reader's mental desktop is a finite area. It can't get bigger. In other
words, the reader's attention span — or short-term memory — is inelastic. No matter how hard readers try (or how much you wish they would
try), they can only concentrate on a relatively small number of things at a
time. This is the way the human brain works. Writers have to learn to
live with this inescapable condition of reading comprehension.

This small, inelastic space for paying attention may make the reader
seem like a limited being, hardly worth addressing with an interesting
paper. Moreover, the limitation does not match other qualities of our
own reading experience: we read articles, chapters, books, and we have a
sense of remembering a lot more than the handful of items that happened to be the last ones to pass across our mental desktop.

According to the theories behind the mental desktop image, readers
manage their desktops — successfully under good circumstances, less successfully under other circumstances. Up to a certain point, it's the *writer*
who is responsible for these circumstances.

To the picture of the reader and desktop we will add a **management device**. The management device arranges and uses mental space. The mental space is furnished with, in addition to the desktop, a sort of side-table for temporary storage, and filing cabinets for long-term storage. To manage the flow of information and make the most of it, the reader operates the management device to assign statements to these different mental spaces. The reader operates the device to detect the following: 1) items that can be combined; 2) items that can be put aside; 3) items that can be neglected; and 4) items that can be sent into long-term memory.

To illustrate how readers can manage their mental desktops, let's consider the following passage.

### "ASIAN CORPORATIONS"

Corporate growth — the development of multiunit firms — can be explained in terms of business response to the conditions of industrialized markets. According to Chandler (1977), when markets grow, businesses need to develop efficient systems of management to handle increased volume and coordinate multiple activities. Another theory also explains corporate development in industrial economies in terms of the market: as the number of transactions increases in the process of transforming raw materials into market goods, uncertainty increases (Williamson 1977, 1981, 1983, 1985). To reduce uncertainty, businesses grow, internalizing transactions and thereby governing them more reliably. These explanations of corporate development, however, do not fully account for corporate growth in Japan and South Korea, where prevailing organizational structures predate industrialization.

The Japanese economy is dominated by large, powerful, and relatively stable enterprise groups. One type of enterprise group consists of horizontal linkages among a range of large firms; these are intermarket groups spread through different industrial sectors. A second type of enterprise group connects small- and medium-sized firms to a large firm. These networks are normally groups of firms in unrelated businesses that are joined together by central banks or by trading companies. In pre-war Japan, these groups were linked by powerful holding companies that were each under the control of a family. The zaibatsu families exerted strict control over the individual firms in their group through a variety of fiscal and manage-

rial methods. During the U.S. occupation, the largest of these holding companies were dissolved, with the member firms of each group
becoming independent. After the occupation, however, firms (e.g.,
Mitsui, Mitsubishi, and Sumitomo) regrouped themselves.

In Japan in the Tokugawa era, from 1603 to 1867, a rising merchant class developed a place for itself in the feudal shogunate. Merchant houses did not challenge the traditional authority structure
but subordinated themselves to whatever powers existed. Indeed, a
few houses survived the Meiji Restoration smoothly, and one in particular (Mitsui) became a prototype for the zaibatsu. Other zaibatsu
arose early in the Meiji era from enterprises that had been previously run for the benefit of the feudal overlords, the daimyo. In the
Meiji era, the control of such han enterprises moved to the private
sphere where, in the case of Mitsubishi, former samurai became the
owners and managers. In all cases of the zaibatsu that began early in
the Meiji era, the overall structure was an intermarket group. The
member firms were legal corporations, were large multiunit enterprises, and could accumulate capital through corporate means.

In South Korea, the chaebol — large, hierarchically arranged sets
of firms — are the dominant business networks. In 1980–81, the
government recognized 26 chaebol, which controlled 456 firms. In
1985, there were 50 chaebol that controlled 552 firms. Their rate
of growth has been extraordinary. In 1973, the top five chaebol controlled 8.8% of the GNP, but by 1985 the top four chaebol controlled 45% of the GNP. In 1984, the top 50 chaebol controlled
about 80% of the GNP. The chaebol are similar to the pre-war

zaibatsu in size and organizational structure. Their structure can be traced to premodern political practices and to pre-World War II Japanese industrial policy which directed Korean development after Japan's colonization of Korea in 1910.

Adapted from Gary G. Hamilton and Nicole Woolsey Biggart 1988 "Market, culture,and authority: A comparative analysis of management and organization in the Far-East." *American Journal of Sociology* 94, 552–594.

As mentioned above, items *can be combined* to form a single item, thus leaving room on the mental desktop for new items to be concentrated on:

"Mitsubishi … Toshiba … Sumitomo …"     *OK, these three examples all show family networks associated with corporate growth … I'll combine them as such. Now there's room for more.*

Items *can be put aside* but kept nearby on the mental side-table as not centrally relevant at this point but liable to be necessary at any moment:

*Hmm … Most of this isn't about* family, *but* family *is bound to come up again. I'll just put the idea of* family *and* corporate growth *here, within easy reach when it's needed.*

Items *can be neglected*, left to fall off the desktop when other material arrives —

*I see. The American market is just an example, not part of the main focus.*

Items *can be sent to long-term memory*, in particular those files which house all we know but aren't thinking about right now:

*Ah, American markets don't seem to be important to this discussion. I won't be needing this. I'll file it.*

When there is no immediate, accessible context for interpreting details, the reader can't *use* them for their contextual implications. Here we see a cognitive outcome of a *structural* feature: a passage that stays low, and doesn't make higher, interpretive levels accessible, can confound a reader.

*Here's Mitsubishi, here's Toshiba, and now here's Sumitomo … hmm … Does this mean cartel? Or some other form of market domination? Is it good? Is it bad? I'm not sure. I'd better keep all this material and these possibilities here on my desk.*

Finally, when the management device is not properly directed to a clear context for interpretation, it may make some very inefficient decisions about long-term storage. Encountering a big claim early in an essay, and finding it neither developed nor repeated in subsequent passages, the device may judge that it is not important enough to keep handy. So the claim gets sent to the long-term memory files — that big, elastic capacity that houses the person's experience and knowledge of the world.

> *American markets haven't come up again. I predict they won't. I'll send this to long-term storage and make room for other things.*

Now the material is not exactly forgotten, but it is no longer in mind. And, stored in long-term files, it is relatively inaccessible compared to items on the desktop and on temporary side-tables. If the device has made a mistake, and it turns out that this material *is* needed, the reader has to go and retrieve the item from the long-term files.

> *Now, what's this about? It seems to presuppose ideas about American markets. Do I have something on that? Maybe in my files ... where did I put that?*

The retrieval takes up attention capacity. During the time the reader spends retrieving something from long-term storage (assuming he *can* retrieve it, and hasn't simply forgotten it), the desktop gets untidy. When he returns, he finds that things have fallen off, and have to be recalled by re-reading.

---

**Exercise 2**

Read the following revised version of the "Asian corporations" passage. The passages in bold attempt to manage a reader's mental desktop. Note that some of these passages belong to the original, while others are new. How do these revisions succeed in addressing your own responses to the original passage? How do they assist a reader's management device to help keep the mental desktop organized (see the four examples of uses above)?

### "ASIAN CORPORATIONS"

**Corporate growth — the development of multiunit firms — can be explained in terms of business response to the con-**

ditions of industrialized markets. According to Chandler (1977), when markets grow, businesses need to develop efficient systems of management to handle increased volume and coordinate multiple activities. **Another theory also explains corporate development in industrial economies in terms of the market:** as the number of transactions increases in the process of transforming raw materials into market goods, uncertainty increases (Williamson 1977, 1981, 1983, 1985). To reduce uncertainty, businesses grow, internalizing transactions and thereby governing them more reliably. **These explanations of corporate development, however, do not fully account for corporate growth in Japan and South Korea, where prevailing organizational structures predate industrialization. While the historical conditions of industrialization may explain why North American and European corporations operate the way they do, Japanese and South Korean corporate structure can be better explained as the result of other conditions: cultural factors which favour family links and which have all along adapted corporate management to older, pre-industrial forms of authority.**

The Japanese economy is **dominated by large, powerful, and relatively stable enterprise groups of business units — groups whose structure can be traced to traditional patterns of authority and family connection. Contemporary corporate structures in Japan are distinguished by characteristic systems of family connection that have persisted throughout this century, re-emerging powerfully in the post-war period. Today in Japan,** one type of enterprise group consists of horizontal linkages among a range of large firms; there are intermarket groups spread through different industrial sectors. A second type of enterprise group connects small- and medium-sized firms to a large firm. The networks of large firms are the modern descendents of the pre-World War II zaibatsu — powerful, family-controlled holding companies. These networks are normally groups of firms in unrelated businesses that are joined together by central banks or by trading companies. In pre-war Japan, these groups were linked by powerful holding companies that were each under the control of a family. The zaibatsu families exerted strict control over the individual firms in their group through a variety of fiscal and managerial methods. During the U.S. occupation, the largest of these holding companies were dissolved, with the member firms of each group becoming independent. After the occupation, however, firms (e.g., Mitsui, Mitsubishi, and Sumitomo) regrouped themselves. **While market conditions can account for some features of the Japanese corporate structure, these persistent network linkages are better explained by cultural frames which influenced the organization of commerce long before industrialization reached Japan.**

**Commercial growth in Japan arose amidst and adapted to traditional authority in a feudal rather than an industrial culture.** In Japan in the Tokugawa era, from 1603 to 1867, a rising merchant class developed a place for itself in the feudal shogunate. Merchant houses did not challenge the traditional authority structure but subordinated themselves to whatever powers existed. Indeed, a few houses survived the Meiji Restoration smoothly, and one in particular (Mitsui) became a prototype for the zaibatsu. Other zaibatsu arose early in the Meiji era from enterprises that had been previously run for the benefit of the feudal overlords, the daimyo. In the Meiji era, the control of such han enterprises moved to the private sphere where, in the case of Mitsubishi, former samurai became the owners and managers. In all cases of the zaibatsu that began early in the Meiji era, the overall structure was an intermarket group. The member firms were legal corporations, were large multiunit enterprises, and could accumulate capital through corporate means. **In Japan, the corporate framework of industrial society preceded the appearance of expanded industrial markets, and that framework — indigenous and culturally specific — persists today.**

**Like the Japanese economy, the South Korean economy depends on large groups of firms which are the descendants**

of traditional forms of authority and commercial cooperation. Today in South Korea, the chaebol — large, hierarchically arranged sets of firms — are the dominant business
networks. In 1980–81, the government recognized 26 chaebol,
which controlled 456 firms. In 1985, there were 50 chaebol
that controlled 552 firms. Their rate of growth has been extraordinary. In 1973, the top five chaebol controlled 8.8% of
the GNP, but by 1985 the top four chaebol controlled 45%
of the GNP. In 1984, the top 50 chaebol controlled about
80% of the GNP. **But this surge of growth — recent and
unmistakable — is nevertheless a phenomenon related to
older patterns of commercial affiliation.** The chaebol are similar to the pre-war zaibatsu in size and organizational structure. Their structure can be traced to premodern political
practices and to pre-World War II Japanese industrial policy
which directed Korean development after Japan's colonization
of Korea in 1910. **Intermarket linkages among business units
coordinated by family affiliation rather than managerial principles are expressions of preindustrial culture as much as they
are responses to expanding markets.**

## 8C Readers Read

In the exercises below, you will hear readers reading passages, thinking
aloud as they go. Their think-aloud responses, which follow the two excerpted passages, were recorded and transcribed. Each of the readers has
long experience reading and writing in the research genres — in language
studies, rhetoric, the social sciences, literary studies.

While there is a lot to be learned from these passages and the responses
they activate, this selection is by no means exhaustive of the occasions of
scholarly writing and reading. Rather, it is intended as a glimpse of what
is usually hidden from writers: the sight (and sound) of readers-at-work.
It may inspire you to conduct your own further inquiries: to ask readers
to read for you — your own work or others' — or to become more ob-
servant of your own reading experiences.

### Exercise 3

You will recognize the passage below: Exercise 5, at the end of Chapter 7, asked you to read this passage — the beginning section of a student-written paper — as a think-aloud practice exercise. You have already offered your own response to it. Having heard the response of your partner, you have begun to estimate the responses of other readers. Hearing readers reading helps us develop an ability to estimate the responses of other academic readers.

Inspect the reader's think-aloud response below: How would you analyze the reader's work on the passage? What conditions seem to be affecting the reader's reception of this writing? Compare your response to the response of this reader, identifying similarities and differences. The reader's think-aloud is followed by such an analysis, to suggest the kind of reasoning you might do to interpret this reader's response.

> Everyone has their own definition of community. For some people it is the place they grew up. For others it is the place they live and work in. Anderson says community is "imagined" (quoted in Chavez 1994).
>
> But what is community? Webster's (1987) defines community as "a unified body of individuals; ... the people with common interests living in a particular area; ... an interacting population of various kinds of individuals ... in a common location." What happens to a community when its original basis, the idea people have of its founding and its reason for existing, is threatened? In this paper I will investigate one such case: coastal communities where fishing has been a way of life and now the salmon stocks are greatly reduced and, in some cases the fishery has been closed.

> READER, *thinking aloud:*
> **Everyone has their own definition of community.** *OK I'm stopping here because I'm thinking this is a definition paper ... because I'm thinking that what's important here is the definition but what I would want is um an indication of why I'm being given this information so I was trying to supply that information in terms*

*of it being a definition paper um OK so I have this general sense that everyone has their own definition of community I'm still at this point not sure of why I'm reading this or why this is important that I get a sense of this generalness of everyone having their own definition* **For some people it is the place they grew up.** *OK so um* **the place they grew up** *so I'm getting further distinctions in terms of definition* **For others it is the place they live and work in** *OK [pause] still don't have a sense OK I guess we're talking about community and different perceptions of community here [pause] that I'm not really sure what to do with these differences they seem so general I need something more focused* **Anderson says community is "imagined"** *OK I have a source here so I'm thinking that the idea of community is confirmed so she'll be paying attention to this um I'm not quite sure I understand what Anderson would mean by "imagined" at this point or the significance of this.* **But what is community?** *OK another question! but still I'm intrigued by this "imagined" and mainly it's because as a reader of scholarly writing I'm interested in scholarly reports of things* **Webster's (1987) defines community as "a unified body of individuals; ... the people with common interests living in a particular area; ...** *OK people with common interests living in a particular area OK so this refers back to the kinds of definition that I read above here* **an interacting population of various kinds of individuals ... in a common location."** *OK so this issue of commonality is always important ... I'm still not sure why I need to answer what is community but I'll continue* **What happens to a community when its original basis, the idea people have of its founding and its reason for existing, is threatened?** *not quite sure what to do with this question and I'm not sure how we go from these sort of general definitions of community to something happening to community this threat and I don't know why this threat is important for the writer and I'm still keeping in mind this idea of imagined so how is that related to any of this* **In this paper I will investigate** *I appreciate this I feel like I'm getting a sense of what um hopefully I'll read on and get an idea of what I'm supposed to be focusing on* **one** such case: coastal communities where fishing has been a way of life and now the salmon stocks are greatly reduced and, in some cases the fishery has been closed. *OK I have to reread [re-reads last sentence]* one such case — *of this threat to community* coastal communities where fishing has been a way of life and now the salmon stocks are greatly reduced *I'm assuming but I'm not being told that [pause] practices in the community are being threatened so I'm assuming that the community will change somehow I'm still not sure what the significance of this is OK so I move from these sort of general definitions of community to [pause] um some questions of what community is and an instance not the operation of community but something happening to a community I don't know how things are adding up here, what I should be focusing on, but I get from the end of it that I should be focusing on changes in communities but I have to infer that this idea of threat and this change in the salmon stocks*

ANALYSIS OF RESPONSE

What do we learn from this encounter between reader and text? The reader looks for the **relevance** of the opening claim: a context in which it would have implications. She hypothesizes that the writer was *assigned* a definition (which suggests a classroom rather than scholarly motivation, possibly). But her inference is not confident: she still wonders "why [she is] reading this." She recognizes the citation as a scholarly move, but dwells on "imagined" — a complex idea. The definition from "Webster's" does not displace "imagined": the reader keeps it on her mental desktop, even though it is not called for again (in this excerpt). Seeking connections, the reader works on connecting the dictionary definition with material from the first paragraph. The writer's question and statement of intention give the reader some confidence, but she still works to find a connection between, on the one hand, the question and statement and, on the other hand, what has gone before. For herself, she constructs the focus on *change.*

THINKING ABOUT REVISION

The writer might focus first on "imagined" community (which at-

tracted the reader's interest), from Anderson, and develop this definition to establish connections which the reader struggled to make.
These connections could be secured by working with Anderson's
definition to involve prevailing ideas like "original basis," "founding," and "reason for being": shared themes in people's *imagina-
tions*. Then the writer might look at connecting these *imaginary*
conditions with the *material* conditions of daily work and "way of
life" (communities not being *imagined* out of thin air). And now
the question stands up: what happens to the *imaginary* when the
*material actuality* changes? The coastal communities the writer refers to offer an occasion for addressing this question.

The reader might also consider leaving out Webster's definition,
and the general claims about "[e]veryone [having] their own definition of community."

### Exercise 4

The excerpted passage below is followed by transcribed think-aloud
responses from two experienced academic readers. Start by reading
the passage, developing your own response to it, and in light of that
response, estimate the response of other academic readers. Now compare the responses of READER A and READER B. What conditions seem to be affecting academic readers' responses? Using the
theoretical material in the beginning of this chapter, look for evidence in readers' think-aloud responses of cognitive needs. What
conditions seem to be affecting readers' reception? Now you might
look for evidence of social needs. In light of academic readers' needs,
what changes would you recommend to the writers of these passages? Write a paragraph, "Thinking about revisions," similar to the
one in Exercise 2 above.

> In Counts and Counts (1992), feelings of equality co-exist
> with discrimination. The RVers say they are all the "same" and
> equal, but they notice and criticize ways that are different from
> theirs. Verkuyten et al. (1994) agrees with this. The residents
> of the old neighbourhood say that equal treatment is impor-

tant but they criticize foreigners for not fitting in. A further questions arises from this; can *community* by defined only in terms of similarity or does community also include ways of interpreting differences? Another question would be: are attitudes towards others more discriminatory when the others are seen as newcomers?

READER A, *thinking aloud:*
**In Counts and Counts (1992), feelings of equality co-exist with discrimination.** [pause] **The RVers say they are all the "same" and equal, but they notice and criticize ways that are different from theirs.** *[pause] this sounds like summary so I get the sense that this is what is going on in Counts and Counts they have feelings of equality and they also discriminate so I would end up if I hadn't read their article thinking that this was what Counts and Counts are feeling or this is what the writer sees them doing ... having* **feelings of equality co-exist with discrimination: they are all the "same" and equal, but they notice and criticize ways that are different from theirs.** *so the RVers themselves are discriminating not Counts and Counts OK* **Verkuyten et al. (1994) agrees with this.** *OK so if I hadn't read either one of these articles I would just automatically assume that they're actually having a discussion or have had a discussion and um but what I think the writer is trying to do is she or he is trying to position these two together so she is making them agree as opposed to um them actually agreeing so she's trying to find points of comparison she's attempting to compare two articles rather than um have them actually agreeing on something or them citing each other, which they don't do so I would use wording that's more comparative or that indicates a comparison between ideas rather than the discourse of agreement* **The residents of the old neighbourhood say that equal treatment is important but they criticize foreigners for not fitting in.** *so the idea here is that there are groups of people that see each other equal or expect equal treatment but in both cases with the RVers and these residents of the old neighourhood they also find ways to um differen-*

*tiate between each other that's the idea that's important* **A further questions** *arises I'm stumbling over the wording a bit here "a further question arises"* **from this** *OK I'm not sure where I see the question above here so I'm going to reread to see if I've missed it* **but they criticize** *OK* **can** *community* **by defined only in terms of similarity or does community also include ways of interpreting differences?** *oh a question is arising from this um and this is the question yeh that's interesting so the writer is asking can we only define community based on similarity or does the notion of community almost always involve this idea of difference as well or incorporates difference* **Another question would be;** *um OK I'm stopping here on this semicolon on this punctuation and noticing above because I thought I had read a colon um pause I might be tempted to just skip over it I just expect certain kinds of sentence structure with these kinds of punctuation it stops me* **Another question would be; are attitudes towards others more discriminatory when the others are seen as newcomers?** *this person based on this observation of how community works has come up with some questions [pause] around community and how it operates so maybe um a kind of discussion of the significance of these questions in terms of Counts and Counts' findings would be helpful yes*

READER B, *thinking aloud:*
**In Counts and Counts (1992), feelings of equality co-exist with discrimination.** *well this disturbs me somewhat because it seems like the equality and discrimination are in Counts and Counts' article and I don't have any recollection of that article being like that so I'm wondering if this writer means "Counts & Counts explain that argue that feelings of equality coexist with discrimination" I suspect it's something like that yes! because as I go on* **The RVers say they are all the "same" and equal, but they notice and criticize ways that are different from theirs.** *so clearly it's the RVers who have these feelings, not Counts & Counts and that unsettles me it makes it hard to concentrate as I go on* **Verkuyten et al. (1994) agrees** *well that's a group so agree-*

*ment thing agree agree* **with this.** [pause] *OK there's something about the way the two sources are being brought together that I find a little bumpy where it makes it sound as though Verkuyten et al. have read Counts and Counts and outright agreeing with them and that's not what's going on I don't think uh so I'd be happier with something that makes a similar point that shows that it's the writer of this paper who is bringing the two sources together OK back* **The residents of the old neighbourhood say that equal treatment is important but they criticize foreigners for not fitting in.** *OK I mean overall I like the fact that these two quite different articles are being brought into the same place I just think that I need a little more help the reader needs a little more help connecting them* **A further questions arises from this;** *now I'm getting a little disturbed — "the questions" — I think the writer knows that it's "question" and these little typos are throwing me off it's hard to concentrate* **can** *community* **by** *see another one* **defined only in terms of similarity or does community also include ways of interpreting differences?** [pause] *OK* [pause] *OK* **Another question would be; are attitudes towards** *well see it's the punctuation thing there's a cumulative effect of small things* **are attitudes towards others more discriminatory when the others are seen as newcomers?** [pause] *well a big jump between those two questions maybe I'd like a little set up for that too I need a sense of things coming together before it opens up to other possibilities that could be addressed they're interesting questions but I'd just like them contextualized a bit*

# 9

# Scholarly styles

Scholarly writing is often ridiculed in the popular media. Like the speech of people who have not internalized schoolroom rules of usage, it is deplored by those who believe in "good" writing. Most scholarly expression goes on out of earshot of the rest of the world — in scholarly journals and at scholarly conferences. But when the sounds of scholarship do leak into more public settings, they can come in for some criticism. In this chapter, we will examine some of the stylistic features that give rise to that criticism.

## 9A Common and Uncommon Sense

Criticism of scholarly expression is sometimes most vociferous where academic research meets public policy. For instance, when a curriculum document reaches the attention of the popular press, those wordings which are traceable to otherwise secluded research domains can leave people indignant or amused. The following example of such "edu-babble" comes from a curriculum report that was presented to Ontario's Minister of Education:

> A certain minimum fluency is required before students are able to reflect critically on their own language use. Attention to language forms and conventions should therefore increase gradually as language skill develops and should arise specifically out of the reading and writing being done. Students are more likely to achieve good

punctuation and spelling and surface correctness through extensive practice in reading and writing rather than conscious attempts to apply rules out of context.

The newspaper article that cites this passage describes it as "bureaucratic babble" and lines up readers who characterize it as "meaningless and offensive," "pretentious," and "arrogant." The article then goes on to report that the passage (along with the 100-page report it came from) was rewritten in **plain language**:

> Students are more likely to learn correct language uses, punctuation, and spelling by reading and writing than by learning rules in isolation.
>
> *Ottawa Citizen*, reprinted in *The Vancouver Province*, July 5, 1994, A14.

Whatever the defects of the original or the virtues of the rewrite, the rewrite gets rid of material like "certain minimum fluency is required," "attention to language forms and conventions," and "through extensive practice in reading and writing rather than conscious attempts to apply rules out of context." Such expressions bear the marks of scholarly activity. Events and attributes are turned into things ("x pays attention to" y = "attention to" y; "x attempts to apply" y to z = "attempts to apply" y to z; "x is fluent" = "fluency"). Verbs and adjectives are turned into nouns, and as a result agents of actions and possessors of attributes disappear (*Who* pays attention or attempts to apply? *Who* is fluent? *Who* requires fluency?). In getting rid of these features, the rewrite might be said to restore "common sense" to the original. But at the same time, it seems to reduce the conceptual complexity of the original: for example, the emphasis on "language forms and conventions" to a set of "rules."

With genre theory in mind, we could argue that it's not that the original is in itself bad, or that the reaction is mistaken. Rather, there has been a series of **genre violations**: the writers of the original transferred the sounds and styles of scholarly research too directly to a non-research document, in this case one meant to be read by government officials. And the ministry officials who objected and the rewriters who responded to these objections failed to acknowledge the fact that the original curriculum document was addressed to professionals: teachers and educational administrators who are familiar with these uses of language. In other words, the situation that the original document served did not include many readers of the *Ottawa Citizen* or the indignant politicians whose consternation was reported.

This example illuminates the conflict between what Halliday and Martin (1993) have called the **common sense** of, roughly speaking, our everyday experience of the world and the **uncommon sense** of the learned domains of research.

From a distance, it seems tempting to vouch for common sense, and deny uncommon sense as unnatural, pretentious, or even deliberately deceiving. Yet common sense has also been the source of some questionable ideas — that whales are fish (to use one of Halliday and Martin's examples) — or less innocent ideas, such as that women are inferior to men, or that children benefit from stern discipline, or that rivers are a good place to get rid of industrial waste. That is to say, sometimes "common sense" is only unexamined assumptions which perpetuate conditions that benefit some people and disadvantage others — or benefit no one in the long run. These assumptions are so widely held — that is, so common — that they appear self-evident.

Research activities seek to subject some of those common-sense assumptions to examination, and this process of examination is represented in the distinctive language of the scholarly genres. For example, in a common-sense world, we all understand the word *think* and use it in various situations:

[Fred and Jane are taking a car trip.]

FRED: When did we get gas?　　JANE: Hmm. Let me *think*.

FRED: We're going an average　　JANE (looking at a map): Wait.
of 85 kph. When will we　　　　I'm *thinking*.
get to Mariposa?

FRED: What are you doing?　　JANE (looking at a map): I'm
　　　　　　　　　　　　　　*thinking* about where we
　　　　　　　　　　　　　　should go next.

But cognitive scientists who want to find out how people think would distinguish amongst these situations, seeing that one is a matter of remembering, another is a matter of calculating an answer to a particular question, and the third is a more complex procedure. For the third case, they might (and have) come up with a specialized term: *nonspecific goal strategy in problem solving*. Rarely would we hear this term outside scholarly circles — or, indeed, outside the even smaller circle of the discipline of cognitive science.

Some advocates of plain language and common sense complain about this kind of wording. They suggest that it is an unnecessarily complicated way of speaking. Why not just say "thinking"? They suggest that, by choosing the specialist term, writers exclude common-sense people and isolate scholars in a false distinction made of elaborate language. And some suggest that this kind of wording is not only pretentious and exclusionary, but also hard to read. Let's examine the grounds for these complaints.

## 9B Is Scholarly Writing Unnecessarily Complicated, Exclusionary, or Elitist?

Later sections of this chapter will offer broader perspectives on this question, looking at how the structure of an expression like *nonspecific goal strategy in problem solving* cooperates with other features of scholarly genres to produce the discourse which typifies and maintains research activities. In the meantime, we could grant that, sometimes, scholars might be advised to say "thinking" instead of "nonspecific goal strategy in problem solving."

But we can make this concession to critics of scholarly style only in light of other considerations. In efforts to reorganize common-sense knowledge of the world into uncommon sense, researchers analyze issues and entities into smaller parts, differentiating those parts into segments which may be scarcely visible to the untrained observer. Those segments — produced by research activity — then become objects of study, and the names for the objects of study are necessary to reporting the results of study.

Be that as it may, our opinion of the wording *nonspecific goal strategy in problem solving* may come down to our opinion of research activity itself. If we believe the results of the research are useful or important, we're likely to identify the inherent complexities of expression as *necessary*; if we don't, we're more likely to dismiss those complexities as *unnecessary*.

This is a big issue, and further inflated by our culture's ambivalence towards "science." On the one hand, we invest heavily – materially and socially – in professional research. Tax and corporate dollars support scholars' activities; experts and scientists are called in as authorities on many matters, from family life to outer space. But, on the other hand, we not only ridicule expert language but also question both our investment in "pure" research (that without any immediately foreseeable use) and the applications of research in new technologies: we complain that they have spoiled cherished aspects of our customary ways of life.

Our judgement about the complications of scholarly language would eventually have to take into account this ambivalence. For now, we might say that, if the activities that appear to depend on wordings like *nonspecific goal strategy in problem solving* have good results, then the wording is not *unnecessarily* complicated — though it may still be complicated. And one of these results might be a clearer picture of how people reason: how certain kinds of schoolroom problem-questions (*If A is travelling at 50 kph and B is going 56 kph in the opposite direction …*) may trigger in children reasoning different from that which the teacher anticipates, or how a doctor's diagnostic questioning may trigger replies that obscure rather than illuminate a patient's condition.

Often accompanying the criticism that scholarly writing is unnecessarily complicated is the accusation that it's elitist. In fact, there can be little doubt that scholarly style excludes many readers. Even within the larger academic community, readers who are members of one discipline can be excluded from the ongoing discourses of other disciplines — paleontologists and cognitive scientists do not tend to understand one another's research very well. While researchers seem to be generally respectful of those working in other fields, smirks and raised eyebrows are not unknown when a researcher comes within earshot of the wordings of another discipline. The "post-modernism" of the humanities and some of the social sciences can inspire ridicule amongst those who do not work in those terms. And, equally, the classifying vocabularies of the sciences and some other social sciences can arouse suspicion amongst those who work with less technical terminologies.

Genre theory predicts that this will be so: the more highly defined and particular the situations which language serves, the more distinctive will that language be, and the more inscrutable to people unfamiliar with those situations. So we might also predict that any social group — skateboarders or pilots or childcare workers — will develop and maintain speech styles which serve and represent the routines which organize their activities. And these styles will, to a greater or lesser degree, exclude people who don't belong to the group and incur the risk of social reactions to that exclusion.

## 9C Nominal Style: Syntactic Density

Criticism of scholarly expression — in particular, the claim that it's hard to read — has sometimes focused on what has been called its heavily nominal style. This characterization refers to its preference for nouns over verbs, and the way that preference results in big **noun phrases** (i.e., a phrase formed by a noun and all its modifiers) like the one that we have been using as our example: *nonspecific goal strategy in problem solving* is longer than *thinking*. This difference is visible to the naked eye, and needs very little grammatical analysis to reveal it. Once nouns are preferred over verbs, noun phrases bear a particularly heavy load, carrying content that would otherwise have been distributed throughout the sentence. These concentrated loads appear likely to challenge readers on two fronts: (1) the syntactic density of noun "strings," and (2) the potential ambiguity of these strings. Let's begin by examining **syntactic density**, the first of these conditions.

In English, the noun phrase is capable of expanding by picking up other sentence elements. In the following series, you will see noun phrases growing by absorbing material from other parts of the sentence.

(a) *the noun phrase absorbs an adjective*
This behaviour is **criminal**.
This **criminal** behaviour…

(b) *the noun phrase absorbs another noun*
The reports record **offences**.
The **offence** reports…

(c) *the noun phrase absorbs a predicate — verb and adverb*
Some strategies **work forward**.
Some **forward-working** strategies…

(d) *the noun phrase absorbs a predicate — verb and (object) noun*
Strategies **solve problems**.
**Problem-solving** strategies…

There are limits to what the noun phrase can absorb, but these examples don't even approach those limits. They exemplify only some of the simplest noun-phrase expansions.

You can see that the capacity of the noun phrase to incorporate other sentence elements provides one of the normal economies of English. For example, by installing "work forward" in the noun phrase (c), the writer leaves the rest of the sentence free to carry other information:

**Forward-working strategies** enable the problem solver to explore the problem space to see what moves are possible.

Speakers of English use the capacity of the noun phrase all the time to achieve economies of expression. Instead of saying —

My car has broken down. It is brand new.

— the speaker can economize, presenting the same information in fewer words:

**My brand-new car** has broken down.

Yet, while this *appears* to be the same information, the choice between the two versions is not entirely free or arbitrary: it has to do with topic development. For instance, if the speaker were to continue reporting his predicament, the second version would tend to lead to development of the "break-down" topic —

My brand-new car has broken down. I was going along and heard this BUMP-BUMP.

— whereas the first version would *tend* to pave the way for development of the "brand-new" topic:

My car has broken down. It's brand new. I just got it last month.

In reflecting on the noun phrase's capacity to absorb material from other parts of the sentence in ways that are patterned rather than arbitrary, let us first take a **cognitive** approach. Consider the effect of the heavy noun phrase on readers' working conditions. How does the decoding of a long noun phrase impose on readers' limited resources for paying attention?

Most theory and research in this area suggests that as readers make their way through sentences, they predict, on the basis of the word they are currently reading, the syntactic category of the following word or phrase. So, if readers encounter a *determiner* like —

**the ...**

— they predict, as most likely but not inevitable, that a *noun* will come next:

the **goal** ...

If their expectations are disappointed, and they find not a *noun* but an *adjective* —

    the **nonspecific** …

— they recover easily, and now predict a noun, since adjectives following determiners have a high probability of being followed by a *noun*:

| the | nonspecific | **goal** |
|---|---|---|
| *determiner* | *modifier (adj)* | *nominal head (noun)* |

This seems to complete the noun phrase, and readers are ready for a *verb* — the goal *is* something, or *does* something. They predict a verb. But what if they encounter another *noun*?

    the nonspecific goal **strategy** …

| the | nonspecific | goal | strategy |
|---|---|---|---|
| *determiner* | *modifier* | *modifier* | *nominal head* |
| | *(adj)* | *(noun)* | *(noun)* |

Now they revise their hypothesis about the sentence and its structure: *goal* is not the head of the noun phrase, but only another modifier. Notice that we have not yet approached the structural limits of the noun phrase. Somebody could conceivably write "the nonspecific goal strategy research innovation project."

    Analysis of the above procedure first isolates noun strings — nouns modified by other nouns — as a site of such failed-then-revised-hypotheses sequences. Then it proposes that these recursive predictions burden readers' attention capacity. (We could see this burden as a micro version of the larger efforts after meaning we explored in Chapter 8, when we inspected that state of readers' mental desktops as they worked to construct the relevance of lower-level information to higher-level concepts.)

    So far, our evaluation of the syntactic density of noun phrases has been **cognitive** only: we have been estimating readers' reasoning as they meet long noun strings. But readers also respond in ways that stem from their **social** experience. And research shows that, while noun strings may cause trouble for some readers, they are no problem for other readers. Are some readers dull and others brilliant?

    In fact, as we saw in Chapter 8, the difference lies in readers' different experience of the world. Readers' social milieu and the background knowledge they have acquired play a big part in their understanding of what they read. It all depends on readers' previous contact with the subject treated by the text. For example, when the primary author of this text was investigating stylistic features in management studies, she came across the term *relationship marketing*. Being unaccustomed to the topic, she didn't know what that was — a dating service? professional matchmaking? Reading on, she was able to infer — from appositives, synonyms, and other elements of the co-text — that *relationship marketing* was a sales strategy which emphasizes techniques for building an enduring relationship with customers: keeping in touch after one sale had been made, building a context for future sales. Presumably, readers more familiar with these aspects of the discourse on management would not have had to experiment with the noun phrase *relationship marketing* in this way.

Conditions people have in mind when they talk about "clarity" and "conciseness" in the scholarly genres may have as much to do with the *identity* and *position* of the reader as they do with the style of the writing. Tracing down this possibility, a student in an undergraduate class in writing in the research genres carried out a small study of readers' level of difficulty in encountering scholarly forms of expression. She selected introductions from three articles, one each from scholarly publications in biomedical science, geography, and literary studies. She asked two readers to evaluate the passages for "clarity." The first subject, a physician, rated the biomedical passage as "most clear," and the literary studies passage as "most unclear." The second subject, a first-year student in a university-transfer program at a college, rated the literary-studies passage as "most clear," and the biomedical article as "most unclear."

Let's put the reader back together as a **socio-cognitive** being, and ask the question again: is scholarly style hard to read? Yes, it is — for some people. Students new to a discipline, for example, may find the nominal style of scholarly writing difficult to read. Perhaps students can benefit from first seeing the scholarly noun phrase as a structure which absorbs other sentence parts, and then methodically unpacking that noun phrase, understanding why it is causing them trouble but not letting it get the upper hand. As *readers*, students can overcome these obstacles once they understand the structure of the obstacle, and where the footholds and handholds are.

As *writers*, students can be wary of all-purpose rules for plain writing — or computer-style checkers — that call for verbs instead of nouns, and deplore noun "strings." Their readers will not necessarily have trouble with a heavily nominal style. But writers can also keep in mind the cognitive load imposed by noun strings. There may be times when unpacking a big noun phrase will offer cognitive relief to the reader. For example, the second passage below may sometimes be preferable to the first (where the target noun phrase is shown in bold):

> **A recent comparative study of multi-family housing development and maintenance costs based on 1986 construction experience** showed that three-storey buildings ultimately provided cheaper housing than high-rises.

> A study recently compared costs of developing and maintaining multiple-family housing. It was based on 1986 construction experience, and it showed that three-storey buildings ultimately provided cheaper housing than high-rises.

---

### Exercise 1

The following noun phrases are taken from published articles in a variety of scholarly disciplines. Analyze them, following the example ("the nonspecific goal strategy") above: what predictive hypotheses would readers first make and then revise as they navigate their way through these noun phrases?

labour supply decision-making
voluntary employee turnover
issues management structures
other-race face recognition
eating pathology scores
risk management science
droplet size distribution measurements

### Exercise 2

The following passage examines "community," a concept whose scholarly sense you have become familiar with from readings in previous chapters. Using the think-aloud techniques introduced in Chapter 8, ask two or more classmates to read and comment on the passage. Do the results differ according to readers' backgrounds —

their area of study, for example? Ask someone from outside the class to read the passage: how does their experience of the passage compare with those of readers in the class?

> I am less concerned with the conceptual aporia of community-capital contradiction, than with the genealogy of the idea of community as itself a "minority" discourse; as the making, or becoming "minor", of the idea of Society, in the practice of politics of culture. Community is the antagonist supplement of modernity: in the metropolitan space it is the territory of the minority, threatening the claims of civility; in the transnational world it becomes the border-problem of the diasporic, the migrant, the refugee. Binary divisions of social space neglect the profound temporal disjunction — the transnational time and space — through which minority communities negotiate their collective identifications.

Homi K. Bhabha 1994 "Now newness enters the world." In *The Location of Culture.* London: Routledge, 231.

## 9D Nominal Style: Ambiguity

We have seen that noun phrases are hospitable to other sentence elements: they will take in just about anything. As these bits and pieces are accommodated in the noun phrase, other elements are left behind. However, when parts get left behind, ambiguity can result. Sometimes the effort required from the reader to resolve the ambiguity is so negligible it is scarcely measurable. The bold-faced noun phrases in the following passage, which appeared in a daily newspaper, make demands on readers that they meet almost automatically.

> The body, discovered in the basement of **a concrete building**, was identified as the remains of **a newspaper boy** who had lived in the neighbourhood in the late 1960s.

*A concrete building* means that the building was made of concrete. But *a newspaper boy* doesn't mean that the boy was made of newspaper: it means that the boy delivered newspapers. The noun phrases don't make these distinctions: they are lost when the noun phrase absorbs other elements.

So, it's *readers* who make these distinctions, by consulting their knowledge of the world (no people are made of newspaper). And readers make the distinctions easily, without significant processing demands.

Other noun phrases can be slightly more distracting. The next passage comes from a news report about social conditions in the United States.

> **Homeless experts** say that the problem will only get worse as the summer goes on.

*What is a "homeless expert"?*

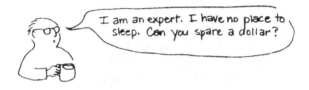

A more likely interpretation soon supersedes the less likely one.

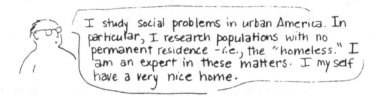

Readers resolve the ambiguity in the noun phrase by consulting their knowledge of the world.

Other noun phrases can be more stubbornly ambiguous. Like the example *relationship marketing*, the following noun string cannot be resolved by simply consulting our knowledge of the world:

> **police arrest information**

Does this refer to information that police use when they arrest people? Or information police compile when they arrest people? Or does it refer to information about police arresting people? Without surrounding context (or maybe even with it), this noun phrase remains ambiguous.

Finally, when style is heavily nominal — that is, when information is concentrated in expanding noun phrases — an accompanying feature appears which can also contribute to ambiguity. This feature, which we have encountered at the beginning of this chapter in the document on Ontario's school curriculum, we will call **agentlessness**. The doers of actions slip away when the actions are turned from nouns to verbs. So, while the verb *attend* requires (in active voice) that the doers of the action be identified —

**Forty-five property owners and six tenants** attended the meeting.

— the noun *attendance* allows these agents of the action to withdraw from the sentence:

**Attendance** was high.

Agentless writing has been condemned as both ambiguous and deceptive, an instrument of concealment. Leaving charges of deception aside for the moment, we must concede that heavy nominals which eliminate agents are liable to be ambiguous. For example, in *labour supply decision-making*, who is making the decision? (and about what?) Someone who has not read the article from which this phrase was taken might be surprised to learn that the decision-makers were Bangladeshi women in London who chose to do piecework at home rather than look for jobs in garment factories.

The ambiguity and syntactic density of a heavily nominal style are both potential troublemakers for readers and writers. Yet scholarly style risks these troubles. This way of speaking must therefore provide some benefits, some important service to scholarly situations. In the next section we will observe these benefits and services.

---

**Exercise 3**

Look in the passage below for dense noun phrases. Rewrite by unpacking them, spreading their elements out into other parts of the sentence and other sentences. For example, "Incarceration-based measures are the most common in national prison-use assessment" could be rewritten as "Some measures are based on the frequency with which criminals are incarcerated. These rates are the measure most commonly used to assess the way nations use prisons." (Note that the rewrite will not necessarily be an improvement — merely another version, less nominal, possibly more friendly to readers in certain situations.)

The Australian basic-wage Royal Commission of 1920, seeking working-class standard-of-living criteria, was chaired by a widely-read and respected living-wage champion, husband of a controversial family-planning advocate. Despite the liberal-reform inclinations of the Commission's chair and its nearly 40% recommended basic-wage increase, one of the main legacies of the Commission was the unquestioned equation of the "family" wage with the male-provider wage.

Adapted from Kerreen M. Reiger 1989 "'Clean and comfortable and respectable': Working-class aspirations and the Australian 1920 Royal Commission on the Basic Wage." *History Workshop* 27: 86–105.

### Exercise 4

The advertisement below appeared in the Career Opportunities section of a national newspaper. Other advertisements in this section included descriptions of positions available in engineering, private- and public-sector administration, personnel and sales management.

Examine the advertisement for features we have identified as belonging to scholarly expression: that is, nouns that represent actions or events, and in doing so lose agents (doers) and the objects acted upon. What questions might someone ask about who does what to whom? Evaluate this passage for its potential ambiguity and syntactic density. Speculate on why these ways of speaking, which seem characteristic of research genres, turn up here in a business genre.

SENIOR CONSULTANT

Automotive marketing

Blackburn/Polk Vehicle Information Services (BPVIS) is Canada's leading supplier of motor vehicle and marketing information services to the automotive industry and its allied businesses. We are looking for a Senior Consultant to work with our clients to market our full range of products and services.

We require an individual with the following skill set:

- knowledge of the automotive market and its information requirements
- general understanding of geo-demographics and market research
- general knowledge of direct marketing.

Our services for the automotive industry include market performance evaluation and benchmarking, network planning and location analysis, customer profiling studies, and support services for direct communication and customer retention programs.

The successful candidate will have strong presentation and interpersonal skills and be self-motivated.

Compensation is performance related and is commensurate with experience. Please apply in confidence to _____.

## 9E Sentence Style and Textual Coherence

Here are three scholarly passages which can arouse questions:

> The insertion of a Fourth World of indigenous populations who have a distinct vision of their place in a world that until recently has ignored them (Graburn 1976) cultivates an awareness of the political potential of submerged nationalities that are emerging once again in the postmodern world. This belated recognition of submerged ethnicities comes in the wake of the demise of the Second World, which no longer provides the paradigmatic base for analyses, as the structures of capitalism, socialism, and imperialism are undermined.
>
> June Nash 1994 "Global integration and subsistence insecurity." *American Anthropologist* 96 (1): 7–30, 8.

Who inserts a Fourth World? Who is aware? Who belatedly recognizes? Who analyzes? What nationalities and ethnicities are these? Who or what submerged them?

> Our study advances and tests a model incorporating both institutional and resource explanations for why firms adopt certain struc-

tural modifications, namely, issues management structures. The study ... provides a model to account for variation in the development of issues management structures across firms.

Daniel W. Greening and Barbara Gray 1994 "Testing a model of organizational response to social and political issues." *Academy of Management Journal* 37 (3): 467–98, 469.

Who explains? Who modifies what? Who manages? What are the issues and what does it mean to manage them? Who develops structures?

This article analyses labour supply decision-making for a particular group of women workers in a particular segment of the London clothing industry. It takes as its starting point the concentration of Bangledeshi women in the homeworking sector of the East London rag trade (Mitter, 1986a).

Naila Kabeer 1994 "The Structure of 'Revealed Preference': Race, Community and Female Labour Supply in the London Clothing Industry." *Development and Change* 25: 307–330.

Who supplies the labour? Who makes decisions? What is supplied? Who labours? Who or what concentrates? What is concentrated?

These samples — all heavily nominal — seem to confirm the view that scholarly writing is difficult. Yet they appeared in respected journals. This style must in some way benefit scholarly writers and readers, and serve scholarly situations.

Halliday and Martin (1993) argue that this "language of the expert" gives priority to **taxonomy**: that is, to schemes for classifying and ordering phenomena. Such schemes depend on *names* for things. So, in the second passage, the action *modify* becomes the noun *modification*, which can then take an attribute ("structural"), which will distinguish it from other "modifications." The action or event stabilized as a noun can then be worked into an arrangement with other named phenomena, "institutions" and "resources." These arrangements, Halliday and Martin argue, are designed to reveal relations of *cause*. This is evident where the authors explicitly ask "*why* firms adopt ... structural modifications." In this ordering search for causes, the grammar of research genres ends up with heavy **nominalizations**.

We might also note tendencies in current scholarship in many disciplines to *integrate* — to bring together theorics, conditions, analyses, dimensions. So, for example, in the third passage, "labour supply decision-making" names an effort to combine — or integrate — analyses of labour supply (availability of workers) with analyses of how people and households make decisions about what jobs they will seek, or keep, or quit. The grammatical outcome of this research initiative is a big noun phrase.

To this social analysis of nominal expressions we can add a cognitive, or socio-cognitive, dimension. In Chapter 8 we imagined readers working with passages of sentences, seeking higher-level terms in which to understand stretches of detail, or to understand the **relevance** of statements in context. Not all genres instruct the reader's efforts after meaning in the same way, and not all genres produce relevance in the same way. The scholarly genres typically maintain coherence and relevance by repeated references to high-level, abstract topic entities. Other genres — like newspaper reports, thank-you notes, or computer manuals — don't do this.

With these conditions in mind, we can begin to see the role of heavily nominalized expressions in supporting these repeated movements between abstract and concrete, generalities and detail. If, over several paragraphs, one were to write about a number of cases where employers preferred to train young employees on the job and tended not to hire people with secondary-school diplomas, one could compress these many cases into *skill requirements in the workplace* and *educational attainment* and specify the relation between them as *not* synonymous. These expressions eliminate the employers who hired and taught and the workers and students who learned or failed to learn. But they also provide an ascent to the high level of **abstraction** that will hold this section of the discussion together, and then serve as tokens for — or efficient reminders of — this section as the discussion develops over 10 or 20 pages. These abstract terms — the nominal versions of actions and events — can be reinstated at each of those points when the academic reader's **mental desktop** needs instructions on managing information. While the details on particular firms and industries and school curriculum can be filed away, the high-level terms should be kept handy.

Scholarly writers seem to need a concentrated expression they can reinstate to bind together parts of their discussion and to manage extensive stretches of lower-level information. These expressions are like elevated platforms from which the extent of the argument can be captured in a glance. There is not much standing-room on these platforms, so, when the arguments are complex, the expression can be dense. In the article on

Bangladeshi garment workers, "labour supply decision-making" has to capture at once the article's distinctions as a contribution to the analysis of labour markets. The author examines labour as offered by workers rather than required by firms — hence "labour supply." And she examines the conditions which determine the decisions people make about work in an immigrant community where husbands' wishes about the wives' work may not coincide with the women's wishes, and where both sets of choices are hemmed in by racial attitudes in the surrounding community. *Labour supply decision-making* is the platform from which expanses of statistical and interview data can be viewed.

These viewing platforms are situated throughout the scholarly article, often working to incorporate summary of other writers' statements. Below, in an article on *voluntary employee turnover* (people quitting their jobs), *employee turnover* is ground shared by the other writers and the current authors, while the expressions *job alternatives* (If I quit will I be able to get another job? Will it be a good one?) and *job satisfaction* (Am I happy in my work? Do I get along with my boss? Will I be promoted?) themselves compress information. And these abstractions not only point back to accumulated reasoning but also can be extracted from the publication and indexed as *key words* — to signal to researchers the site of scholarly conversation on a topic shared in a research community. Abstractions sum up previous research attention and the current episode — and they point forward, too, as reference or orientation for other researchers' future work:

> In a major conceptual advance from previous research directions, Hulin and colleagues (1985) recognized that job alternatives and satisfaction could have substantially different effects on employee turnover across various populations. For example, job alternatives but not job satisfaction might have a substantial and direct effect on turnover among marginal and temporary employees (often described as the secondary labor market). In contrast, both alternatives and job satisfaction might have significant effects on turnover among permanent and full-time employees.
>
> Thomas W. Lee and Terence R. Mitchell 1994 "An alternative approach: The unfolding model of voluntary employee turnover." *Academy of Management Journal* 19 (1): 51–89, 54.

Nominal expressions also tend to appear as writers end one section of argument and move on to the next stage. Here, the writer concerned with

subsistence economies concludes a three-part account of the "world cri-
ses" affecting the "submerged ethnicities." She uses three expressions which
nominalize verbs (and remove their agents) to compress the preceding
discussion and make it portable, able to be carried forward compactly to
the next section:

> These world trends of **integration of economies, dependence on
> finance capital**, and **erosion of subsistence security** have profound
> consequences for the societies we study, whether they are located in
> core industrial countries or in developing areas. I shall illustrate their
> implications in three case studies of integration into the **global
> economy** where I have carried out fieldwork.
>
> Nash 1994: 13 (emphasis added).

Unlike many other genres, scholarly genres must live up to demanding coherence requirements, hinged on abstraction and spread through
deep descents to specifics and sharp ascents to generality. We could say
that these large patterns of abstraction and specificity at text level determine smaller patterns at sentence level.

Earlier in this chapter, we asked what benefits come from long expressions which many measures would estimate as cognitively costly (hard to
read). Now we have the answer: cognitive cost at the level of sentence
and phrase brings a profit at the level of textual coherence.

Yet the model of the reader's mental desktop warns us that those sen-
tence-level costs can be high — to readers who give up, and to writers
who can't get through to exhausted readers. So you will find academic
writers stopping to unpack a passage and relieve some of the congestion
on the desktop.

> Pleck suggests that Afro-American women worked more as a reac-
> tion to their greater long-term potential for income inadequacy than
> to immediate economic deprivation. It was as if they were taking
> out insurance against future problems.
>
> James A. Geschwender 1992 "Ethgender, women's waged labor, and economic mobility."
> *Social Problems* 39 (1): 1–16, 7.

Sensing perhaps that "immediate economic deprivation" (being poor? not
having enough money?) and "long-term potential for income inadequacy"
(worry about not having enough money later?) are complicated ways of
speaking, the author rephrases these expressions in everyday language.

In other words, while the research genres privilege the heavily nominal phrase — for reasons we have just examined — they also privilege corrections to the socio-cognitive conditions produced by their own styles. We practiced one of these stylistic correctives in Chapter 5: the appositive expression. The appositive says it again, in other words, giving the reader a second chance at an important but difficult concept. For instance, the writer in the passage immediately above says again "long-term potential for income inadequacy." Seeded throughout research writing we find two tiny expressions which signal writers' efforts to say it again: *i.e.* and *e.g.* The expression *i.e.* (an abbreviation for *id est,* a Latin expression meaning "that is") signals that an element in the preceding statement (or statements) will be repeated: *i.e.* works *laterally,* putting an additional expression next to the one which the writer estimates as important but difficult, or important and complex, and deserving further attention. Synonymous with *i.e.* are *that is, namely, in other words, that is to say.*

On the other hand, *e.g.* (*exempla gratia,* another Latin term, meaning "for example") signals that an element in the preceding statement will be exemplified, at a lower level of generality; *e.g.* works *vertically,* descending from high levels to lower levels of specificity. Synonymous with *e.g.* are *for example, for instance.* Both *i.e.* and *e.g.* can work as appositives — enriching readers' understanding of a term, inviting their cooperation in its use in the particular context.

By these means, writers can reduce cognitive costs of heavy nominal expressions to the reader. But what can readers do when they face imposing clumps of nominals? Rather than give up, they can unpack those clumps for themselves, finding the everyday wordings that would represent the ideas at stake, and trying to think of examples of what the writer is talking about.

---

**Exercise 5**
Take the three passages at the beginning of this section and unpack them for yourself. In each case try to construct concrete examples of what the writers are talking about. Using i.e and e.g., rewrite the passages, incorporating answers to the set of questions immediately following each passage.

## 9F Messages about the Argument

In the previous sections we saw that the research genres are distinguished by nominalizaton and the superstructure of abstraction that it builds. Both nominalization and abstraction can appear in other genres. But they do not work in the same way they do in the research genres, where they consistently enforce the special coherence of scholarly writing and attach individual research contributions to an ongoing scholarly conversation. The features we will inspect in this section — **messages about the argument** — also distinguish the academic genres.

The following passage, which appeared in a geography journal, exhibits several features we will investigate:

> … the study of gender issues generally in rural areas remains relatively neglected (Little 1991).
>
> This paper is an attempt to begin to redress the balance by concentrating on the gender divisions apparent in the material collected by the Rural Church Project, and aims also to highlight the need for further specific study of gender and the rural church. After a brief discussion of the history of staffing in the Church of England, we consider recent published studies on gender roles in the Church and our own material from the Rural Church Project survey on the staffing of parishes in five dioceses. We then turn to rural parishioners and consider the influence of gender on church attendance and religious belief, together with attitudes towards women priests. Our conclusion is an attempt to reconcile the very different pictures of the rural church which emerge from the information on staffing on the one hand and attendance, belief and attitudes to women priests on the other.
>
> Susanne Seymour 1994 "Gender, church and people in rural areas." *Area* 26 (1): 45–56, 45.

This passage refers to itself ("This paper"); it refers to the author ("We"); it forecasts the argument to follow; it situates itself in relation to what other studies have said —or not said.

To sharpen your sense of these features as distinctive, call to mind other genres, familiar from everyday life. Would you find a newspaper report or a thank-you note referring to itself?

| | |
|---|---|
| This report provides information on protest at the legislature. | This thank-you note expresses gratitude for two gifts received last week. |

Probably not, although instances of some other genres (very formal business letters, for example, or legal documents) can refer to themselves. Would you find a newspaper report or thank-you note referring to the author in this (limited) sense?

| | |
|---|---|
| I/we present a series of quotations from participants at the protest. | I/we describe the gift in favourable terms. |

Probably not, although the thank-you-note writer may refer to himself in other senses ("I have been very busy at school and look forward to the holidays"). Would you find a newspaper report or thank-you note forecasting its discussion?

| | |
|---|---|
| These quotations will be followed by quotations from political figures responding to the protest. | Following the description of the gift, brief news about the recipient's family will be presented. |

Again, probably not. And it is hard to construct a situation where either of these everyday genres would situate the current utterance, what is being said, in relation to what others have said, or not said.

| | |
|---|---|
| Little information about this event has been published, since it only happened yesterday. | No one has so far expressed gratitude for this gift in writing. |

Later we will look at this last feature, which situates the utterance in relation to other utterances. In the meantime, we will examine the other features which distinguish the cited passage from — at least — newspaper reports and thank-you notes.

---

### Exercise 6

Inspect essays you have written recently or are currently drafting: do you find expressions which refer to the essay itself? (Keep in mind that such wordings appear at points where writers make major claims or promises.) How do you feel about saying, "This study focuses on three explanations for …"? Would you feel better saying, "This paper …" or "This essay …"?

## 9G **The Discursive *I***

One feature in the above passage on gender roles in rural churches (p. 183) that sometimes surprises students is the author's tendency to refer to herself. Although the first-person singular *I*—and the plural *we*— occurs in the scholarly genres with nowhere near the frequency that it does in daily conversation (where it is a favoured sentence-opener), it is by no means absent from published scholarship.

Sometimes students ask their teachers if they want them to use *I*, or to avoid it. This question is often accompanied by a question as to whether the teachers are interested in the students' own opinions. In the long history of the teaching of writing, *I* and "opinion" have become connected.

However, in conventional, mainstream scholarship, it would be hard to connect *I* with the ordinary sense of "opinion," in light of the constraints under which it occurs. We will now examine these constraints.

Here are some occurrences of *I* in published scholarship. See if you can infer the constraints which control the use of *I*. (Analysis follows, but try to make this out for yourself before looking at the analysis.)

> Lesbian theory and feminism, I want to suggest, are at risk of falling into a similar unhappy marriage in which "the one" is feminism.
>
> Calhoun 1994: 573.

> ... I shall focus upon expectations and evaluations regarding the participation of married women, with husband present, in the waged labor force. I begin with a discussion of the "cult of domesticity," explore ethnic variations in commitments to the cult, examine the causes and consequences of its decline in influence, and evaluate the consequences for ethnic groups of difference in rates at which married women work for wages. I close with a consideration of policy implications.
>
> Geschwender 1992: 1.

> This article has two purposes. The first is to show that ability grouping in secondary schools does not always have the same effect, and therefore it is worth seeking ways of using it more effectively than commonly occurs. A brief review of earlier studies, and a reinterpretation of the conclusions of an earlier synthesis, provide the support for this claim. The second goal is to explore instances of

relatively successful uses of ability grouping, in the sense that high-quality instruction fosters significant learning among students assigned to low-ability classes. What characterizes such classes? To address this question, I draw on evidence from earlier studies by other authors, and I provide two new illustrations taken from a larger study of eighth- and ninth-grade English classes in 25 midwestern schools.

Adam Gamoran 1993 "Alternative uses of ability grouping in secondary schools: Can we bring high-quality instruction to low-ability classes?" *American Journal of Education* 102: 1–22, 1.

On the one hand, the *I* of the writer in these passages seems to hover on the vanishing point. In virtually every case, the *I*-construction could be eliminated without depleting content. It could simply disappear ("Lesbian theory and feminist theory are at risk of …") or be replaced by one of the text-referring words like "study" ("this study focuses"), and the last passage mixes such words ("article," "review") with instances of *I*.

Given the frequency with which *I* makes its appearance in the scholarly genres, we might look at the typical habitat of the first-person pronoun: what does it occur with? Then we notice that all the verbs that have first-person subjects refer to some **discourse action**, something the writer is doing:

**I want to suggest**
**I begin with**
**I shall focus**
**I explore, examine, evaluate**
**I close**
**I draw on evidence**
**I provide**

Analysts who specialize in the study of the research genres would distinguish among these verbs, finding different categories of discourse action. But, for our purposes, it is enough to note their general similarity: they all describe the speaker in his or her capacity as a writer/researcher. Let us call the *I* of the scholarly genres the **discursive *I***.

As a writer in the scholarly genres, you can refer to yourself, pointing yourself out to your reader. But, as we have seen, your identity is limited, and attitudes to these limitations run to extremes. So many students report that their teachers and professors have instructed them not to use *I* that there must still be some *I*-avoidance afoot. Perhaps this can be explained by the limitations on *I* when it occurs in scholarship. Those who would disallow *I* translate the limits into a blanket prohibition.

Taking a different view, some scholars criticize the research genres for the limits they put on *I*. Conventions which limit writers to the discursive *I* erase elements of identity that are, in fact, relevant to research and its results. Such criticisms propose that who we are, as social and political beings, influences what we choose to study, how we gather information, and how we interpret that information. The discursive *I* obscures those influences and limits not only the surface expression of scholarship but its deeper character as well. In the next chapter we will look at instances in which *I* preserves a greater degree of the researcher's identity, but for now we should recognize the frequency with which the discursive *I* appears in the research genres.

---

### Exercise 7

What do you think of the reference to the "author" in the following passage? Does it help you to know that this paper was written by a psychologist? Can you devise any other way of writing this passage — without using the first person singular?

> The author decided to investigate the academic achievement levels of the teenage mothers with whom she was working after being told repeatedly that their favorite subject in school was math — an unexpected and perplexing finding because girls are generally reported to feel they are not good at, and thus dislike, math (Parsons, Adler, and Kaczala, 1982).

Rauch-Elnekave 1994: 97.

### Exercise 8

Inspect essays you have written recently or are currently composing: how do you represent yourself when you write an academic paper? Are you happy with this representation? Would your friends and family recognize you? What options do you feel you have? Do the options vary according to the discipline you are working in?

## 9H Forecasts and Emphasis

Like references to the text itself, the discursive *I* of scholarly writing often occurs along with **forecasts**: statements about how the argument will be organized, what readers can expect.

> **First**, I will summarize prior research indicating that instruction is typically inferior in low-ability classes. **Second**, I will briefly show that new data from a study of midwestern secondary schools mainly conform to this pattern. **Third**, I will give four examples — two drawn from past research, and two original cases taken from the study of midwestern secondary schools — that illustrate that high-quality instruction can occur in low-ability classes. **Finally**, I will consider the limitations and implications of these illustrations.
>
> Gamoran 1993: 4–5 (emphasis added).

Forecasts can also show up in agentless forms — that is, without either the text itself or the discursive *I* promising a particular course of discussion.

> Before proceeding to a more precise description of **the research methods used** and a detailed discussion of sample matched reader-writer protocols, **the relevance of this study** to current theoretical disputes over appropriate rhetorical techniques and planning processes for appellate advocates **should be put into sharper focus. Two basic issues will be addressed:**
>
> 1) What rhetorical techniques in briefs do current brief writing theories recommend appellates use, and what conflicts exist between these theories?
>
> 2) What problems has empirical research investigating these theories encountered?
>
> James F. Stratman 1994 "Investigating persuasive processes in legal discourse in real time: Cognitive biases and rhetorical strategy in appeal court briefs." *Discourse Processes* 17: 1–57 (emphasis added).

This passage achieves its agentlessness by using the **passive voice**: "the research methods used" (*who* used the methods?); "the relevance ... should be put into sharper focus" (*who* should do this?); "two basic issues will be addressed" (*who* will address the issues?).

The passive voice has been condemned by many, and defended by few. Despite its bad reputation amongst people who compose rules-for-writing, however, it is very common in scholarly expression, as well as elsewhere. In the three passive constructions listed above, for example, the themes of the sentences ("the research methods," "the relevance," and "two basic issues") are more important than *who* is "using," "addressing," or "putting them into sharper focus." The passive voice enables this focus on sentence themes.

While we do not run across forecasts (either with or without passive constructions) so often in everyday life —

| | |
|---|---|
| MATTHEW: What have you been up to? | MARK: In addressing your question, I will first express my philosophy of life. Next, I will show that philosophy operating in my recent activities. Finally, I will describe my plans for the future. |

— they are extremely common in the scholarly genres. It seems that forecasts play an important role in helping readers manage the contents of their mental desktops. Forecasts instruct the mental desktop's information-**management device**. They guide readers in determining when one section is finished and another beginning — determining, that is, when to file lower-level information, compacting its gist into higher-level statements that can be kept handy as the discussion goes on to other areas.

Readers are also served by statements of **emphasis**. Here are some examples.

The **crucial point** for this essay is that between 1939 and 1944 the organization attracted *popular support.*

*

Our **main interest** here is the style of the printed language — how did it reconcile with the everyday language of the predominantly oral world?

Thiathu J. Nemutanzhela 1993 "Cultural forms and literacy as resources for political mobilisation: A.M. Malivha and the Zoutpansberg Balemi Association." *African Studies* 52 (1): 89–102, 92–93 (bold emphasis added, italic emphasis in original).

*

The **general point here** is that there are instances — this [campaigns for non-sexist language] is one — where we can locate the specific and concrete steps leading to an observable change in some people's linguistic behaviour and in the system itself.

Deborah Cameron 1990 "Demythologizing sociolinguistics: Why language does not reflect society." In *Ideologies of Language*, ed. John E. Joseph and Talbot J. Taylor. London: Routledge, 91 (emphasis added).

*

What I want to **highlight** in Wittig's explanation of what bars lesbians from the category "woman" is that it claims both too much and too little for lesbians as well as reads lesbianism from a peculiarly heterosexual viewpoint.

Calhoun 1994: 563 (emphasis added).

A common means of achieving emphasis is to use the **cleft** form of a sentence (i.e., a sentence that begins "It was X that …" rather than "X …") Many guides to "good" style disallow sentences beginning with *it*. These sentences are said to be boring or "empty." Yet *it* in English serves a built-in grammar of **emphasis**, known as the cleft. Notice how *it* works in these ordinary, conversational sentences to stage the importance of a particular part of the sentence.

| Julie brought the cookies. [not anybody else] | It was Julie who brought the cookies. |

A speaker could use intonation — "*Julie* brought the cookies" — to achieve emphasis. Writers can't use intonation — but they can (and do) use the cleft form of the sentence. (Notice how, if you say the second sentence above, stress falls on "Julie.") If the speaker or writer wanted to emphasize the contribution rather than the contributor, they could say or write:

It was the cookies that Julie brought [not the lasagna].

In research writing, cleft sentences beginning with *it* can accomplish emphasis, e.g.,

It was Foucault's work that mobilized research of institutions under the "surveillance" theme.

And, while we are thinking about sentences beginning with *it*, we can also observe that on many occasions the tendencies of English will use the **end-weight principle** to shift heavy material to sentence-end, leaving the sentence beginning "empty." Of the following pair, the first is more likely to be produced by English speakers and writers.

It may be argued that this neglect is due to a lack of scholarly interest in the rural church rather than in gender relations in the Anglican Church as a whole.

That this neglect is due to a lack of scholarly interest in the rural church rather than in gender relations in the Anglican Church as a whole may be argued.

The reason that the first is usually preferred is that it obeys the "end-weight" principle in English: a tendency for sentences to tilt, letting heavy material slide to the end, and producing what's called **anticipatory-it** or **it-extraposition**. Like the passive voice, sentences beginning with *it* have been criticized by authorities on "good" style, but there seems to be little basis for these criticisms.

The use of emphasis is not, however, universal in academic writing. Some research articles provide neither forecasts nor emphasis pointers. Movements along the hierarchy of generalization — from high-level abstraction to specifics and back again — themselves convey implicit messages about the argument, messages that will alert experienced readers to important points in the text. Nevertheless, many do use expressions of emphasis, and most seem to offer some kind of forecast.

Similarly, most instances of the discursive *I* could be removed, and the expression in which they occur adjusted to get across equivalent information. But *I* occurs nevertheless, with some frequency. Perhaps both techniques not only benefit readers' desktop-management devices but also provide writers with greater control over the use that readers make of their texts. Perhaps forecasts and emphasis pointers would have, on some occasions, controlled some of those unruly readers/instructors who missed your point. While we could speculate that both forecasts and emphasis (and the associated references to the text itself and its writer) are signs that scholarly genres are domineering or overpowering in their measures for controlling readers' interpretive work, we can perhaps also sympathize with writers' desires to overrule the hazards of misunderstanding.

The scholarly genres can seem aloof productions, remote from the personal contact and proximities of more mundane genres or of everyday conversation. Yet the features we have looked at in this section all summon writer and reader to the same spot, putting the writer in close touch with the reader.

### Exercise 9

Imagine a reader from outside the academic community encountering the passage below (which is the first paragraph of an introduction). How could you prepare that reader for contact with this example of scholarly expression? How would you explain the features of the passage so the imagined reader would understand them as functional expressions of the academic community's routines and procedures? (It might help to imagine a particular reader — a friend, family member, neighbour, co-worker, or maybe yourself at an earlier stage of your education.)

## PASSAGE A

Recent research in the history of nineteenth century psychiatry has explored the expanding powers of the medical profession and the proliferation of the asylum, that "magic machine" for curing insanity. This medicalization of madness has usually been portrayed as a "top-down" process: "social control imposed from above with greater or lesser success on a population now the unwitting object of medical encadrement." But as historians have begun to study individual asylums and the complexities of committal, more emphasis is being placed on the role played by families in the process. Asylum doctors, it has been suggested, merely confirmed a diagnosis of insanity already made by families, by neighbors, or by non-medical authorities. Consequently, as the American historian Nancy Tomes has argued, "the composition of a nineteenth century asylum population tells more about the family's response to insanity than the incidence or definition of the condition itself." Such arguments imply a more "dynamic and dialectical" interpretation of the process of medicalization, one that requires a careful assessment of family demands for medical services and the degree to which these demands were met, willingly or unwillingly, by the emerging psychiatric profession. In the present stage of research on mental illness and its treatment, it is vital to expand the range of institutional studies.

Patricia E. Prestwich 1994 "Family strategies and medical power: 'Voluntary' committal in a Parisian asylum, 1876–1914." *Journal of Social History* 27 (4): 799–818, 799.

## 91 Presupposing vs. Asserting

Another feature of academic writing that may pose particular difficulty for student writers is the way that writers sometimes provide almost introductory explanations and at other times seem to assume that their readers already know apparently obscure matters. As we noticed in Chapter 5, explaining a term, defining it appositionally or even more elaborately, does not necessarily mean that you take your reader to be uninformed. Instead it can be a means of negotiating or confirming common ground. Sometimes things should not be taken for granted, and should be attributed, defined, or explained, to show that the writer respects certain ideas as having been painstakingly constructed by the research community. In such cases we detect writers **asserting** claims. But at other times writers appear to satisfy their readers by representing things as understood, and by not explaining — in other words, **presupposing** knowledge on the part of the reader. In these cases, terms like *of course* and *obviously* project the writer's interpretation of the **state of knowledge** – the distribution of knowledge, its rarity or commonness. *Of course* draws boundaries around **discourse communities**: people who belong to these communities know the topics marked with *of course* and other signs of **obviousness**; they don't need to have things explained.

As if it were not already challenging enough for newcomers to estimate the distribution and obviousness of knowledge in the disciplines, we find that *of course* and the other signs of a statement's obviousness are not the only ways of signalling that knowledge is shared. In the example which follows, the writer makes several assumptions about readers' knowledge of the topic, through **definite expressions** — *the* or *this* phrases that are heavily nominalized.

> Recent research in **the history of nineteenth century psychiatry** has explored **the expanding powers of the medical profession** and **the proliferation of the asylum**, that "magic machine" for curing insanity. **This medicalization of madness** has been portrayed as a "top-down" process ....
>
> Prestwich 1994: 799 (emphasis added).

An alternative version of these sentences shows just how much the original takes for granted and assumes as already known by the reader.

> Psychiatry was practised in the nineteenth century. In the nineteenth century, the powers of the medical profession expanded, and asylums proliferated. Madness was medicalized.

Whereas the original version presupposes this knowledge, the alternative version asserts it. Perhaps you can hear how the first version constructs the reader as *knowing*, and the second constructs the reader as *unknowing*, and needing to be told.

In any social situation, the choice between presupposing and asserting can be tricky, for, as we see, it conveys messages about the speaker's ideas of the addressee's state of knowledge. It can also convey messages about the speaker: by always asserting, the speaker can seem naive or can appear to have just learned something that is in fact well known. In the research genres, the choice between presupposing and asserting can be particularly tricky in that "knowingness" is crucial to status and power. And it seems that students can sometimes make the mistake of starting too far back, explaining too much, and thereby offending their expert readers. John Swales (1990) reports a case study of just this situation, where a PhD student's dissertation in the biological sciences explained too much, presupposed too little, and excited sarcastic and impatient comments from her readers. At the same time, however, readers can react negatively to a writer's offhand mention of a complicated concept, and can appreciate an explanatory account of it. (In the sample above, for example, what does it mean, exactly, for something to be "medicalized"? These days, lots of people are finding instances of "medicalization" here or there, but we may have been neglecting the concept itself, taking too much for granted.)

Presupposing expressions can take many forms: proper nouns, for example. (To say simply "Chomsky" rather than "Noam Chomsky is a transformational linguist" presupposes that readers know who Chomsky is, and can identify him for themselves. It also presupposes that we know what Chomsky does — what a transformational linguist is.) We will not go into all these forms here. Nor can we come to any conclusions about what kinds of knowledge students should presuppose and what kinds they should assert, for, at this point, we don't know a lot about this aspect of the style of the research genres — or any other genres. What we do know, however, is that readers are sensitive to patterns of presupposition, and that these patterns signal information about the state of knowledge and its distribution.

**Exercise 10**

The following statements are opening sentences from articles in a variety of disciplines. Some (but not all) presupposing expressions in each are shown in bold-face type. To develop your awareness of the effect of these expressions, rewrite each passage to **assert** what the original presupposes. You may find yourself resorting to *there* expressions (e.g., "the three aspects of readability" becomes "there are three aspects of readability"); *there* expressions in English are specially designed for asserting. You may also notice that many of the bold expressions are **nominalizations**: a stylistic feature we have become familiar with in our study of the research genres.

### PASSAGE A

Scholars have long noted, often with disapproval, **the tardiness of the introduction of printing to the Muslim world**, but **the consequences of that introduction on the production, reproduction, and transmission of knowledge in Muslim societies** are now only beginning to be understood.

Adeeb Khalid 1994 "Printing, publishing, and reform in Tsarist Central Asia." *International Journal of Middle East Studies* 26: 187–200 (emphasis added).

### PASSAGE B

**When Margaret Fuller's *Woman in the Nineteenth Century* first appeared in the winter of 1845,** few readers were prepared to accept **her uncompromising proposition that "inward and outward freedom for woman as for man shall be as a right, not yielded as a concession".**

Annette Kolodny 1994 "Inventing a feminist discourse: Rhetoric and resistance in Margaret Fuller's *Woman in the Nineteenth Century.*" *New Literary History* 25 (2): 355–82 (emphasis added).

### PASSAGE C

During the 1980s and 1990s a number of factors emerged in various countries of western Europe to raise anew questions about **the meanings of national identity. The finally acknowledged presence of settled immigrant populations** (as opposed to transient-worker populations), **the arrival in western Europe**

**of large numbers of asylum-seekers from southern and east-
ern Europe and from the Third World** and, most recently,
debates in the countries of the European community about
some of **the provisions of the Maastricht Treaty** have been
among the most significant factors that have fuelled contro-
versies about national identity.

Christopher T. Husbands 1994 "Crisis of national identity as the 'new moral panics':
Political agenda-setting about definitions of nationhood." *New Community* 20 (2):
191–206 (emphasis added).

# 10

# Making and maintaining knowledge

When research findings are reported to the public, in the broadcast media or the general-circulation print media, they are normally "popularized." That is, specialist or technical terms are translated and replaced with everyday ones. We can expect that, thereby, some meanings are lost — careful distinctions produced by technicality itself. But we might also expect that some other meanings, equally important, are also lost in popularizations since research genres not only report findings but also represent the knowledge-making process itself.

In Chapters 2–4 and Chapter 6 in particular, we saw that summary and orchestration of voices are central features of scholarly writing. When academic writers introduce and orchestrate other voices, they indicate and make audible a **state of knowledge**: its limits, the conditions under which it was produced, the positions from which statements issue. Through such orchestration of others' voices, academic writers can establish a position in the scholarly conversation that opens up possibilities for their own contribution to knowledge. The position they establish by citing others defines what hasn't been said, what needs to be said, or even what has been mistakenly said. In short, it identifies what we will call a **knowledge deficit**. As we will see, knowledge deficits are about the making of knowledge, about how new knowledge can be made.

Chapter 11 focuses explicitly on the state of knowledge and knowledge deficits, the most concentrated expressions of which often appear in introductions and conclusions. This chapter extends the study of summary and orchestration, and so begins to sketch ways in which the state of knowledge and knowledge deficits find expression in the research genres. The following sections focus on features which mark statements for their status as knowledge — and distinguish research discourse from popular genres and also from some forms of school writing.

## 10A Making Knowledge

Consider for a minute what it means to make knowledge. Say Matthew felt a need to know, on a particular summer day, if that day was warmer or cooler than the day before. He might consult his own sensations, and find that, yes, this day was hotter. Reporting his sensations, he gets some corroboration.

MATTHEW: Whew. It's hot.     THOMAS: Yes. A real scorcher.
This is the hottest day.     This is the hottest day.

We could say that Matthew and his corroborator have in an informal way begun to make some knowledge of the relative temperatures of the season in question. (They might go on to compare this season to others, and generalize about climatic conditions.)

But say both Matthew and his corroborator had, the day before, gone for a long swim in a mountain lake. The swim cooled their bodies, and they found the air temperate, not scorching. You could say that their position — their point of view, their experience of the world — had affected their findings about relative temperature. Aware of variables like swimming in glacial waters, the next time Matthew constructs knowledge of relative temperatures he looks for some sign outside himself and his closely positioned corroborator.

MATTHEW: This is the hottest     THOMAS: Yes.
day. The butter's melting. It
didn't melt yesterday. This is
the hottest day.

Now they could be said to have made knowledge by consulting a sign (butter), reading it (it's melting), and citing this evidence. But Thomas might question Matthew's evidence.

THOMAS: *Our* butter melted a bit yesterday, too. Where do you keep your butter? How much did it melt?

So Matthew has made some knowledge of relative temperature (it's hot enough to melt butter), but it is vulnerable to criticism. Or, to put it another way, this knowledge is not conclusive: it provokes further knowledge-making.

Finally, if Matthew wanted to make knowledge that was independent of his position — his swimming experience, his habits in storing and observing his butter — he might consult a widely recognized and respected instrument of measurement: a thermometer.

MATTHEW: This is the hottest day. It's 33 degrees Celsius. It was only 31 degrees yesterday.

This may seem to put an end to knowledge-making on this topic, but someone could go further (claiming a **knowledge deficit**), questioning Matthew's instrument or its use.

THOMAS: Are you sure? Did you move the thermometer? I keep mine in the shade. Have you had your thermometer checked?

Or someone could question the use of the instrument itself and emphasize the importance of subjective experience.

THOMAS: Yesterday was hotter for me. I was tarring a roof. I've never been so hot in my life. It's very well to say it's the hottest day, but you aren't taking into account the experience of roofers.

In this sequence of knowledge-making actions, we have, very roughly, travelled through the range of **methods** of the research disciplines, from "soft" (so-called "subjective" interpretations of data corroborated by members of a community occupying similar positions) to "hard" (so-called "objective" interpretation sustained by research instruments which produce quantitative readings of the world) and back to what we might call "critical" (sort of "reflexive-soft" interpretations which question whether any knowledge can ever be produced independent of the interpreter's position).

Even without the critical techniques of current theory, we can see that knowledge-making procedures differ from discipline to discipline. These differences are reflected in stylistic differences: different ways of representing the production of knowledge. The most conspicuous of these differences is that which distinguishes publications with lots of numbers from those with no numbers. This difference has been characterized as the difference between **quantitative** and **qualitative** study.

**Quantitative** method aims to approach knowledge-making as objectively as possible: that is, it seeks to set aside biases caused by an individual's beliefs or immediate experience of the world by observing and quantifying controlled studies or experiments using as broad a sample as possible. A classic example of the success of quantitative study is the Copernican revolution, in which the earth-centred view of the solar system was gradually replaced with the sun-centred model. The invention of the telescope and the observations of planetary motion by Galileo provided empirical evidence that the earth revolves around the sun, despite deeply ingrained beliefs to the contrary and the apparently obvious evidence of our senses when we observe the sun rising and setting on a daily basis. In another famous example of the quantitative method, James Watson and Francis Crick used studies showing that in DNA adenine was always present in the same amount as thymine, with the same holding true for guanine and cytosine. These ratios helped invalidate previous three-strand models of DNA and confirm Watson and Crick's hypothesis that DNA is structured as a double helix. This sort of method, which you probably associate with the sciences, attempts to quantify empirically reproducible findings. In the example above, when Matthew uses a thermometer to observe the temperature, he is taking the first step toward quantitative study. Of course, meteorologists would approach Matthew's question in a more systematic and sophisticated manner, by referring to temperature readings in a number of established locations recorded over years. So, a meteorologist might point out that while an average temperature of 33 degrees Celsius is the hottest day of the year where Matthew lives, in fact, it was several degrees hotter on the same day twenty years ago, and is often hotter on many days in some countries closer to the equator.

A significant part of undergraduate education in the sciences and social sciences is devoted to learning established methods for quantitative study. These methods vary according to discipline and the phenomena studied, but the central importance of quantitative study to making knowledge should lead us to expect stylistic expressions that reflect it in the research genres (see Section 10B below, for example). However, these methods are not without their critics, even within disciplines that favour quantitative research.

Critics of scholarly practice have suggested that research with a strictly quantitative emphasis produces distorted versions of people's experience of the world. Once phenomena — events and attitudes, and the people who are involved in those events or harbour those attitudes — are translated into units which can be counted, and the numbers are subjected to routines of statistical interpretation, they get separated from the meaningful complexities of real-life contexts. So a study of, for example, "learning outcomes" in a hundred classrooms might identify three relevant conditions: the socioeconomic identity of the learners (as measured by a standard scale), their learning styles (as measured by a standard method of classifying learning styles), and their performance in a subject area (as measured by a standardized test). The results could lead to changes in curriculum or teaching strategies. Critics of this kind of research argue that such quantifications erase the classroom moment, the experience of students and teachers, the complex interactions amongst them. Research quantifications produce a limited or possibly skewed version of the world, and their applications can be unrealistic. In place of or in addition to quantitative research they propose **qualitative** research.

**Qualitative** research can take various forms. One way to look at it is to say that it distinguishes itself from quantitative research by replacing the *many* instances (open to statistical interpretation) with *one* instance or a few instances. The one instance is examined in detail. The long-distance panoramas of quantitative research are replaced by close-up views. So, in the qualitative version of the learning-outcomes study, researchers would locate themselves in one classroom and watch — for days, months, even years. They would record what they saw, taking notes, using video or audio tapes; they would collect documents and artifacts (the teacher's lesson plans, tests, students' work, and so on); they would talk to the teacher and to the students. Unlike quantitative researchers, who arrange measurable situations (controlled instruction, perhaps; tests administered solely for the purpose of the study), qualitative researchers try to leave things as they are. The only change is the presence of the researchers themselves. Back at their desks, the qualitative researchers interpret the material they have gathered. Surveying their data, they look for patterns and regularities, and, consulting the theoretical tools available to them, they develop explanations for what they have observed.

Both quantitative and qualitative techniques seek generalizations, but they establish the *authority* of their generalizations by different means.

While quantitative studies represent their validity by numerousness and recognized means of manipulating numerous instances to coax out statistically significant results, qualitative studies have only the one instance (as in a "case study") or the one group (such as a group of young women who read teen romance fiction). So, while the "objective" style of quantitative research and the rhetorical force of that style are very important (consider, for a moment, the implications of our discussions on limits of the discursive "I" in Chapter 9G), qualitative research may actually be even more dependent on *style of reporting* to persuade readers to accept generalizations developed from limited instances. Moreover, as qualitative study generates an abundance of detail, the means of controlling these data, and transforming them into text that readers can understand, are perhaps more demanding for writers than the customary techniques used for producing text to report quantitative research.

Qualitative techniques show up in various disciplines, and, while many scholarly journals are exclusively quantitative in the submissions they publish, and some tend toward qualitative research, many others publish both quantitative and qualitative work. You will also find articles that are themselves a mix of quantitative and qualitative techniques. Given this variety in form and occurrence, it would be rash to list rules for reporting research. Nonetheless, the shared concern for the sources of knowledge and an interest in tracing the production of knowledge lead to some features common to both quantitative and qualitative research. The prominence of **reported speech** is an obvious sign of these interests and concerns (see Chapters 2, 3, and 11), but it is not the only sign of them. Appearing with some regularity throughout reports of research are typical expressions which signify that knowledge is under construction and in the process of being made, and that it comes from a **position** in the research community. In Sections 10D and 10E we will inspect some of these expressions, including **modalizing** and **limiting expressions** and try to arrive at generalizations about their use. Finally, we will consider the relation between tenses and knowledge-making, specifically looking at how **tenses** may represent the history of research. First, though, in section 10B, we will glance at the research genres' most explicit demonstration that knowledge is made. Along the lines that distinguish quantitative from qualitative study, research genres are also distinguished by whether they make provision for a "**Methods**" section — an explicit account of how the researchers produced the knowledge they are now reporting — or leave method implicit.

**Exercise 1**

Consider how knowledge is made in different disciplines. Drawing on your experience of different courses you have taken, reading you have done, and the experiences of friends, compare knowledge-making practices or methods in the natural sciences, social sciences, and humanities. Which would you identify as primarily qualitative? Which are quantitative? Which seem to combine both methods? In what ways do features such as individual observation and interpretation, quantification of data, statistical analysis, experiments using control groups, and so on define each discipline's knowledge-making practice as qualitative or quantitative?

## 10B Method Sections

Method sections expose the procedures by which knowledge has been produced.

> MATTHEW: I used the following method. I placed a thermometer on the east-facing wall of my house. I took readings from the thermometer on two days in a row at noon. I compared the readings.

The rhetoric of method sections has been much studied, for these sections show some interesting stylistic features. For one thing, they tend towards **agentless expressions** (see Chapter 9D and 9H). So you will find in one of the samples in the exercise below these wordings: "[t]he conversations to be examined here ..."; "[t]he groups were formed after consultation with the children's teachers." In these cases, the people who examine, form groups, and consult with teachers are missing from the statement. If Matthew was to explain his method in this way, it might look like the following:

> MATTHEW: Method: A thermometer was placed on an east-facing wall of an average-size dwelling. Readings were taken from the thermometer on two successive days at midday. The readings were compared.

This feature of style has excited a lot of commentary, and sometimes it is interpreted as a way of persuading readers that the researchers' methods were very "scientific" and "objective," and not open to personal bias. The importance of reproducing results in quantitative study may also explain the emphasis on actions rather than on the agents of that action.

Another interesting feature of method sections is their unusual pattern of coherence: although sentences are all, roughly, about "method," sometimes the relation between sentences is obscure. So, in the first sample in the exercise below, you will find:

> The participants in this study were educationally and socially advantaged, middle-class, urban children who were predominantly white. The children attended the day-care centre for full days, year round, and had known each other for 1–3 years.

If this were not a method section, a reader could very well ask, "What is the connection between, on the one hand, race and socioeconomic status and, on the other hand, full-time attendance in daycare? Is it a causal connection? And what does any of this have to do with the topic of the article?" But it is a method section, so readers don't ask these questions.

---

### Exercise 2

Three samples of method sections appear below. (Only Passage 3 is complete.) Analyze these samples for agentlessness and connectedness. Then consider the overall function of these passages: If you were to generalize from these limited data, what would you identify as the main concerns of researchers composing an account of their methods? What kinds of questions are the researchers answering about their work? Can you detect differences in these questions in different disciplines?

### PASSAGE 1

The sample consisted of adult patients (over the age of 18 years) who met one of the selection criteria: (a) surgery in the past 24–72 h and pain in the last 24 h, or (b) diagnosis of cancer, care in oncology units or hospice units, and pain in the last 24 h as assessed by the research assistant. Two hundred thirty-four patients were recruited for this study, including 100 postoperative patients, 100 oncology patients, and 34 hospice patients. The response rate was 94% for the surgical group, 89% for the oncology group, and 68% for the hospice group. The sample size of the hospice group is small because some hospice patients were too fragile or even cognitively impaired at the time this study was conducted. Of these 234 patients, 49% (n = 115) were male and 51% (n = 119) were female. The age range was from 18 to 87 with a mean (SD) of 52.8 (15.9) years. Sixty-five percent of the participants (n = 152) were married. Their religious affiliations included Buddhist (51.7%), Taoist (12.4%), Catholic (1.0%), Jewish (7.7%), and none or other (27.2%). Twenty-seven of these patients had a high school-equivalent education and 44% had completed college education. Demographic characteristics of the patients in each of the study groups are presented in Table 1.

### 2.3 Instrument

The outcome questionnaire of this study was adopted from the study by Ward and Gordon (1994). This questionnaire was translated into Chinese by using a translation and back-translation method to ensure correct translation. The questionnaire was based on the American Pain Society Standards (Max et al., 1991). This questionnaire included (1) patients' assessment of pain severity and satisfaction with how pain was managed by physicians and nurses, (2) patients' perceptions of the time between a complaint of pain and receipt of medication, and (3) patients' perceptions of the time between a complaint of inadequate medication and the receipt of different or stronger medication. Patients were asked if their doctors or nurses discussed with them the importance of pain management. The specific items in the outcome questionnaire, based on the PAS standards, are listed in Table 2. Finally, a one-page demographic sheet covering basic information, such as age, gender, and education was included in the questionnaire.

### 2.4 Procedure

Patients who met the selection criteria were approached individually by the research assistant. Patients who met criterion (b) (diagnosis of cancer) were approached within 72 h of admission to the unit. The research assistant described the study and obtained oral consent. Special emphasis was made that the patients' confidentiality would be protected and that their care providers would not know any individual's answers. Patients were asked to complete the questionnaire without assistance from others. If a patient […]

Chia-Chin Lin 2000 "Applying the American Pain Society's QA standards to evaluate the quality of pain management among surgical, oncology, and hospice inpatients in Taiwan." *Pain* 87: 43–49, 43–44.

## PASSAGE 2

The conversations to be examined here are from an extensive research project with 3- to 5-year-old children at a day-care center in a large midwestern city. The children were grouped into 12 same-sex triads on the basis of friendship and age. The groups were formed after consultation with the children's teachers. The participants in this study were educationally and socially advantaged, middle-class, urban children who were predominantly white. The children attended the day-care center for full days, year round, and had known each other for 1–3 years.

The triads were videotaped during the regular day-care day in one of the children's usual play areas, which was separate from the larger group. The only children in the room were those being filmed. They were not supervised by an adult, although an assistant and I sat somewhat out of sight in a play loft above and behind the children's play area. The children knew we were there. They were videotaped on three separate occasions, each time playing at one of three types of activities. Each group was videotaped for a total of approximately 75 minutes (25 minutes per session).

Amy Sheldon 1990 "Pickle fights: Gendered talk in preschool disputes." *Discourse Processes* 13: 5–31, 12–13.

## PASSAGE 3
*Subjects*
The subjects were 64 girls, ranging in age from 12 to 17, who voluntarily enrolled in a comprehensive program for teenage

mothers and their infants that was provided by the local public health department in a large city in North Carolina. Of
the 64 girls, four were white and 60 were African-American.
They had been sexually active from a young age, the average
age at first intercourse having been 13.3 years (range 10 to
16, median 14). Average age at the time of first birth was 15.5
years (range 12.5 to 17; median 15). One girl who gave birth
at the age of 12 1/2 years had been raped by her mother's
boyfriend. Less than half of the girls' mothers had been teenage mothers themselves. Although 43% of the fathers frequently participated in the care of their infants, 19%
maintained only minimal contact, and 38% had none. Half
contributed to the support of their child. Although school attendance by parenting teenagers was encouraged in the school
district, 12 of them (18%) were not attending school at the
time of initial intake into the program.

*Procedure*
Girls were required to attend the clinic at regular intervals,
depending upon the age of their infant (i.e., mothers of
younger infants attended more frequently), although many
appointments were not kept. Efforts were made to administer
a structured interview and a measure of self-esteem (Piers-
Harris Children's Self-Concept Scale). In addition, the records
of some of the girls' performances on the California Achievement Tests (CAT) were obtained from local public schools ($N$
= 39). The scores reported were those most recently completed
by each girl. They include the results of testing done in the
sixth ($N$ = 9), seventh ($N$ = 8), eighth ($N$ = 20), and ninth ($N$
= 2) grades between 1984 and 1988.

The Mental Scale of the Bayley Scales of Infant Development was administered to infants at their 9th and 18th month
clinic visits, where possible. Because of logistical difficulties
(e.g., missed appointments, attrition) all data are not available for every girl.

Helen Rauch-Elnekave 1994 "Teenage motherhood: Its relationship to undetected
learning problems." *Adolescence* 29: 91–103, 93.

## 10C **Qualitative Method and Subject Position**

Not all disciplines use method sections. Research in disciplines in which scholars do not share recognized instruments and procedures do not explicitly expose the means by which knowledge has been made. So, in literary criticism, you will not find:

> The novel was read and notes were taken. Annotation took place at each point where the annotator could detect mentions which might signify something.

But even in disciplines where methods are tacit — generally but silently understood, and not much talked about — there can still appear implicit traces of method. In these disciplines, theories and concepts take the place of instruments and procedures, producing knowledge by operating on a particular set of data. Sometimes the implicit method can be seen most clearly in the **abstract**, the brief summary that sometimes precedes an article or accompanies bibliographical information found in an index. For example, consider the following abstract of Gregg Hurwitz's article "Freud, Jung, and Shakespeare's *Pericles*":

> This essay applies a Freudian psychoanalytic and Jungian archetypal narrative analysis to Shakespeare's first and oft-criticized romance. The author argues that key structural and thematic elements of Pericles are best illuminated when viewed through a psychological interpretative lens, and that the play is best comprehended when examined in the context of its associative, rather than linear, richness. Masculinity and femininity, central themes of the narrative, are explored both in relation to the Oedipal complex and psychological individuation. Pericles also provides an excellent basis to examine key differences between Freud's and Jung's approach, particularly Jung's widening of the primarily sexual psychoanalytic approach to encompass broader archetypal meaning.
>
> Gregg Hurwitz 2002 "A tempest, a birth and death: Freud, Jung, and Shakespeare's Pericles." *Sexuality & Culture* 6 (3): 3.

In the case of this article, the method involves a way to read the play. Hurwitz applies a technique borrowed from psychology to look at Shakespeare's *Pericles* in terms of associations rather than plot or dramatic development in order to isolate certain themes. In turn, reading the play this way allows him to compare different psychoanalytic techniques. In the article proper, this method is explained, but it is not done so in such a compact manner. The introduction begins by introducing *Pericles* and comparing it to other works by Shakespeare, before gradually explaining how psychoanalytic issues can be seen in the drama. The abstract brings the method into focus.

In disciplines that use qualitative method instead of quantitative method (see Section 10A above) an explanation of method can be more explicit, sometimes resembling the style of the quantitative methods section but without the clear demarcation of a section. Consider, for example, the following introduction from Sue Jackson's article "To Be Or Not To Be? The place of women's studies in the lives of its students."

> In considering the experiences of women students in higher educa-
> tion, it was important to me that I enabled the women to develop
> their thoughts, ideas, feelings and opinions over a period of time.
> This would also enable me to consider any changes that took place
> in their experiences and perceptions during this period. I eventu-
> ally interviewed 14 women although, because of their changing cir-
> cumstances, I was not in the end able to interview all of the women
> through all of the three years. I interviewed the women four times
> during the period of their degrees: in the first semester; in the sec-
> ond semester; halfway through their second year; and halfway
> through their third year. Each interview lasted between 45 minutes
> and an hour. From the start, I wanted to centralize the students'
> voices and experiences.

> Sue Jackson 2000 "To Be Or Not To Be? The place of women's studies in the lives of its
> students." *Journal of Gender Studies* 9 (2): 189–197, 189.

You will notice that in explaining her method, Jackson places considerable emphasis on her own role in the knowledge-making process. Earlier, in our examination of quantitative methods sections in Section 10B,
we noted that the researchers were largely missing from the explanation.
Why does Jackson think it is important to include her own position and
role as a researcher? She answers this question later in the article:

> From the outset it was important to me to locate myself in my re-
> search. Indeed, how could I not? I did not want to pretend to be a
> disembodied researcher, nor that the research was somehow 'out-
> side' of me. I am not an unseen and unmarked voice, but a person
> situated in my own complexities and lived realities. [...] From the

outset, then, I identified my research as feminist, taking a feminist standpoint which engages in political struggle and centralizes women's experiences....

Sue Jackson 2000: 190.

The example from Jackson provides a good illustration of how genre responds to changing social situations. It could be argued that it was **feminist reasoning**, at the end of the twentieth century, which most sincerely invited the *subject* — the thinking, feeling being, experienced in the complexities of daily life — back into scholarly writing. Feminist reasoning has criticized research practices for being carried out from a *masculinist* **position** or point of view, and then representing that position as *universal*. So feminist research would be inclined to dismantle the form of knowledge constructed by traditional research practices, and expose that knowledge as not only not "objective" but also as serving the interests of those who work at it. But some tracks of feminist research would also do more than expose the subjectivity of established regimes of knowledge. They would acknowledge the impossibility of the independent "fact" (and possibly even deny its desirability), and require that the researcher identify himself or herself.

Fleshed out beyond the **discursive *I*** we met in Chapter 9G, the "subjective" researcher would expose the relevant social and political — *personal* — elements of his or her experience of the world. These elements would constitute the full **subject position** from which the researcher speaks. The "knowledge" which the researcher then offers would be contingent on that position: not absolute or universal, but relative to that position.

It is hard to say how far this project for remodelling scholarly writing has advanced. Publications in disciplines which deal with gender-related topics are still perhaps the most likely to invite the fleshed-out subject to the page (and even then, in the presence of gender issues — as we have seen from the excerpts from articles on gender-related topics in previous chapters — the traditional scholarly voice can still prevail). But, even among articles which are not about gender issues, we can also find writers stepping out from traditional styles and saying who they are, and what happened to them, personally, to make them think the way they do now:

In the forty years that I have been doing fieldwork in Latin America and the United States, my own awareness of how the events I recorded are related to the world around them has expanded along with (and sometimes belatedly to) that of my informants. This follows trends in the field as the unit of investigation has progressed from one of bounded cultures where the task was to recapture a traditional past to a multilayered, historically situated inquiry where the authoritative stance of a privileged observer was no longer condoned. In tracing my own enthnographic journey, I shall try to capture some of those experiences in which I was forced to encounter the world dimensions of everyday struggles for survival. (13)

\* \* \*

I found interpretation of these events [homicides in a village in the Mayan area of Chiapas, Mexico] difficult, given the dominant paradigm of structural functionalism in the field of anthropology. (14)

\* \* \*

When I completed the monograph on the Maya, I felt the need to escape the involuted conflicts of Mayan semisubsistence farmers and work in a society where the hostility was turned outward against class enemies. I visited the mining communities of Bolivia in the summer of 1967, just three weeks after the massacre of San Juan in Siglo XX-Catavi. (17)

\* \* \*

I borrowed some books from my informants and acquired a library of publications by current Latin American theorists to cope with the confusion of ideological currents and social movements that I found in the mining community.

\* \* \*

Clearly, all of this turmoil [coup, debt crisis] exceeded the anthropological models available for analysis of field data. I tried to keep the life of the community at the center of my thinking about what was coming in, allowing it to be filtered through the people's sense of what was happening. The life narratives that I undertook with a few of my informants provided the ballast that kept me from sliding into metatheories concerning the consciousness of workers. (19)

Nash 1994: 13–19.

This article is not about gender issues, yet perhaps its style has been influenced by the feminist reasoning which suggests that researchers identify themselves. It's interesting, too, that this researcher represents herself as changing — as a thinker and observer — over time. She knows things now that she didn't know before; she has been influenced by others, she has changed her mind. Just as knowledge is located in time and changes over time, so are knowledge-makers located in time, and subject to its influences. It's worth noting further that Nash is writing in the discipline of anthropology — for, besides feminist reasoning, the other radical interrogation of scholarly authority in the late twentieth century has come from **post-colonial** positions. Post-colonial reasoning has challenged the authority of Western researchers to produce knowledge of other cultures, and exposed traditional anthropological knowledge as saturated with colonial values.

---

### Exercise 3

Examine the following abstracts from scholarly articles. Note how the first abstract, which was written by the writer of the article, uses complete sentences and functions like a compact summary of the article, but the second is more fragmented and seems to survey the topics of the article in the order that they are covered. Based on these abstracts, describe the method by which knowledge is being made in each article.

### ABSTRACT 1

Although late nineteenth century and early twentieth century Canada, the United States, Australia, and New Zealand were all settler societies with a predominantly British ethnic heritage, a comparison reveals intriguing differences in attitudes and practices related to "racial" mixing during this period. The relation to land was the underpinning of the dominant discourses concerning miscegenation in all four countries, and these discourses were grounded in an international pan-European discussion of social and physiological difference. However, constructions of sexuality, class, race, gender, and national values, as well as previous experiences of inter-ethnic contact, all played roles in determining attitudes and policies toward racial mixing in any particular circumstance. The actual forms of mixing that took place, and to a certain extent the discourses about them, were shaped by indigenous as well as European attitudes and agency, and in some instances were shaped as much by male patriarchal authority and male gender solidarity across cultures as by the interests of settler colonialism.

Victoria Freeman 2005 "Attitudes Toward 'Miscegenation' in Canada, the United States, New Zealand, and Australia, 1860–1914." *Native Studies Review* 16 (1): 41–70.

## ABSTRACT 2

Studies the parallelism of the English play 'Mary Magdalen' preserved in the Bodleian Library MS Digby 133 and William Shakespeare's 'Pericles.' Summary outline of 'Pericles'; Narrative source of relevant parts of 'Mary Magdalen'; Possible guests that make up saints' legends — conversion, martyrdom, miracle and withdrawal from the world.

Peter Womack 1999 "Shakespeare and the sea of stories." *Journal of Medieval & Early Modern Studies* 29 (1): 169–188.

### Exercise 4

Examine the two excerpts from scholarly articles below to determine how each writer steps beyond the traditional role of the discursive *I*. (Passage 2 comes from a co-authored article innovatively structured as a dialogue.)

### PASSAGE 1

About 2 years ago, I conversed with an American businessman in Mexico about how difficult replacement parts were to come by in that country. Over the next several months, he formed an alliance with Mexican and American partners and investors and formed a company, one with a more specific business goal, namely, to provide rebuilt engine parts from the U.S. to commercial transportation fleets in Mexico.

During meetings over the following year, the American and Mexican partners saw me in action, doing what linguistic anthropologists naturally do — mediating worlds — sometimes in English, sometimes in rusty Spanish, sometimes in both. We mutually decided that I would spend the summer in

Mexico City to help start up the company. I dealt with Mexican and American partners, government offices, lawyers, and customers. I worked in the cracks between two different "cultures," cracks described in recent books on Mexican-American relations, books whose titles foreshadow the examples to come: *Distant Neighbors* (Riding, 1985) and *Limits to Friendship* (Pastor and Castaneda, 1988).

Kismet turned me into something I had never been before — an "intercultural communicator." The rest of this article is dedicated to figuring out what, in light of that experience, the phrase might mean.

*Intercultural Communicator*

After my baptism by fire, I returned to the university in the autumn and approached the library with a naive question in mind: "What is the field of intercultural communication all about?" The question was naive because the literature is huge, diverse, without agreement on any particular unifying focus (see Hinnenkamp, 1990, for a related concern with the fundamentals of the field).

Michael Agar 1994 "The intercultural frame." *International Journal of Intercultural Relations* 18 (2): 221–37, 221–22.

## PASSAGE 2

### I. Introduction: Multiple openings with(in) a dialogue

What, then, are the limitations of our practice? How is our practice complicit with certain established societal structures?
— Ming-Yeung Lu

MING-YUEN S. MA: This quote brings up many of the questions that keep coming up in my mind as I work on this project, and I think that they point out the uncertainties in my motives: who am I, a first generation Chinese gay man, who was born but did not grow up in the United States, whose higher education was enabled by my privileged, upper-middle-class background, to write about Asian lesbian and gay writers? What is my placement in the text? What does it mean for us to be writing about works by persons of Asian and Pacific Islander descent in a language that is not our own — though most of us communicate by it?

ALICE Y. HOM: As a second-generation Chinese American, raised in a working-class immigrant family but educated in an Ivy League college, I think there are some complexities to the language issue. Many second-, third-, and fourth-generation Asian Americans do not feel their native language is an Asian language. When talking about Asian Pacific Islander lesbian and gay writing, we have to address the definition of "Asian Pacific Islander." In this case we are speaking of Asian and Pacific Islander immigrants and those born in the United States. The diaspora is limited to the United States although some of the Asian Pacific Islander lesbian writings are coming from Canada. For the most part, we will concentrate in this United States-centred context because most of our research and experiences are from here.

Alice Y. Hom and Ming-Yuen S. Ma 1993 "Premature gestures: A speculative dialogue on Asian Pacific lesbian and gay writing." *Journal of Homosexuality* 26 (2/3): 21–31, 22.

## 10D Modality

In Chapter 9 we met the **discursive *I***: the being who arranged and forecast discussion, who pointed to parts of the text, summing up and emphasizing. We also met a more radically personal **subject position** (discussed above in Section 10C) which seems to make appearances when researchers feel compelled to emphasize their personal role in the knowledge-making process. As we noted, this need may be due to the discipline (for example, women's studies or ethnographic disciplines like anthropology) or it may arise from a general questioning of the knowledge-making process itself. Below we meet a variant of the discursive *I* — the **knowledge-making *I*** — that is pervasive, albeit more shy than the arranger and forecaster of discussion. This "I" is not as personal as the expression of subject position, but it is similar insofar as it marks the presence or role of the researcher in the knowledge-making process.

For example, in summarizing the views of another writer (Wittig), this writer (Calhoun) appears in the surface of the text as a reasoning being, evaluating the statements of others:

> Because lesbians and heterosexual resisters must have, on [Wittig's] account, the same relation to the category "woman," there can be no interesting differences between the two. This, **I think**, is a mistake, and I will argue in a moment that lesbians are in a quite special sense not-women.

Calhoun 1994: 564 (emphasis added).

You will note that the second appearance of the "I" in this passage is the discursive, forecasting "I" organizing the argument: "I will argue...." But the first appearance — "I think" — asserts Calhoun's own judgement on the issue under discussion. Since the scholarly genres impose so many restrictions on the presentation of the writing "self," we might well scrutinize this special appearance of the writing self to find out what conditions permit it.

What we will find is that the "I think" in the passage above is by no means an isolated case. Rather, it is a variation on a set of expressions that are in fact abundant in the research genres, and that tend to occur in just such situations as the passage above exemplifies: situations where the writer is taking a step beyond established knowledge, moving to offer new statements to the research community. To develop some perspective on this set of expressions and their range of occurrence, we will first see how the grammar of "I think" is related to the grammar of some other expressions which are akin to it in function.

Say Matthew is inside on a dark night. He hears a sound on the roof. He reports to Thomas:

> It's raining.

Since he is inside, where it is dry, he is *inferring* that it is raining. Matthew could report his finding as a product of his own easoning — an **estimate from a position of limited knowledge**.

> **I think** it's raining.

Matthew doesn't know if it is raining for sure, so he emphasizes that the statement is based on his own perception. He could mark his statement as such an estimate by other means. He could say:

It **seems** to be raining. It **must** be raining.

Or, if the speaker and his companion are new to the area, and less certain about local night sounds, he could express his estimate with less certainty:

THOMAS: What's that noise?  MATTHEW: It **could** be rain.

It **might** be rain.

**Maybe** it's rain.

"Seems," "must," "could," "might," "maybe" are all expressions embedded in the statement that identify it as the product of inference from a position of limited knowledge. Along with other expressions like "evidently," "apparently," "perhaps," "possibly," "appears," these expressions **modalize** statements. Roughly, they are equivalent to "I think." Although **modality** erases "I" from the surface of the expression, it nevertheless maintains the sense of the statement in which it occurs as being knowledge under construction from a certain location: the speaker's or writer's position in the world.

These traces of reasoning from positions of limited knowledge are typical of scholarly expression. They signify the research community's persistent interest in the production of knowledge. On the one hand, they permit the individual researcher to move into unconfirmed territory — a lone explorer, estimating and reckoning — and, on the other hand, they signal respect for the community's cooperative work of corroborating and recognizing established positions.

So strong is this tradition of respect for properly established positions that even when the current researchers are evidently impatient with the dominance of accepted views, and when their own research defies those views, they still identify knowledge deficits through modalized statements. So, when two researchers report extensive evidence to overturn the standing idea that trade-union activities have a lot to do with Britain's post-war economic circumstances, they nevertheless approach the standing view with signs of respect, expressed through **modality**. Here they treat the work of a distinguished and widely cited scholar:

Olson's work demands to be taken seriously, yet it, too, **seems** to be flawed. Olson has attracted considerable support from economists and economic historians because his methodology conforms to the tenets of individual rational action theory inherent in neo-classical economics. However, this choice of approach **can** be criticised because it encourages a misleadingly simplified view of reality.

* * *

It **may** be right to conclude about Olson, therefore, that what he has produced is not an explanation, but merely an historical set of abstractions. His theory **seems** to provide little more satisfaction than the offerings of far less sophisticated analysts.

At this point, it **appears** wise to turn from the current literature and re-examine the contemporary evidence. Many recent authorities have argued, as we have shown, that restrictionism was strongly evident on Britain's shopfloor after 1945, but not much of what has been written, it **seems** fair to conclude, is very persuasive.

Nick Tiratsoo and Jim Tomlinson 1994 "Restrictive practices on the shopfloor in Britain, 1945–1960: Myth and reality." *Business History* 36(2): 67, 69 (emphasis added).

Using modalized expressions allows Tiratsoo and Tomlinson to question established positions on the topic and to politely suggest an alternate approach, in this case to return to the "evidence."

You will notice that in the example about rain above, Matthew follows the observation that it "seems" to be raining by saying that it "must" be raining. This confident assertion may seem to contradict the expression of uncertainty conveyed by "might." And yet, while "must" can seem like an expression of certainty, it is in fact a sign of strong but not infallible conviction attending an inference. For example, "It must be nearly 4 o'clock" suggests that the speaker does not have a watch and so can't say for sure what time it is. Along with "must," "obviously" can seem like an expression of certainty, but the next examples show that speakers can use "obviously" (like "must") in the presence of doubt, or **uncertainty**:

> ... obviously you grew up, although this might not be the case, in a family that encouraged this interest [in music].

Rex Murphy, *Cross-Country Check-up*, CBC, 23 April 2000, talking to a constitutional expert about music.

From a distance, we might think that the research genres would be the ones without these markers of *limitation*, which indicate *possibility* rather than certainty, *maybe* rather than yes or no — and even **subjectivity** in that these expressions indicate the writer's reasoning, inference, speculation. If we think of research and the sciences — particularly the "hard" sciences — as sources of authority and ultimate fact, we would not expect these traces of *indeterminacy* in the research genres. But in fact they are abundant.

Perhaps we would not be surprised at this indeterminacy in the research genres if we thought of the research genres' distinctive dependence on reported speech. In a way, the expressions which make a statement indeterminate by showing that it is the speaker's inference from incomplete evidence are something like the statements which are reported as coming from someone other than the writer. So, to return to our rain example, the speaker could also make a claim about the weather by reporting the speech of someone else.

MATTHEW: Tanya says it's raining. THOMAS: Oh.

If Thomas knows that Tanya has just come in from outside, then he is likely to credit the statement as valid. It seems to come from a reliable position. On the other hand, if Tanya has not been out, and is only speculating, and tends to interpret all noises as rain, Thomas might not be convinced. The context in which the reported statement was produced — the speaker's identity and situation, the timing of the statement — helps the listener to evaluate the statement. Similarly, reporting expressions, documentation, characterization of the source — all these features of scholarly citation help readers evaluate reported statements.

---

### Exercise 5

Identify the modalizing expressions in the following passages. How do they limit the speakers' claims for the knowledge they will produce?

### PASSAGE 1

Human representations offer archaeologists the possibility of investigating ancient social categorization and differentiation from within. Of course, we are given only a very partial view. Figurines do not provide maps to complete social systems. Instead, they encode only very selected themes. The anthropomorphic figurines of Early Formative Paso de la Amada [Mexico] appear to be stylized human images depicting idealized social categories or roles (Lesure 1997). Their specific uses are unknown. Most were deployed, broken, discarded in household contexts. They were probably grouped into sets or scenes in which not only the individual representations but comparisons between them became important (Flannery and Marcus 1976, 382; Marcus 1989, 1996). It therefore seems likely that the message conveyed by the use of figurines involved statements not only about social categories, but about relationships between categories.

Lesure 1999: 209.

**PASSAGE 2**

An objective way to determine the current nature of the field of personality psychology is to examine what gets published in various journals over a fixed period of time. This is not a foolproof system, since more papers are rejected for publication than are accepted. The ones that do get accepted might thus represent a biased sample. Journal editors serve as "gatekeepers" and therefore what is accepted might not necessarily be the best but rather may reflect the biases of journal editors and referees or the zeitgeist of psychology.

Nevertheless, what is published in personality journals is probably the closest approximation of the true nature of research in the area, and is certainly a good indicator of what is currently being disseminated.

Norman S. Endler and Rachel L. Speer 1998 "Personality psychology: Research trends for 1993–1995." *Journal of Personality* 66 (5): 621–69, 621.

## 10E Other Markers of the Status of Knowledge

As we have seen, modality and reporting expressions both mark statements as issuing from a position of limited knowledge. In this section we will look at other expressions that mark statements for their status as knowledge. First, we will examine **limiting expressions.** These can resemble modality by indicating a lack of certainty on the part of the writer. Or they can qualify or place other limits on statements, especially generalizations. Second, we will look at **agentless expressions** with specific attention to how they indicate consensus about whether a statement is obvious or not. The function of these different expressions may sometimes seem to overlap, and generally speaking we can regard them as establishing writers' attitudes toward or opinions of the statement they are offering.

By definition, **generalizations** may seem to defy limits. The opening generalization of the passage below appears at first to ignore the modalizing and reporting tendencies we have been observing in the last section:

> During the course of the twentieth century relationships between minorities and dominant societies have fundamentally altered in wartime....

However, on closer inspection we will see that it in fact conforms to traditions of marking statements for their status as knowledge:

> During the course of the twentieth century relationships between minorities and dominant societies have fundamentally altered in wartime, an assertion which applies to all states. The position of minorities usually deteriorates, particularly if they represent a group which has acted as the traditional scapegoat for the dominant society, or if they are identified with the state facing their land of settlement in war. In such a situation the minorities almost invariably face persecution, varying from controls on movement and expression to internment and even genocide. The response of the dominant group varies according to the political traditions upon which it is grounded. A liberal democracy will usually retain traces of tolerations, while an autocratic state will exercise more arbitrary anti-minority policies (Panayi 1990b). Few exceptions exist to this state of affairs, although in some cases opportunities may arise that allow a minority to make some socio-economic progress. The experience of Afro-Americans and American Indians in the first world war provides an example (Dippie 1982, p. 194; Grossman 1989).
>
> Mark Ellis and Panikos Panayi 1994 "German minorities in World War I: A comparative study of Britain and the U.S.A." *Ethnic and Racial Studies* 17(2): 238–59.

The writers seem to be aware of the risk they take in offering a generalization that is neither reported nor modalized, for they quickly move to characterize it and insist on its generality:

> ... an **assertion** which applies to **all** states.

Then, as they develop this generality, they gradually and slightly reduce the application of its parts: "all" gives way to "usually," "almost invariably," "usually," "[f]ew exceptions exist," and "some cases." Each of these expressions conditions the statement in which it occurs as in some way *limited*. The writers do not commit themselves to saying that any given statement is universally true. That would be too much.

The following statement is from an article reporting results of an experimental study of the ability to remember and learn a written style:

> [T]he subjects **demonstrated a trend toward** mentioning more rules for the marked forms than for the unmarked forms for all three style characteristics.

Jennifer Zervakis and David C. Rubin 1998 "Memory and learning for a novel written style." *Memory and Cognition* 26 (4): 754–67, 764 (emphasis added).

How would this statement sound without the **limiting expression**?

In effect, expressions like these control the extent of a statement's application. They reduce and monitor how the generalization is applied to cases or instances. They place limits on knowledge by conditioning where and under what circumstances it is valid. While by no means exhaustive, the following list gives a good sense of the range of limiting expressions:

| | |
|---|---|
| usually | in part |
| most | at least |
| some | partly |
| many | often |
| generally | sometimes |
| roughly | typically |

Notice the effect that the insertion of appropriate limiting expressions can have in conditioning a broad statement for use in a research setting. Consider this statement:

> Family-wage campaigns supported both patriarchal and corporate interests.

Compare it with this statement:

> Generally, family-wage campaigns supported patriarchal and corporate interests.

Given the scholarly genres' preoccupation with the status and production of knowledge, we could expect limiting expressions to cooperate with reporting and modality to sketch the limits of knowledge. In the following example, a writer offers an interpretation of evidence she has presented as to the conditions of labour after the abolition of slavery in Brazil. Identify and compare modalizing, reporting, and limiting expressions in the passage (note that all three are in bold-face):

> It was this process that **Peter Isenberg called** "modernization without change" and that **has generally been interpreted** as implying a crushing continuity of dependence and poverty for former slaves. While this is **in one sense quite** accurate — indeed, rural northeasterners **may** have been even more malnourished after emancipation than before — an overemphasis on continuity **may** obscure the importance of the access to land that **many** former slaves did achieve....
>
> Even though the physical work performed by labor tenants **might** differ little from that performed by slaves, the orbits of their lives now had a **somewhat** different shape. While slaves had lived in a centralized set of quarters under direct supervision, moradores **usually** built their huts "at scattered points on the estates." An even more general dispersion of the population was **probably** prevented by the development of central mills, but the small-scale dispersion within estates **could** be of crucial importance to the development of a life oriented toward family and neighbors rather than employer. And, to the extent that freedom of movement **could** be maintained, it provided **some** constraint on the exactions that **could** be imposed on rural dwellers.
>
> Rebecca J. Scott 1994 "Defining the boundaries of freedom in the world of cane: Cuba, Brazil, and Louisiana after emancipation." *American Historical Review* February: 70–102, 96 (emphasis added).

Reporting expressions include the citation of Isenberg ("called") and the obscured reference "generally interpreted." Note that Scott continues by calling the reported statements into question. She does so by first using **limiting expressions** ("in one sense" and "quite") and allowing for the validity of this "one sense" with the **modal expression** "may." As she proceeds, note how modality is used again ("may," "may," "might," "could," "could") and coupled with different limiting expressions: "many former slaves," "somewhat different shape," "usually built," "some constraint." All these expressions limit the scope of the statement. In that respect, they are pointers to the statements' status as knowledge, and to the writers' limited position: they are not in a position to say such-and-such is true for all cases.

In addition to limiting statements, we also find scholarly writers expressing attitudes about the **obviousness** of statements. Alongside words like "possibly," "may," "might," or "could," we see them saying things like the following:

**Certainly,** *x*
**It is evident that** *x*
**Surely** *x*
**Apparently** *x*
**Undoubtedly** *x*

They can even combine apparent confidence with seeming reservation. For example, summarizing the research of "social investigator Ferdinand Zweig," these writers say:

> He concentrated on five main sectors (building and civil engineering, cotton, engineering, iron and steel, and printing) and found that restrictive practices of various kinds were **certainly sometimes evident.**
>
> Tiratsoo and Tomlinson 1994: 70 (emphasis added).

They don't say:

> He ... found restrictive practices of various kinds.

This complex trace of reasoning — the phenomenon is "evident" (to an observer/interpreter), but only "sometimes," but then "certainly" — indicates the status of this statement as knowledge.

To say that something is evident — or apparent, or observable, or recognizable — is to say that it is so *to someone*. Remembering that scholarly writing makes big efforts to attach statements to their sources, we might confront wordings like these and ask, well, *who* finds something evident or apparent, or *who* observes it or recognizes it? At first, these wordings might seem vague, and at odds with other features we have been looking at. But we can account for these typical wordings by noticing how they resemble some other forms we have seen. *Observable, evident, identifiable* are **agentless**: they take away the person who observes, identifies, or finds something evident. So they are like other agentless forms we have seen, for example:

**it is known that** *x*
*x* **is acknowledged as ...**

In the following passage, which expressions are agentless?

> The problem of deep oceanic convection induced by localized sur-face cooling has received considerable attention in the last years. Results from field observations (e.g., in the Greenland Sea or the Gulf of Lions), laboratory experiments, and numerical simulations have led to some theoretical predictions concerning the structure of the convective region like plume scale, chimney scale, and rim cur-rent by, for example, Klinger and Marshall (1995), Send and Marshall (1995), and Viseck et al. (1996). The comparison of these scaling arguments with real ocean data on deep connection is some-what restricted due to the lack of detailed measurements of convec-tive plumes and chimneys, although field experiments have provided very impressive cases of deep ocean convention (e.g., Morawitz et al. 1996; Schott et al. 1996).
>
> S. Raasch and D. Etling 1998 "Modeling deep ocean convection: Large eddy simulation in comparison with laboratory experiments." *American Meteorological Society* 21: 1786–1802, 1786.

Who attends? Who observes? Who experiments? Who designs simulations? Who produces results? The answers to these questions are not given. In the passage, "attention" and "observations" are agentless. They take away the person who attended and the person who observed. Notably, if we ask *who* uses theory to predict, examples are given: Marshall (1995), Send and Marshall (1995), and Viseck et al. (1996). Why are Raasch and Etling so imprecise about some things and so precise about others? Apparently they assume that readers are generally familiar with the earlier findings that led to the work of Marshall and others.

Expressions like "it is known that ..." seem to distribute knowledge: it is not just the present speaker who sees this or knows it. Similarly, in the case of expressions like "evident" or "observable," the commentary on the status of knowledge includes not so much an estimate of its probabil-ity (as "possibly" or "may," for example, would provide), or not only a trace of its source (something someone reported), but a measure of the position from which x is known. As —

**it is known that x**
**x is acknowledged as ...**

— suggest that more than one person knows this, so —

evident
apparent
observable
identifiable

— suggest that, from any reasonable position, people would see this. "Reasonable position," however, by now should occur to us as a social rather than purely cognitive (and universal) measure. And we can now recognize the role of **presupposition** in such expressions (see Chapter 9I). In scholarly circles, reasoning goes on in social contexts, among people of similar experience.

These markers of **obviousness** can take the form of "evident," "apparent," "recognized/recognizable," or "observed/observable," or the more pronounced forms of "surely," "certainly," "clearly," which insist that the statement should be acceptable to reasonable readers. Most compelling, perhaps, of these forms is "of course." "Of course" signals that the statement is so evident that readers are only being reminded of what they already know.

> It is now well-established, of course, that the majority of British employers looked to the apprenticeship system rather than formal education in the classroom as the appropriate training for the bulk of their employees.
>
> Keith Burgess 1994 "British employers and education policy, 1935–45: A decade of 'missed opportunities'?" *Business History* 36(3): 29–61.

"Of course" signals that the writer takes his readers as already knowing that it is known that British employers favoured apprenticeship training. "Of course" describes that status of this knowledge as widely distributed in the community which forms the audience for this article.

In a way, "of course" is an expression of politeness: it constructs readers as knowledgeable, as not needing to be told something they already know. But what if you *didn't* know that apprenticeship was the preferred form of training? In this case, "of course" would inform you that the topic is common ground for the intended audience, a well-known consensus in that community.

Yet, while markers of obviousness can create the impression of consensus, they can also suddenly alienate a reader. On the one hand, you should be aware of the power of certain expressions to appear to distribute knowledge: you can use them in your own writing to signal to your readers that you know you are not delivering brand-new ideas, but, rather, ideas that are broadly entertained in the community. On the other hand, these expressions incur some risk that your reader may not find something as clear, evident, or matter-of-course as you suggest.

| MATTHEW: Clearly, Dickens' verbal art is a precursor of cinematic art. | THOMAS: Wait a minute. That's not clear at all. |

While "of course" and related expressions say "This statement is in keeping with what you and I (and others like us) know about the world: it's what we would expect," words like "surprisingly" say "This statement is *not* in keeping with what you and I (and others like us) know about the world."

> Most analyses of the various proposals to date (including the so-called Flat Tax, a national sales tax, the "USATax," etc.) have concentrated on the distributional impact of the plans, along familiar lines of progressivity and regressivity. **Surprisingly** little critical attention has been paid to the macroeconomic implications of these tax reform plans, particularly to the claims about saving.
>
> Neil H. Buchanan 1999 "Taxes, saving, and macroeconomics." *Journal of Economic Issues* 33(1): 59–75 (emphasis added).

"Of course," "obviously," "surprisingly" signify a solidarity amongst those convened by what we called writer's orchestration (see Chapter 6). They reflect a kind of identification on the part of the writer with the scholarly community: shared attitudes and experiences in research disciplines.

We could also see expressions like "of course," "obviously," and "surprisingly" as expanding the identity of the **discursive *I***, for they emphasize a **position** — from which something is well known ("of course") or clearly to be seen ("obviously") or never seen before ("surprisingly"). Although academic writing is often considered impersonal, or neutral, or anonymous, in fact there are many markers of **subjectivity** in scholarly style: expressions of attitude — and even feeling (of a sort). Here two economists are "astonish[ed]" by something which might not stir such feeling in people who do not share their position in the world.

> From 1929 to 1932, Argentina imported severe deflationary pressures and adverse terms-of-trade shocks from the international

economy: the external terms of trade declined by 24 percent and the foreign (U.S.) price level fell by 26 percent.

In this context it is **astonishing** that the Argentine Great Depression was so mild and short-lived by international standards.

Gerardo della Paolera and Alan M. Taylor 1999 "Economic recovery from the Argentine Great Depression: Institutions, expectations, and the change of macroeconomic regime." *Journal of Economic History* 59 (3): 567–98, 569 (emphasis added).

---

### Exercise 6

In the passage below, the writers begin to reinterpret evidence. Identify the modal and limiting expressions they use as they begin to evaluate available knowledge.

> Taken together, these various accounts appear to constitute a formidable indictment, yet closer inspection once again exposes flaws. Some industrial correspondents did, of course, have good contacts in business and may have accurately reported what they were told. Nevertheless, it is not certain what employers' complaints really added up to: grumbles from the boardroom were, of course, nothing new. Moreover, some of the press accounts have a formulatory ring and may well have been shaped more by the pressure to grab the reader's attention than the desire to present accurate facts.

Tiratsoo and Tomlinson 1994: 69–70.

### Exercise 7

Inspect essays you have recently written or are currently drafting. Do you find the modalizing and limiting expressions we have been examining in examples of published scholarship? If you find them missing, can you explain their absence? (That is, does your writing situation differ from that of professional scholars in ways that lead you away from such expressions of position and limitation? Or have you been unaware of the role these expressions play in making statements in the research genres?) If you find modalizing and limiting expressions missing from your academic writing, try introducing them at appropriate points, and observe the effect.

---

## Exercise 8

Identify in the following passages signs of attitude (something is good, or bad) and feeling (something has taken the writers by surprise).

### PASSAGE 1

In many less developed countries the government resorts to minimum wage laws in a bid to raise the living standards of the workers. In India, for example, the Minimum Wages Act of 1948 laid down standards of minimum wage. The objective was "not merely ... the bare sustenance of life but ... for some measure of education, medical requirements and amenities."[1] In other countries also, such laws and regulations were motivated by similar concerns.

Unfortunately, however, there is little concern about the possible detrimental effects of such laws on the level of employment, as these laws may induce the firms to cut down on the number of workers employed.

*Note*

1 Committee for Fair Wages appointed by government of India, 1948.

Saikat Datta and Prabal Roy Chowdhury 1998 "Management union bargaining under minimum wage regulation in less developed countries." *Indian Economic Review* 33 (2): 169–84, 169–70.

### PASSAGE 2

The complex and often fitful transition from central planning to the market in China and the Warsaw Pact countries has been a hot topic during the past decade. Notably, the United States made a similar transition after World War II. Indeed, the reconversion from a wartime command economy to a market-oriented postwar economy, a transition accomplished with astonishing speed and little apparent difficulty, constitutes one of the most remarkable events in U.S. economic history. Nevertheless, economists and economic historians have devoted little attention to that episode, and their explanations of it are, on close inspection, extremely problematic.

Robert Higgs 1999 "From central planning to the market: The American transition, 1945–1947." *The Journal of Economic History* 59: 600–23, 623.

---

**PASSAGE 3**

Unfortunately, this methodological assumption treats the media as passive "channels" of communication or neutral and objective observers and recorders of events, a view that for some time now has been rejected by scholars of the media (e.g., Gans 1981; Herman and Chomsky 1988; Shoemaker and Resse 1991), as well as refuted by studies of the media coverage of collective events (Danzger 1975; Franzosi 1987; McCarthy, McPhail, and Smith 1996; Meuller 1997a; Snyder and Kelly 1977).

Pamela E. Oliver and Daniel J. Myers 1999 "How events enter the public sphere." *American Journal of Sociology* 105(1): 38–67, 39.

---

## 10F Tense and the Story of Research

Although simple present is the most common form for reporting expressions in the research genres, it is joined by other forms of the present tense, and also by the past tense. With this array of tenses, scholarly writers tell the story of statements occurring, staging or dramatizing the making of knowledge. In this story, knowledge is not timeless and immutable, but historical, located in time.

Most of the **reporting verbs** we have been looking at seem to prefer the simple present form in the research genres.

> Rouse **presents** a novel challenge to spatial images, highlighting the nature of postmodern space. He **points out** that members of a "transnational migration" circuit can be parts of two communities simultaneously. However, he **argues** ....
>
> Chavez 1994: 55 (emphasis added).

Although, clearly, the speech actions of arguing or pointing out occurred in past time (before Chavez wrote the above), they are presented in present tense.

In a sample summary in Chapter 3, we followed the trend and used the simple present too:

> To explain the means by which heterosexual society produces heterosexuality as "natural," and produces "negative social reality" for

lesbians and gay men, Calhoun (1994) **catalogues** the social practices (e.g., dating, sex education, erotica) which construct sex/gender dimorphism, and the social conventions (e.g., joint gifts and invitations to husband-and-wife) and legal and economic structures (e.g., adoption procedures, spousal health benefits) which produce the "single unit" of intimately bonded man and woman.

Consider how this would sound if we changed the verb from simple present to simple past:

To explain the means by which heterosexual society produces heterosexuality as "natural," and produces "negative social reality" for lesbians and gay men, Calhoun (1994) **catalogued** the social practices ....

An academic reader could stop, or misstep, noting the past tense. Later, we will consider how such a reader might interpret this way of talking about Calhoun's research. What is important for the moment is that the simple present tense appears to be an important way to bring scholarly conversations to life. Why is this so?

Consider the role of the simple present in this example of everyday conversation:

So this guy comes over and **says** is that your car and I'm like yeah and he **goes** you gonna leave it there and I'm like — *what?*

Studies of simple present (e.g., Chafe 1994) in conversational citation suggest that it coincides with speakers' evaluation of what they are saying as particularly impressive: they dramatize their report of important moments by switching to simple present, creating an effect of immediacy. Scholarly "conversation" may be borrowing some of this immediacy in its preference for the simple present.

However, this is not the whole story of tense and citation. Simple present can be, in some instances, overtaken by present progressive ("ing" forms of the verb):

Here $x$ **is questioning** the ....

This may be likely to occur with **direct-speech** citation — where the other speaker is quoted in their own words — and the present progressive intensifies the moment of the conversation, improving even on the immediacy provided by the simple present. But it occurs in other situations too, like this one:

> ... the latent structure of childhood negative emotions **is** only **beginning** to be conceptualized in detail (e.g., Joiner, Catanzaro, and Laruent, 1996).
>
> Bruce F. Chorpita, Anne Marie Albano, and David H. Barlow 1998 "The structure of negative emotions in a clinical sample of children and adolescents." *Journal of Abnormal Psychology* 107(1): 74–85 (emphasis added).

More common than present progressive is present perfect.

> The bulk of the empirical work on migration determinants **has studied** how wage and unemployment differentials affect migration flows under the Harris-Todaro (1970) hypothesis of risk neutrality of an individual migrant. [...] The role of other factors than expected wages **has been emphasized** in the new migration literature.
>
> Francesco Daveri and Ricardo Faini 1999 "Where do migrants go?" *Oxford Economic Papers* 51: 595–622 (emphasis added).

Present perfect is a sensitive form in English — second nature to speakers of English as a first language, perhaps, but difficult to explain — and called on to execute speakers' perception of what is close or distant in time. In conversation, it says something is done, but only *just* done — recent enough to be still an aspect of the present situation (and often occurs with "just"). Writers in the research genres sometimes select the present perfect, as we see above and in the next example:

> Premack and Woodruff (1978) asked "Does the chimpanzee have a theory of mind?" Since it was posed 20 years ago, Premack and Woodruff's question **has dominated** the study of both social behavior in nonhuman primates [...] and cognitive development in children, but progress in the two fields **has been** markedly different. Developmentalists have established empirical methods to investigate children's understanding of mentality, and forging links with philosophy of mind and philosophy of science, they **have mustered** the conceptual resources for disciplined dispute about the origins [...], on-line control [...], and epistemic stance [...] of human folk psychology (e.g., Goldman 1993; Gopnik 1993; Gopnik and Wellman 1994). In contrast, those working with primates **have continued** to struggle with the basic question of whether any primate has any capacity to conceive of mental states.
>
> C.M. Heyes 1998 "Theory of mind in nonhuman primates." *Behavioral and Brain Sciences* 21: 101–48, 101 (emphasis added).

The first sentence of the example above shows that writers in the research genres can also pick the simple past for reporting verbs: "Premack and Woodruff (1978) *asked* 'Does the chimpanzee have a theory of mind?'" The next writers begin their article on a new model of social interaction by citing a prominent contributor to such study, and use the simple past in conjunction with a positive evaluation ("celebrated") of the work's reception:

> In his celebrated essay on "The Architecture of Complexity," Herbert Simon ([1962] 1969) **developed** the argument that all complex systems shared certain structural features. These features emerged, he **showed,** by virtue of what appeared to be a universal partitioning principle — the tendency for strongly interacting entities to group together into subsystems.
>
> Thomas S. Smith and Gregory T. Stevens 1999 "The architecture of small networks: Strong interaction and dynamic organization in small social systems." *American Sociological Review* 64: 403–20, 403 (emphasis added).

Similarly, writing about undocumented immigrants in the U.S., Leo R. Chavez cites the ancestral, founding statements of social theorists:

> Classical theorists **wrestled** with the notion of community, particularly the forces that held together complex societies. For Marx (1967 [1867]), the community or society **was** the arena within which interest groups defined by their relation to the means of production, competed .... Early anthropological work on tribal societies, the "classic" ethnographies of Malinowski (1961 [1922]), Evans-Pritchard (1972 (1940]), and others **were concerned** with issues of social solidarity and village life, social structure, and organization. It was Redfield (1956) who ... **brought** the notion of the "little community" into full anthropological gaze.

Eventually, the record emerges from history and touches the present (in the perfect aspect):

> The subfield of human anthropology, drawing on both Redfield and the Chicago School, **has produced** a wealth of interesting research on communities around the world (Hannerz 1980).
>
> Chavez 1994: 52 (emphasis added).

But when does the present begin? In 1980? Or in 1950, as in this article from meteorology?

By combining surface observations, cloud-motion winds, and up-per-air observations from kites and balloons, Bjerknes (1919) and Bjerknes and Solberg (1922) **set forth** the conceptual framework for understanding three-dimensional air-flows and associated weather within cyclones and about fronts by establishing the "Norwegian frontal-cyclone model." Inspection of even earlier observational analyses over North America (e.g., Bjerknes 1910; Rossby and Weightman 1926; Palmn and Newton 1951; Sanders 1955), how-ever, reveals that frontal-cyclone evolutions over the central United States do not always mirror the conceptual model developed in Northern Europe. Recognition of the differences in topography and land-water distribution between northern Europe (where the Nor-wegian cyclone model originated) and the central United States **has** subsequently **led** to more complex conceptual models of surface fron-tal-cyclone evolutions and their attendant precipitation systems (e.g., Newton 1950, 1963; Carlson 1980; Hobbs et al. 1996).

Paul J. Neiman et al. 1998 "An observational study of fronts and frontal mergers over the Continental United States." *Monthly Weather Review* 126: 2521–52, 2521 (emphasis added).

Inspecting the example below, we might notice that the simple present emerges with the research question — when the current writer *replies* to the reported statements, and initiates a new stage in the conversation.

The subfield of human anthropology, drawing on both Redfield and the Chicago School, **has produced** a wealth of interesting re-search on communities around the world (Hannerz 1980) ....

Suffice it to say that despite all the work that has been carried out on communities, the question still **remains**: What **underlies** a sense of community? Anderson (1983) **examined** this question and **suggested** that communities are "imagined." Members of modern nations ....

Such a view allows for a redefinition of *community*. Since it is imagined, a sense of community is not limited to a specific geo-graphic locale (Gupta and Ferguson 1992). Immigrants **are said** to live in "binational communities" (Baca and Bryan 1980), "extended communities" (Whiteford 1979), "transnational communities" in "hyperspace" (Rouse 1991), and "transnational families" (Chavez 1992). These concepts **highlight** the connections migrants main-tain with life in their home communities ....

Chavez 1994: 54 (emphasis added).

What can we learn from the example above? Past tenses seem to occur in reporting expressions as a writer represents founding statements which led to other statements: so, after reaching the present in 1980 (and the chance to ask a question), we are back in the past with "Anderson (1983) examined." With this in mind, let's reconsider our question concerning the use of the past tense in the summary of Calhoun above ("Calhoun (1994) **catalogued** the social practices..."). A reader might interpret Calhoun's cataloguing as preliminary or foundational work, rather than the immediate motivation of the present research. Reporting expressions in scholarly writing may favour the present tenses, because these tenses signal an essential motivation for scholarly work: the scholar listens to what is being said; then, from his or her position, has a question to ask, and takes a turn in the conversation. The present tenses cue the *writer's* motivation.

Sometimes, markers write in the margins of student papers

**Watch your tenses!**
**Tense!**
**Be consistent in tense**

— suggesting that academic readers are sensitive to these signals which indicate the story of knowledge being made. Staging the construction of knowledge, the verb forms writers use also indicate *their* version of this story: their sense of the sequence of knowledge, its contexts of production, the remoteness in time of some statements (remote but still audible, and enduring or echoing despite the passage of time) and the proximity of others (some so nearby in time that they are re-spoken as if in the present moment). On the one hand, the staging of statements in time is a dimension of a writer's particular perspective on the scholarly conversation. On the other hand, it displays the writer's familiarity with the progress of knowledge in the discipline. This perhaps explains readers' sensitivity to tenses, and to (what may seem to them) misrepresentations of the progress of knowledge, and may also explain the difficulty that newcomers to the disciplines can have in locating statements in time — choosing among present and past tenses, simple and perfect aspects — in ways that make sense to readers very familiar with the scholarly conversation.

# 11

# Introductions and conclusions

In the schoolroom essay, introductions and conclusions are often determined by models relating to a number of elements of the social situation, including the need for students to do well on standardized, provincial essay-writing exams. For example, think of the advice high school students are routinely given for writing introductions for five-paragraph essays: begin with a generalization, narrow the topic, and end the paragraph with a thesis statement identifying the three main points of the essay. But genre theory tells us that introductions and conclusions are likely to serve quite different purposes in research writing, and so it is particularly important to consider how the scholarly context shapes the beginnings and ends of research essays. Obviously, in both schoolroom and research writing, introductions and conclusions share the need to begin and end, and this need will bring some similarities. However, there are crucial differences that arise because of the knowledge-making demands of the research genres that we studied in the last chapter. This chapter will focus on generalization, citation, and documentation practices in order to identify some of these differences. In particular, it applies our knowledge of **summary** and the **orchestration** of voices, discussed in Chapters 2–6, to these specific locations in the academic paper. We'll consider how **citation** leads to estimates of the **state of knowledge** and **knowledge deficits**, features of academic writing that make an appearance in both introductions and conclusions. We'll also take a close look at reporting style and the accompanying conventions of **documentation**. But first, let's consider the role of **generalization** and citation in establishing how a topic has been discussed before, and what this implies in terms of **common** versus **uncommon** sense (see Chapter 9A).

## 11A **Generalization and Citation**

Most people would probably agree that introductions typically begin at and sustain a relatively high level of generality. For the schoolroom essay, generality itself is often enough to get the essay under way.

> Throughout history, humans have sought to understand who they are.

Or:

> Imagination is a powerful force in our daily lives.

But if we transfer this habit of generality directly to the academic essay, we might find that academic readers' expectations are not entirely satisfied by generalities like these. Academic readers are used to beginnings like the following passage, taken from an article:

> In the last 20 years, business organizations have been increasingly held accountable for their corporate social performance in a variety of areas (Wood, 1991). Firms have been confronted by an organized, activist, and concerned set of stakeholders (Ansoff, 1975; Freeman, 1984) clamoring for improved corporate performance on a wide range of social and political issues, from clean air and nutritional labelling to equal employment opportunities.
>
> Greening and Gray 1994: 467.

It seems likely that most people — including the writers — already know that public consciousness of business and industry has changed, and corporate spokespersons appear on TV, and are often quoted in the print media to answer complaints about their products and practices. But, even though these circumstances seem to be part of common knowledge, the academic writer attributes their mention to particular sources. Why are statements that could easily be justified as belonging to the present writer attributed to other writers?

Recent research into academic discourse has shown that one of the moves writers typically make is to confirm that they are carrying on a **tra-**

**dition of inquiry**. Parenthetical citations show that a particular topic has been discussed in published research, which attests to its relevance and importance. In the academic community to which an article is addressed, people recognize this topic as something to be studied. So, we could say that Greening and Gray include these citations in order to show that other scholars have discussed the issue. In turn, we should expect that they will extend this discussion. We will explore this use of citation in more depth in the following sections. First, however, let's focus directly on what is at stake in terms of "common knowledge." If attaching a citation to a common-sense generalization seems odd, how does it affect our understanding of the common-sense version of that generalization?

This next example begins to explain how. It is taken from the eugenics article introduced in Chapter 1:

> Eugenics theory powerfully influenced late nineteenth- and early twentieth-century U.S. policies concerning the groups then known as "the dependent, defective, and delinquent classes" (Henderson 1901, U.S. Department of the Interior 1883). In essence, eugenicists held that the "fit" should be encouraged to reproduce ("positive" eugenics) and the "unfit" prevented from doing so ("negative" eugenics).
>
> Rafter 1992: 17.

Here too, the writer begins with some general statements about the influence of eugenics theory on public policy and scholarly views, but these statements also carry the exact words of other speakers. We might not be surprised by the generalization, because the ideas seem to be part of our common knowledge, but we will probably react negatively to the words used to describe the groups: "dependent," "defective," and "delinquent." In this sense, we may very well recognize why it is important for the parenthetical citation to identify who characterized these groups in this way. Even without consulting Henderson or the U.S. Department of the Interior, just by looking at the dates, we can guess that they are examples of the influence and the policies mentioned in the generalization. The writer is not just generalizing: he is locating the generalization in terms of exact speakers and social actors (Henderson and the U.S. Department of the Interior). Recalling our study of **levels of generality** in Chapter 3B, we see that the generalization is being secured by a particular example, and that the quotation marks signal something about this example: namely that the assumptions or beliefs of these speakers (e.g., Henderson) are at issue. While it may once have been common knowledge that certain groups are "defective," researchers have since questioned this way of looking at the world. In this sense, the citation suspends a common-sense assumption on the part of the cited speakers.

As well as putting a check on **common sense** — on unexamined though widely held views — attributing generalizations to others can also put a check on personal perceptions. We may notice, in our daily life, that the servers at fast-food outlets are elderly people. So we construct a generalization: "The fast-food franchise industries hire elderly people." But what if it is only the one or two outlets that serve the fried chicken we like that actually do hire elderly people? What if, in the next district or province, most servers are adolescents? Our limited experience — our particular position in the world — has distorted our knowledge of the situation. And what if our experience is limited in some other way, for example, by attitudes and interests? Maybe we have a grudge against elderly people, and feel the world is overrun with them. We see them everywhere. Our unchecked personal perception would produce an unwarranted generalization, a stereotype, one which reflected our point of view but might not stand up to rigorous scrutiny. So, in academic writing, we find generalizations that typify sections of the population secured with citation to demonstrate that these categories are products of research and not stereotypes or untested personal perception:

> Some investigators have attributed ... low rates of delinquency and other behavior disorders [among "people of Asian descent in North America, particularly those of Chinese heritage"] to culture-related factors. That is, Asian culture emphasizes conformity, family solidarity, harmonious relationships, and respect for authority, especially the unconditional respect for parents, or filial piety (Fong, 1973; Hsu, 1981). The North American culture, on the other hand, emphasizes freedom and individualism. Consistent with this notion of cultural differences, Kelley and Tsang (1992) reported that Chinese parents in North America used more physical control over their children and more restrictive child-rearing practices than did their non-Chinese counter-parts.
>
> Siu Kwong Wong 1999 "Acculturation, peer relations, and delinquent behavior of Chinese-Canadian youth." *Adolescence* 34 (133): 107–19, 107–08.

As suggested by the terms of this example — "people of Asian descent in North America, particularly those of Chinese heritage" — the generalization has been produced in a context of scholarly research and exchange and is therefore less susceptible to the criticisms that can be leveled against untested "common knowledge."

---

### Exercise 1

Here are two examples of generalization occurring in opening sections of research articles. What would be the "common-sense" versions of these generalizations?

#### PASSAGE 1

To combat racism effectively it is necessary to understand its complex features and underlying themes. In Britain it has recently been argued that such understanding is lacking in many anti-racism strategies (see Gilroy 1990; Rattansi 1992). Anti-racist understanding of racist thinking and arguing is not very sophisticated. Cohen (1992), for instance, typifies anti-racism as the disavowal of complexity for the sake of pursuing moral certainties. Anti-racism appears to be lacking in effectiveness because of its doctrinaire form and its lack of powerful arguments.

Verkuyten et al. 1994: 253.

#### PASSAGE 2

Gender is one of the most important categories — if not the most important category — in human social life. The dichotomy between female and male is of crucial relevance to virtually every domain of human experience (Bem, 1981; Huston, 1983; Ruble and Ruble, 1982). All known cultures specify that female-male is a fundamental distinction. They provide terms to distinguish boys from girls and men from women. More importantly, they associate men and women with different sets of characteristic features and with different sets of behavioral expectations (see Williams and Best, 1990).

Thomas Eckes 1994 "Features of men, features of women: Assessing stereotypic beliefs about gender subtypes." *British Journal of Social Psychology* 33: 107–23, 107.

## 11B Reported Speech

As we have observed, introductions in the schoolroom-essay genre and in the research genres share a tendency for high-level — i.e., general — beginnings. Both genres, it seems, strive thereby to establish a common ground of understanding with readers. The difference between them is that "common understanding" extends in different directions. In the schoolroom essay, introductory generalities seem to cast such a wide net as to grab any reader in sight. The research genres, on the other hand, compose introductory generalities to cast a narrower net in order to initiate a scholarly conversation — to resume the collaborative consideration of topics that research communities are working on. Accordingly, **reported speech** is an important (and very common) way to start a scholarly conversation.

As we saw in Chapter 2, reported speech is so crucial a feature in scholarly discourse that the research genres have developed their own distinctive ways of incorporating the speech of others. And, although the rules vary from discipline to discipline, supporting systems of documentation — footnotes, endnotes, lists of works cited, parenthetical clusters of names and dates — are intricate and rule-governed.

Equally intricate are the systems that direct writers to quote a lot, or not much, or quote directly, or to paraphrase, or to put other writers' names in the reporting sentence, or to put them in parentheses, or even to leave some speakers unidentified. As we proceed to examine the roles played by reported speech, we may find some *guides* to this system, but we will not find the kind of *rules* that govern, for example, the preparation of a "Works Cited" or "References" page or the punctuation of a parenthetical citation in a certain discipline. Instead, we will find patterns that indicate the preferences and habits of academic communities.

First, let's think about how we incorporate the speech of others in everyday conversation. We can use **direct speech**, the exact words the other person used:

> JANE to FRED:  FRED to CATHERINE:
> "I'm so sorry. I forgot  And then Jane said, "I'm so sorry. I forgot
> your birthday."  your birthday."

While in writing, direct speech is supposed to be verbatim, in talking, as some research has shown, people are often not accurate in their repetition of others' words. Instead of direct speech, we often substitute our own words — **indirect speech** — which can be more or less close to the original:

| JANE to FRED: | FRED to CATHERINE: |
|---|---|
| "I'm so sorry. I forgot your birthday. | And then Jane said she regretted it. She was sorry she had forgotten my birthday. |

When we are summarizing, we often find ourselves using indirect speech: that is, we transform the exact words of another speaker/writer to fit into a smaller space, and a different context.

Like everyday speakers, academic writers make decisions as to what they will quote directly and what they will incorporate indirectly. It appears that there are tendencies in how much direct versus indirect speech is used. These tendencies follow the function of the summary: to confirm what has been said, to dispute it, to go further. Moreover, there is a fairly good chance that indirect speech in scholarly writing will appear in a **nominalized** form (see Chapter 9C). To continue with the example above, the writer might change "regretted" into the noun "regrets" (Jane said she had regrets). Reported speech, mostly in indirect form, can take a step toward nominal style by transforming the **reporting verb** itself into a noun. This pattern is very common. For example,

$$
\text{she} \quad
\begin{array}{l}
\text{suggests} \\
\text{assumes} \\
\text{argues}
\end{array}
\quad \text{that ...}
$$

— can become:

$$
\text{her} \quad
\begin{array}{l}
\textbf{suggestion} \\
\textbf{assumption} \\
\textbf{argument}
\end{array}
\quad \text{that ...}
$$

So, "Jane expressed regret…" could become "Jane's expression of regret…." Based on our observations about nominal style in Chapter 9, we might predict that reporting expressions will tend to appear as nouns when a writer is compressing or classifying statements.

Let's consider some of the most common patterns of reported speech in academic writing. The simplest, baseline case of reported speech — both direct and indirect — is "*x* said *y.*" Or "*x* said" can be replaced by a characterization of the original speech, and followed by the gist, sometimes with a bit of direct speech retained.

> FRED to CATHERINE: Jane expressed regret about forgetting my birthday, saying she was "sorry."

Research writing can often depart from these baseline cases. Commonly, the reported speaker can leave the sentence itself and relocate in parentheses.

> Heartfelt regret is an important element in ongoing relationships (Short 1996).

This form can eliminate the speech verb (*say* and its many substitutes, such as *report, suggest,* etc.) as above, or retain it:

> It has been reported that the expression of regret is a key factor in ongoing relationships (Short 1996; Gross 2000).

Sometimes the speaker or speakers can disappear entirely: the act of speech is represented as agentless:

> It has been reported that the expression of regret is essential, and should be done regularly.

This way of speaking seems to defy the research community's practice of attributing statements. On non-scholarly occasions, agentless reports of statements may tend to make the statement seem more valid — coming from not just one person (who may or may not be reliable) but from more widely distributed sources.

> It is widely known that the expression of regret is essential in ongoing relationships.

So the agentless report of speech can suggest some consensus. Inspecting the samples of reported speech below, you will have a chance to see if this is the case in scholarly publications.

In a variation on the agentless report of speech, statements can sometimes be attributed to a **typified group** — "informants," "researchers," "eugenicists," for example, in the scholarly genres; "experts," "officials," or "business leaders" in other genres. So our example, in a "group-speaker" form, could be rewritten:

> Interviewees report that the expression of regret is a key factor in friendships.

When statements are presented as reported speech in any of these forms, their quality as knowledge is indicated: the statement has been produced

— somewhere. At first it may appear that, in the scholarly genres, to present a statement as coming from a position other than that of the present speaker may implicitly affirm that the statement is true: "this is not just my idea." But, as we saw in Chapter 6 ("Orchestrating Voices"), things are more complicated than this. Statements are reported not simply to ensure that only true things get down on paper. Writers also report statements to establish common ground, to sketch a community of speakers producing knowledge in a particular area. Reported statements produce a map of that knowledge domain. And a main concern of scholarly writers, as we will see, is to locate themselves on that map — maybe close to some speakers, or far away from others, maybe starting in densely populated locales where a lot has been said, but heading out into sparsely settled regions from which few statements have been transmitted so far.

We have called the baseline case of reported speech "*x* says *y*." In one of the variations on our example, we picked up the verb "expressed" (which we turned into a noun). Although "express" can be used in reporting the speech of our friends, it is by no means the most effective verb for reporting the speech of academic writers. In Chapter 2, we noted the importance of choosing verbs that characterize the action of the original, such as s*tate, propose, suggest, maintain, claim.* Associated with verbs of speech are a set of verbs we could call "knowledge-making." Among the knowledge-making verbs, we find words like *analyze, investigate, examine, discover, find, identify, observe.*

> **Analyzing** shopping opportunities, Smith (2000) **found** that bargains were available.

Like the verbs of speech, these verbs can be turned into nouns, as in

> **Analysis** of shopping opportunities has led to the **identification** of bargains (Smith 2000).

Where a range of wordings presents choices, the different choices tend to be associated with different functions. So, in everyday speech, to use *claim* as a reporting verb may in some situations have the effect of discrediting the statement, or at least suggesting that it needs review.

> THOMAS to MARK: Well, Matthew claims to have found bargains.

It is not clear whether *claim* — as just one example — works the same way to express doubt in scholarly writing. But research has found some correlation between the choice of reporting verb and the position of the writer vis-à-vis the sources reported.

Choice of reporting verb can also be influenced by the discipline in which the writer is working. In his study of citation practices in eight disciplines (molecular biology, magnetic physics, marketing, applied linguistics, philosophy, sociology, mechanical engineering, and electronic engineering), Ken Hyland (1999) found diversity in reporting expressions used. For example, marketing is distinctive for its "particularly high degree of author tentative verbs, with *suggest* accounting for over half of all instances" (350); philosophy and marketing are more likely than the other disciplines in the sample to name the cited author outside parenthetical references (358–59); physics favours the reporting verbs *develop, report, study*, while sociology prefers *argue, suggest, describe, note, analyze, discuss*. In the sample, none of the science papers used direct quotation (348). Hyland suggests that part of what people learn when they become part of a research community is a discipline-specific understanding of how scholarly work is organized, and how knowledge is made. Techniques for reporting the speech of others display this understanding.

---

**Exercise 2**

Examine the following samples of scholarly writing which report the statements of others. Identify the extent to which the samples illustrate the range of expression and function described above: the summoning of the voices of others to gesture to an important issue or established line of research; the variation between direct and indirect speech; the naming, obscuring, or typifying of other speakers; the characterization of the production of statements with various words for speaking and/or making knowledge.

From these limited data, can you generalize your results? What do you notice about the reporting of statements in scholarly prose? Can you see any correlation between the features you identify and the disciplines in which the writers are working?

**PASSAGE 1**

In the second paradigm, gender is construed as a global personality construct. The concepts of masculinity, femininity and

---

androgyny exemplify this approach (see, e.g., Archer, 1989; Cook, 1985; Morawski, 1987). In reviewing the literature concerning the sex-differences and the gender-as-a-personality-construct approaches, Deaux and Kite (1987) come to the following conclusion: "The scientific record on questions of sex differences, based on either biological or psychological distinctions, is shaky at best [...]. Yet despite evidence of considerable overlap and situational specificity of gender-related behaviors, beliefs in sex differences are held tenaciously" (p. 97).

Researchers adopting the third and most recent approach conceive of gender as a social category, that is, as a category on which perceivers base judgements, inferences and social actions. The central research issue here is not "how men and women actually differ, but how people think that they differ" (Deaux, 1984, p. 110).

Eckes 1994: 107–8.

## PASSAGE 2

Many commentators on post-war Britain have suggested that the workforce and its unions must accept a large part of the responsibility for the country's continuing economic ills. British workers may or may not have been unusually strike prone, but they have certainly long colluded, it is believed, in a range of restrictive practices on the shopfloor, thus increasing costs, curtailing output and drastically limiting the scope for necessary industrial modernisation. As the distinguished Anglo-German academic Ralf Dahrendorf has recently put it, working people in Britain have tended to "stretch their work so that it begins to look like leisure".[1] In this situation, the inevitable consequence has been economic stagnation.

Over the following pages we aim to challenge this view and demonstrate that restrictive practices of this type have been nowhere near as common or serious as some have argued.

*Note*
1  R. Dahrendorf, *On Britain* (1982) p. 46.

Tiratsoo and Tomlinson 1994: 65.

## Exercise 3

The distinctive appearance of the following is characteristic of publications in history. Describe the ways it departs from what we have
come to regard as typical of scholarly introductions. Describe the
distinct ways this writer establishes the generalities that frame research contributions.

In October 1888 the Colonial Office expressed deep disquiet
at news that an officer of the Gold Coast Constabulary, In-
spector Akers, while involved on an expedition to subdue
Krepi, had inflicted harsh sentences of flogging upon men
under his command who were accused of attempting to strike
an NCO, drunkenness and cowardice. The nine accused Hausa
constables were flogged publicly before the whole force, the
worst offender receiving 72 lashes. Both the method of flogging and the number of lashes given were extremely severe
and contrary to the standing orders of the Constabulary. In
an enquiry that consumed a considerable amount of Colonial
Office time and paper, the matter was thoroughly investigated
and Akers, an officer with "many good qualities" but "having
a violent and hasty temper," was invalided home.[1]

European use of physical violence, even excessive violence,
against African subordinates was not particularly unusual in
the late nineteenth and early twentieth centuries. However,
the Akers case, coming less than ten years after flogging had
been abolished in the British Army, marks an approximate
point at which the Colonial Office began to exercise concern,
and seek to regulate, the extent and severity of officially sanc-
tioned corporal punishment inflicted on African soldiers and
also labour. A discussion of official and colonial attitudes to
the use of corporal punishment in British Africa is a large subject and beyond the compass of a brief article. What is attempted here is much more manageable: a discussion of the
attempts by the Colonial Office, over a period of more than
sixty years, first to regulate more closely and then to bring to
an end corporal punishment in the African Colonial Forces.
Colonial Office officials were agreed on the need to regulate

corporal punishment; those advocating abolition steadily increased with the progress of the century. Both regulators and reformers in London had to contend with military officers and colonial administrators who argued that corporal punishment was necessary for the control and discipline of African troops, especially when on active service, and the steady pressure from various humanitarian lobbies in Britain denouncing severe practices in the colonies.

*Note*

1   Public Record Office, Kew [PRO], CO96/197/3064, 31 Dec. 1888; and CO96/197/3080, Griffith to Knutsford, conf., 30 Nov. 1888.

David Killingray 1994 "The 'rod of empire': The debate over corporal punishment in the British African colonial forces, 1888–1946." *Journal of African History* 35: 201–16, 201.

## 11C Documentation

Reporting expressions — direct and indirectly reported speech of other speakers, and the echoes of reporting in the nominalized style we have been considering — summon a community of voices, and position the present writer amongst them. But everybody knows that these expressions are only part of the system that situates research amidst other research. These reporting expressions are secured by a system of **documentation** — footnotes, endnotes, lists of "References" and "Works Cited."

It is also well known that styles of documentation differ from discipline to discipline. Most disciplines use some variation on a system of parenthetical expressions in the body of the text which are keyed to an alphabetical list at the end. For example, the name of each writer (each source) listed at the end of this sentence —

> The idea of using assessment as a lever for school change is not a new one: many accountability tools in the 1970s and 1980s tried to link policy decisions to test scores (Linn, 1987; Madaus, 1985; Wise, 1979).

— signals an entry in a list called "References" at the end of the text:

Linn, R.L. (1987). Accountability: The comparison of education systems and the quality of test results. *Educational policy* 1 (2), 181–198.

Madaus, G., West, M.M., Harmon, M.C., Lomax, R.G., and Viator, K.A. (1992). *The influence of testing on teaching math and science in grades 4–12.* Chestnut Hill, MA: Boston College Center for the Study of Testing, Evaluation, and Educational Policy.

Madaus, G.F. (1985). "Can we help dropouts? Thinking about the undoable." In G. Natriello (Ed.), *School dropouts: Patterns and policies* (pp. 3-19). New York: Teachers College Press.

The parenthetical "(Linn, 1987)" sends the reader to the first entry above, while "(Madaus, 1985)" sends the reader to the third rather than the second entry under "Madaus." (If Madaus had two entries, both by himself only and both from 1985, the writer could have distinguished them as "1985a" and "1985b.")

While documentation systems vary in detail, they all operate to achieve one principal effect: the reader's easy movement from the body of the text to the full documentation in the "References" or "Works Cited" pages. Let's compare the above example from a journal in education to the following passage from an anthropology journal:

> Although many examples exist, a recent example was presented by Rouse (1991), who carried out ethnographic research among immigrants from the Mexican community of Aguililla living in Redwood City, California. In developing the notion of "transnational communities," Rouse presents a novel challenge to spatial images, highlighting the social nature of postmodern space.
>
> Chavez 1994: 56.

Although it looks a little different — instead of a parenthetical cluster of names and dates, we find the name of the writer and date of publication incorporated into the sentence — it nevertheless operates in the same way. If the reader is interested, he or she can find relevant information about the source (Rouse 1991) in the "Reference" list:

Rouse, Roger
    1991 Mexican Migration and the Social Space of Postmodernism. Diaspora 1:8–23.

Variation in systems of documentation can be found both in styles of reporting, in the body of texts, and styles of listing, at the end of texts. Yet, with slight distinctions in the ordering of information, documentation provides three important items of information: the name of writer, the title of the work, and publishing information necessary to distinguish the publication from all other publications. Making arrangements for the readers' "easy movement from the body of the text to the full documentation" is part of the writer's larger orchestration of the scholarly conversation. Most obviously, it enables readers — if they choose — to find the source in a library or elsewhere, read it, and join the conversation themselves.

Less obviously but equally important, the full documentation provides more information about the circumstances under which the cited statement was produced. A reader who may not in fact get the original and read it can still find relevant information about the conditions of the statement's production: Did the cited statement appear in a book or an article? If it was in a book, was it a chapter in a collected edition? Who edited the book? If it was an article, in what journal did it appear? What was the title of the book or chapter or article (i.e., how did it announce what it was about)? And, most important, when was the statement produced?

---

**Exercise 4**

Below are four samples of entries from reference pages at the end of articles in scholarly journals. Inspect these samples to determine the points at which they are similar and at which they vary (e.g., punctuation, use of capitals, order of information, and so on). How do scholars document a source that is (a) an article in a journal? (b) a book? (c) a chapter in a book? (d) an article in a book? Can you see any correlation between the features you identify and the disciplines in which the writers are working?

**From a "Works Cited" list in *PMLA* (a literary-critical journal, *Publications of the Modern Language Association of America*):**
Baudrillard, Jean. *For a Critique of the Political Economy of the Sign.* Trans. Charles Levin. Saint Louis: Telos, 1981.
Eisenstein, Sergei. "Dickens, Griffith, and the Film Today." *Film Form.* New York: Harcourt, 1949. 195–255.

Geertz, Clifford. *The Interpretation of Cultures*. New York: Basic, 1973.

Gilbert, Elliot. "The Ceremony of Innocence: Charles Dickens's A Christmas Carol." *PMLA* 90 (1975): 22–31.

**From a "References" list in *Environment and Planning*:**

Frobel F, Heinrichs J, Kreye O, 1980, *The New International Division of Labor: Structural Unemployment in Industrialized Countries and Industrialization in Developing Countries* (Cambridge University Press, Cambridge)

Johnson H T, 1991, "Managing by remote control: recent management accounting practices in historical perspective," in *Inside the Business Enterprise: Historical Perspectives on the Use of Information* Ed. P Temin (University of Chicago Press, Chicago, IL) pp. 41–70

Monden Y, 1981, "What makes the Toyota production system really tick?" *Industrial Engineering* (January) 36–46

**From a "References" list in *Language and Communication*:**

AUDEN, W.H. 1962 Dingley Dell and the fleet. In *The Dyer's Hand and Other Essays*, pp. 407–428. Random House, New York.

JAYNES, J. 1976 *The Origin of Consciousness in the Breakdown of the Bicameral Mind*. Houghton Mifflin, Boston.

JAYNES, J. 1986 Consciousness and the voices of the mind. *Canadian Psychology* 27, 128–137.

LAWSON, L. 1989 Walker Percy's prodigal son. In Crowley, J.D. (Ed.), *Critical Essays on Walker Percy*, pp. 243–258. G.K. Hall, Boston.

**From a "References" list in *Genetic, Social, and General Psychology Monographs*:**

Eisenstadt, S. (1989). *Israeli society* (2nd ed.). New York: Stockten.

El-Sarrag, A. (1968). *Psychiatry in northern Sudan: A study in comparative psychiatry*. British Journal of Psychiatry, 114, 946–948.

Spiro, M.E. (1983). Introduction: Thirty years of kibbutz research. In E. Krause (Ed.), *The sociology of the kibbutz: Studies in Israeli society II*. New Brunswick, NJ: Transaction Books.

## 11D Introductions: State of Knowledge and the Knowledge Deficit

Investigating the role of reported speech in getting the scholarly discussion under way, we observed that, when statements are presented as issuing not from the present writer but from other writers, they include an implicit comment on their status as knowledge. They were produced by someone; they came from a site in the research community. If we take this perspective on scholarly statements, we can see **reported speech** as mapping a set of **positions** in the territory of knowledge producers. In Chapter 10, we used the term **state of knowledge** to name this mapping activity: the ways a writer indicates the limits of knowledge, the conditions under which it was produced, and the positions from which statements issue. And we used the term **knowledge deficit** to talk about how writers can define what hasn't been said, what needs to be said. These indicators occur throughout a given piece of scholarly writing, but they often appear in a compressed form in introductions.

The state of knowledge in compressed form should be familiar because we have examined several examples already (consider the passages in Exercise 2 above). Here is another example:

> There have been several well-conducted efforts to understand childhood disorders of emotion in terms of distinct and meaningful components (e.g., Fox and Houston, 1983; Ollendick and Yule, 1990; Papy, Costello, Hedl, and Spielberger, 1975). In particular, several investigators have found considerable overlap between the constructs of anxiety and depression (e.g., Lonigan, Carey, and Finch, 1994; Norvell, Brophy, and Finch, 1985; Tannenbaum, Forehand, and McCombs-Thomas, 1992; Wolfe et al., 1987) and have suggested a higher order construct of negative affect (Watson and Clark, 1984). Although the evidence for this relation is compelling, the latent structure of childhood negative emotions is only beginning to be conceptualized in detail (e.g., Joiner, Catanzaro, and Laurent, 1996).
>
> Chorpita et al. 1998: 74.

In this passage, Chorpita et al. provide a summary of certain research activities. You will notice that the overall pattern begins by identifying the area of study ("childhood disorders" in terms of "components"). It then focuses on a type of finding ("overlap" of "anxiety and depression") and how it has been interpreted ("higher order construct"). Following this, some caution is exerted ("only beginning to be conceptualized"). At each step, these research activities are located by way of parenthetical citation that usually names more than one research publication. Without advancing an explicit position or comment of their own, Chorpita et al. have told the story of the research that precedes their own. They have created a map on which we might expect they will locate their own work.

One way researchers can locate themselves on the map is by claiming to add to existing knowledge: a space that has been recognized as unoccupied or only tentatively claimed gets filled up with new data and further reasoning. Sometimes the space has not yet been recognized: it has gone unnoticed by others. Another way scholars get title to a position on the map is to evict the current occupant: they show that previously established knowledge cannot hold that ground because it is faulty or incomplete in some way.

In making moves on the knowledge map, the writer identifies a **knowledge deficit**. There is something we don't know, some space on the map where there is a gap, a spot where no one has so far settled to take careful account of the place. Or there can be some error in what is held to be true. The only way such a deficit can be identified is through a review of what is known, or taken to be known. Reported speech — the whole practice of citation and summary — *constructs the deficit*. On the one hand, reported speech provides a positive rationale for the current writer to speak, because it shows that the research community is already talking about an issue. On the other hand, by allowing the current writer to respond to a deficit, reported speech provides a negative rationale by indicating why the discussion so far is not complete.

When the current writer responds to a knowledge deficit, we can expect to find a distinct change in style of expression. **Modal expressions** emerge, overtaking reporting expressions, and the **discursive *I*** often appears alongside. We've observed that the modalized statement is an inference or estimate of knowledge (Chapter 10D).

One such estimate of knowledge can be found in writers' formal statements of their **hypothesis**: the statement which is deemed plausible, but which is, so far, untested and will be shown to be tested in the course of the article. Modalized expressions, without the discursive I, show up in statements such as this one:

Two main hypotheses are addressed in this study: (1) that unidentified and untreated learning difficulties **may** be related to teenage girls becoming pregnant, deciding to raise their children, and dropping out of school, and (2) that teenage pregnancies **may** *not* be characteristically "unintended."

Rauch-Elnekave 1994: 92 (italic emphasis in original, bold emphasis added).

But many research publications do not specify the hypothesis in this way, and still make use of modal expressions and the discursive *I*. So rather than attach these features simply to the hypothesis, it may be better to locate them in the larger process of constructing a **knowledge deficit**. Here we spot it showing up as a writer poses his research question about "low ability" classes where "high quality instruction fosters significant learning among students":

What characterizes such phrases? To address this question, **I draw** on evidence from earlier studies by other authors, and **I provide** two new illustrations taken from a larger study of eighth- and ninth-grade English classes in 25 midwestern schools. Although these examples are far from conclusive, common elements emerge that, taken together, **may** help to characterize effective instruction in low ability classes in secondary schools.

Gamoran 1993:2 (emphasis added).

The question identifies an as yet unoccupied location on the knowledge map: we don't know what goes on in these classes. Plotting his approach to this space, the writer moves speculatively. Conceding the limits of the evidence available to him, he says his work "may help" to make this unknown area known. Compare the unmodalized, unqualified version of the same statement:

Common elements emerge that characterize effective instruction in low ability classes in secondary schools.

The unmodalized version may actually be more in keeping with the traditions of the schoolroom essay. Students are often advised to take a stand, state their opinion, be decisive in their writing. As readers of newspapers, we expect journalists to take a decisive stand. Yet, in scholarly writing, where knowledge is laboriously constructed, the modalized version is more typical. Scholarly statements leave traces of their sources and their status.

To identify the knowledge deficit, the writer of the above example must show that the current state of knowledge is inadequate.

> According to this view, observed differences among studies in the effects of grouping are due to chance; taken together, the studies indicate that no real effects on achievement exist. Another interpretation **seems** equally **plausible**. The inconsistent findings **may** have resulted from uncontrolled differences in the way ability grouping was implemented in the various school systems under investigation.
>
> Gamoran 1993: 3–4 (emphasis added).

In moving to show that a published view from a respected source comes up short, and leaves the state of knowledge in this area unfinished, the writer does not simply deny the view ("This interpretation is wrong"). He doesn't even say that "another interpretation is equally plausible," or "more plausible." It only "seems equally plausible." And the reinterpretation is itself modalized: "inconsistent findings may have resulted from uncontrolled differences" rather than "inconsistent findings resulted from uncontrolled differences."

---

### Exercise 4

The samples in the exercise below show two distinct ways that writers identify knowledge deficits. Inspect these passages and identify the ways each one establishes the writer's (or writers') right to speak positively (i.e., by connecting the present work with established concerns) and negatively (i.e., by identifying a knowledge deficit).

### PASSAGE 1

In this article, we examine the cultural categories and the conceptual logic that underlie the orthography debates about kreyòl that have taken place over the last 50 years. In Haiti, as in many countries concerned with nation building, the development of an orthography for vernacular literacy has been neither a neutral activity nor simply about how to mechanically reduce a spoken language to written form. The processes of transforming a spoken language to written form have often been viewed as scientific, arbitrary, or unproblematic. However, the creation of supposedly arbitrary sound-sign (signi-fied/signifier) relationships that constitute an orthography al-ways involves choices based on someone's idea of what is important. This process of representing the sounds of language in written form is thus an activity deeply grounded in frame-works of value.

Shieffelin and Doucet 1994: 176.

**PASSAGE 2**

In many ways, the influenza pandemic of 1918–19 is the "for-gotten" epidemic; forgotten, at least, by scholars studying Brit-ish Columbia's First Nations. Much attention has been paid to the timing and severity of late eighteenth- and early nine-teenth-century epidemics for what they tell us about the proto-historic and early contact culture and population change. Scholars have argued the significance of these epidemics in softening up indigenous societies for the onslaught of coloni-zation. Few, however, have examined later disease patterns for what they tell us about the nature of cross-cultural relations in the early twentieth century.

Mary-Ellen Kelm 1999 "British Columbia First Nations and the influenza pandemic of 1918–19." *BC Studies* 122 (Summer): 23–47, 23–24.

## 11E Student Versions of the Knowledge Deficit

As a student writer, you may be reluctant to say that nobody has ever stud-ied this before, or that everybody has got it wrong so far. But, with some adjustments, you can still replicate the move which identifies a knowledge deficit. Consider the following example from a scholarly article:

> There are several studies which have analyzed the discourse func-tions of quotation. Some researchers have analyzed languages other than English (e.g., Larson 1978; Besnier 1986; Glock 1986). Others have analyzed English, but most did not examine discourse samples to determine if their analyses are actually supported by data (e.g., Wierzbicka 1974; Halliday 1985; Li 1986; Haiman 1989). Addi-tionally, these studies have not addressed the question of whether

direct quotations are really quotations. In other words, how authentic are direct quotes? Do they represent actual previous utterances, or are they inventions of the speaker? This paper focuses on these questions as well as on the functions of quotation in informal spoken English. Unlike these other studies, my analysis is based on discourse samples.

Patricia Mayes 1990 "Quotation in spoken English." *Studies in Language* 14 (2): 325–63, 326.

A student writer could recast this knowledge deficit to show that there is something interesting to be found out:

> Although speakers often resort to sayings which they attribute to other speakers, and listeners accept these sayings as appropriate elements of conversation and other speech genres, we might still ask what role such quotations play in these speech acts. What conditions motivate speakers to repeat others' claims? Is the repetition exact or approximate? authentic or fictionalized? In short, how and why do we represent our own speech as originating with someone else?

Or it could be recast to mark the writer's position in relation to one other speaker (instead of seven):

> Halliday (1985) provides a useful account of the functional grammar of reported speech, but his analyses do not explain the role of quotation in conversation and other speech acts. What conditions motivate speakers to repeat others' claims?

That is, where a professional version of the statement of the knowledge deficit would summarize many (if not all) published claims about a research entity, the student version can summarize one or two.

In some situations, student projects may cite no other speaker. In those cases, the introduction can instead propose plausible ideas about the object of inquiry and then show that these ideas, reasonable as they seem, are problematic: they leave some questions unanswered. The example below in effect invokes possible statements about the object of inquiry, bringing these statements into a kind of conversation with one another, and allowing a question to emerge from this conversation.

> *As For Me and My House* can be read as a system of concealment: Mrs. Bentley skips days at a time, shifts her focus suddenly to the

weather, offers little information about her own background while she relentlessly exposes her husband's personal history. Yet the idea of concealment suggests an audience — and *As For Me and My House* is represented as a diary, a genre which assumes no audience but the writer herself. If the narrative is indeed a pattern of withholdings, how can we reconcile this condition with the book's generic presuppositions about audience? From whom is the missing information being concealed? Perhaps by revising the idea of concealment, and recasting it as a system of attention to painful matters, we can understand Mrs. Bentley's diary on its own terms, as a diligent, deliberate — and sometimes desperate — personal inquiry into the circumstances of her life.

You will see from these examples that a question tends to follow the problematizing activity, or the identification of a knowledge deficit.

For student writers and professional scholars alike, arrangements for speakers — those schemes of scholarly conversation we investigated in Chapter 6 — can take the writer to the verge of a knowledge deficit, and incite questions. Introducing *speaker x* to *speaker y*, and summarizing the statements of each one, the writer arranges for a new exchange between these positions.

## 11F  Conclusions: State of Knowledge and the Knowledge Deficit

How do conclusions contribute to the reader's understanding of research writing? Certainly, the conclusion is the writer's last chance to make sure that connections between parts of the discussion are secure in readers' minds; it is the last chance to invoke the complex, high-level abstractions which motivated the discussion, made sense of its specifics, and contributed to the ongoing scholarly conversation. It is therefore best to think of conclusions as not concluding so much as *confirming* what has gone before.

While conclusions which merely restate the introduction are a common feature in the high school classroom essay, they can be troubling for readers of the research genres. This isn't to say that repetition does not occur in scholarly writing in general or conclusions in particular. As we saw in Chapter 8, reinstating abstractions can help readers manage their mental desktops by interpreting detail and bringing material back to attention. However, exact repetition in a conclusion can sound strange, because the reader who is addressed at the end of an essay is not exactly the same reader who is addressed at the beginning. At the end, the reader is familiar with the details and course of the argument: he or she has just been through it. To simply repeat the introduction suggests that the reader hasn't heard what the writer said.

So conclusions in research writing tend to address the reader as *a different reader* from the one who read the introduction. In the intervening pages, the reader has encountered detailed analysis and illustration, the claims and supporting evidence. The reader at the end of the paper needs reminders of key **abstractions** and important findings to confirm the results and significance of the essay. The conclusion essentially advances the writer's claim in its final — rather than preliminary — form.

But scholarly writers also go beyond confirming claims in conclusions. They indicate the *limits* of new knowledge. In our discussion of introductions earlier in this chapter, we noted that signs of limited knowledge come with **modality**. In conclusions, where writers locate new **knowledge deficits**, we might expect to find modality and other signs of limits. This concluding section from an article on plain language shows the researchers still speculating and inferring:

> As in the case of consultation between health-care professionals and consumers, it is **possible** that legal concepts are difficult to understand because, even when explained in plain language, they are complex or because they are in conflict with folk theories of the law. The subjects in this study (and lay people in general), **may** have been relying on inaccurate prior knowledge of the law or on their own intuition about justice, which **frequently** does not reflect the legal reality. These results **suggest** that plain language drafting alone will take us only part way to the goal of making the law more broadly understood. It must be supported by other measures such as public legal education and individual counselling of persons faced with legal obligations.
>
> Michael E.J. Masson and Mary Anne Waldron 1994 "Comprehension of legal contracts by non-experts: Effectiveness of plain language redrafting." *Applied Cognitive Psychology* 8: 67–85, 79 (emphasis added).

As well as using modality, writers can point to a new knowledge deficit by explicitly remarking on what we don't know. In the following example, the writer confirms the main point of the essay and the knowledge deficit it addressed, then directly refers to the study's "limitations" and indicates what remains to be done:

> Through his association of writing with speech, Malivha immersed *Inkululeko* in the pre-existing forms of communication, and thus ensured the paper's accessibility to its audience. As *Inkululeko* was read some fifty years ago, we are at a disadvantage in getting a clearer picture of how readers interacted with the newspaper. Questions about how the paper was distributed, read and discussed among the people would undoubtedly enrich our understanding of the role played by *Inkululeko* in mobilising for the ZBA, but what is left of these today will certainly be general impressions and memories.
>
> In spite of these limitations, it is hoped that this essay has highlighted issues otherwise largely overlooked by existing social-historical studies seeking to understand questions of popular responses to political mobilisation in the countryside. The processes of forced removal, dispossession, and community destruction undoubtedly generated political consciousness which varied with region and time. But a focus on these processes alone, this essay argued, ignores a host of other factors which can also help explain questions of popular responses to political mobilisation in the countryside. Using the ZBA as a case study, the essay focused on how ideas about these process were communicated to the Zoutpansberg people by looking at the language and style of mobilisation, and the methods as well as the media of communication the organisation used. We believe that a more detailed and thorough research in this direction will enrich our understanding of how some organisations are able to attract popular following in the countryside.

Nemutanzhela 1993: 100–01.

As well as confirming the main point of the essay, and the knowledge deficit it addressed, this conclusion directly refers to its own "limitations" by mentioning them, and indirectly refers to limitations by saying what still has to be done. As the example also shows, conclusions not only gesture toward the future, making a promise for greater knowledge still, they also tend to return the reader to the highest level of **abstraction**: here, such terms as "dispossession" and "political consciousness." This move makes sense because these abstractions are often the high-status terms that gave the introduction rhetorical force — the Big Issues which warrant claims on readers' attention and identify the writer as someone in touch with established concerns.

Accordingly, it is mainly in conclusions that we see the rather rare appearance of what we could call **moral statements**. While the research genres are generally relatively free of statements of moral obligation like this —

> People **should** learn to respect the environment.
> We **must** preserve our neighbourhoods.

— there are nevertheless some occasions when obligation is expressed. Sometimes these obligations are about research itself. Something needs to be examined more closely; something should be explained in relation to something else. We can see an example of such an expression of obligation here, in the last sentence of an article on the experience of German minorities in Britain and the U.S. in World War I (notice as well the major abstractions — *xenophobia, control, intolerance* — that are invoked by this ending):

> In each case, the experience of the German minority **needs** to be placed within traditions of xenophobia in the two countries, but, more especially, the war atmosphere which led to increasing control of all citizens towards and a growth of more general intolerance towards all perceived outgroups.
>
> Ellis and Panayi 1994: 255–56 (emphasis added).

Sometimes the expression of obligation extends to the *application* of the research, as the following example shows. Plain language redrafting is not enough to make legal documents understandable:

> It **must** be supported by other measures such as public legal education and individual counselling of persons faced with legal obligations.
>
> Masson and Waldron 1994: 79 (emphasis added).

And, sometimes, researchers can conclude with statements that resemble the calls to specific action or attitude we find in other genres, such as newspaper editorials or partisan political briefs. This is from a conclusion the writer has labelled "Policy implications":

Human capital differences may be addressed by establishing programs to help women complete their education. We **should** offer scholarships and financial aid for women at both the high school and college levels. We **must** also establish programs to allow women who were forced to drop out of school to return and complete their education. These educational programs **must** be supplemented by others that provide job training and retraining. Many women worked prior to leaving the waged labor force to bear and/or rear children. Their occupational skills often became outdated during their absence and **must** be brought up to date. Other women may never have developed relevant occupational skills because they grew up in an era or community where it was not expected that women would work for wages and will need to develop initial job skills. Programs of job training and retraining will be expensive without any possible source of funds other than the federal government.

My own analysis has revealed that young children in the home are a major barrier to married women's participation in the waged labor force. It is possible that this reflects a negative evaluation of mothers with young children working outside the home, but it could also reflect the absence of safe, affordable day care. We cannot or perhaps **should** not do anything about the former possibility, but we can certainly address the latter. We **must** establish federally funded and federally supervised day care centers. It would be especially desirable if these day care centers could combine custodial with educational functions to provide a "head start" where needed.

Geschwender 1992: 12 (emphasis added).

This conclusion seems strongly stated. It goes further toward real-world action/application than many research genres would permit. But the preceding (and following) examples show that "moral" statements are not entirely missing from the scholarly genres — although they may occur in different degrees and with different focus in different disciplines.

Different disciplines have different kinds of connections with the world beyond the research domain — and the variations in "moral" statements (what *should* be done) that we have observed in the samples in this section are signals of these different connections. In the conclusion to an article from the journal *Estuaries*, for example, "marsh creation" is a positive goal — a *good* — and conditions which "retard" advance towards this goal are *ills*.

The recent decline in fur demand has depressed the industry so that nutria [an aquatic rodent]-trapping in Louisiana's coastal marshes is no longer economical, yet control of nutria populations is essential to maximize growth of newly created marshes. Marsh creation is a major policy objective of the state of Louisiana and of the Federal government. Dealing with the population size of an introduced mammalian species is a part of that policy issue.

We have shown that an introduced species — the nutria — alone or in combination with native migrating waterfowl can seriously retard marsh development in the deltaic environment. This demonstration of the importance of herbivory in the Atchafalaya Delta has practical applications for the northern Gulf of Mexico coast where coastal wetland loss rates are the highest in North America ($65 \text{ km}^2$ year, Britsch and Dunbar 1993).

Elaine D. Evers, Charles Sasser, James Gosselink, Deborah Fuller, and Jenneke Visser 1998 "The impact of vertebrate herbivores on wetland vegetation in Atchafayala Bay, Louisiana." *Estuaries* 21(1): 1–13, 12.

As the passage indicates, nutria population is an obstacle, so "control of nutria populations is essential to maximize growth of newly created marshlands" (nutria *should* be reduced in numbers). Did you notice that the arguments recommending marshland as *good* are presupposed rather than reviewed? This presupposed positive understanding is captured in the claim that "[m]arsh creation is a major policy objective of the state of Louisiana and of the Federal Government."

As this example shows, research interests in some disciplines or subdisciplines involve a direct connection with interests in the public domain. You might analyze your discipline's internal way of thinking about what is desirable or undesirable. Each discipline's ethos — its set of values and beliefs — contributes to disciplinary "moral" statements or imperatives, such as claims about what research should be done or claims about what interventions should be undertaken in the world beyond research domains.

**Exercise 5**

The passage below comes from the conclusion of the article on the effects of "low-ability" grouping. In this passage, "Mrs. Turner" and "Mrs. Grant" were two of the successful teachers of low-ability classes observed by the writer. Identify the expressions that limit the researcher's findings.

Yet another limitation of this study, also a form of narrowness, is that it relied on higher-than-expected achievement as a sign of effectiveness without considering other sorts of outcomes. Critics of ability grouping, however, maintain that low-track assignment is stigmatizing, producing harmful social outcomes apart from effects on achievement (see, e.g., Schwartz 1981; Oakes 1985). Cases studied by Valli (1986) and by Camarena (1990) seemed to open the possibility of counteracting this problem. However, in this study, Mrs. Turner commented in the year-end interview that assigning students to a remedial class stigmatizes them and depresses their motivation, and she views this as reason to avoid assigning them to a separate class. In fact, both Mrs. Turner and Mrs. Grant told us that, although they see the ability-grouping question as complex and multisided, on balance they both prefer mixing low-track students with other students. Thus, our examples of teachers who succeeded with low tracks — at least with respect to instruction and achievement — would actually prefer to end that arrangement. Perhaps, then, these are simply examples of good teachers, who would be effective regardless of how students were assigned. In any case, given the likelihood that ability grouping will continue to be used, we need to know much more about how to use it well.

Gamoran 1993: 18–19.

### Exercise 6

Examine the moral obligations or "imperatives" in the passages below. What *should* be done? What is good or bad? What kind of outcomes are in sight?

### PASSAGE 1

There are at least four reasons why studying gaze aversion and disengaging from the environment may be of more than passing interest. First, the behavior is so frequent as to be characterized as "commonplace" (Kundera, 1996). Second, the results bear a family resemblance to the irrelevant speech effect (LeCompte, 1994) and to the analysis of attentional demands on retrieval (Craik, Govoni, Naveh-Benjamin, and Anderson, 1996). Third, this sort of behavior has been noted as relevant by investigators in at least two other domains: social behavior (Argyle and Kendon, 1967), and law enforcement. In the latter context, Fisher and Geiselman (1992) recommend closing the eyes as a component of the cognitive interview designed to facilitate accurate recall of information from eyewitnesses to crimes.

Finally, Glenberg (1997) has proposed that disengaging from the environment may be a significant source of individual differences in cognition. That is, planning, recollective memory, and language all seem to require some ability to disengage from the current environment. If there is reliable variability in the capacity or skill needed to disengage (see Ehrlichman and Weinberger, 1978, for data on this), this variability ought to be systematically related to the execution of a wide variety of cognitive and behavioral skills.

Arthur M. Glenberg, Jennifer L. Schroeder, and David A. Robertson 1998 "Averting the gaze disengages the environment and facilitates remembering." *Memory and Cognition* 26 (4): 651–58, 657.

### PASSAGE 2

The rewards of working with TEK are commonly expressed using the future tense. While improvements are certainly possible, available methods of documenting TEK, such as the one used in this study, are effective. What remain to be developed are better means of integrating TEK approaches with those of Western science, better ways of using TEK in resource management, and a better understanding of how TEK can help conservation, including sustainable use of living resources.

This research shows that an effective methodology used in a collaborative research process with elders and hunters can document a wide range of useful land detailed information. The benefits of such research include a better understanding of the ecology of a region or a species, as well as cooperation in research, which aids the cooperative management strategies that are increasingly common in Alaska and elsewhere in the Arctic. Effective processes for applying documented indigenous knowledge to management, conservation, and biological research, however, remain elusive, and require additional investigation.

Huntington et al. 1999: 59.

# Glossary

**abstract** the brief summary that sometimes precedes an article or accompanies bibliographical information found in an index.

**abstractions, abstract words** concepts, ideas, and entities which could be said to have essentially mental existence, for example, "power" or "racial antagonism." We develop abstractions from concrete data and generalizations. Abstractions occupy the highest levels of generality and perform a cognitive function: that is, they play an important role in reasoning. "Prestige" abstractions also perform important social functions: high-value abstractions attract the attention of members of a particular academic community; display the writer's allegiance to the interests and knowledge-making methods of that community; and establish the writer's right to speak as a member of the community, just as, for example, "voluntary employee turnover" or "relationship marketing" can establish a speaker's position as a member of the management-studies community (CH. 3, 4, 8).

**agentless expressions** expressions that highlight the activity rather than the actor, by eliminating the person (or "agent") doing the activity. *See also* PASSIVE CONSTRUCTIONS and FORECASTS.

**ambiguity** the capacity for a word or phrase to be interpreted in two or more ways. Ambiguity is associated particularly with noun phrases containing two or more nouns, for example, "huge pot sale."

**anticipatory-it, it-extraposition** the use of "it" at the beginning of a sentence as a means of deferring important material to the end of the sentence. *See also* END-WEIGHT PRINCIPLE (CH. 9).

**apposition/appositive** a grammatical structure, signalled by commas, dashes, colon, parentheses, "or", and "i.e." (*id est*), that puts an equivalent expression next to a term which the writer estimates as important but difficult for a reader. The appositive may define and narrow the meaning and application of an important word or it may expand and amplify the sense of the term (CH. 5).

**assertion** the speech action of making a statement for the new information of the reader — as if the reader did not know this information. *See also* PRESUPPOSITION (CH. 9).

**citation** the customary practice of attributing words, phrases, or statements to another speaker (CH. 2).

**cleft sentence, cleft construction** a syntactic construction commonly used for emphasis. Cleft constructions take the form "It was X that did such-and-such" rather than "X did such-and-such" (e.g., "It was geological evidence that supported the Alvarez hypothesis" rather than "geological evidence supported the Alvarez hypothesis") (CH. 9).

**cognitive response vs. social response** the response of a reader based on understanding or reasoning vs. the response based on social expectations, though the distinction is blurred in actuality. Social expectations come from shared habits of reasoning and preferred procedures for constructing knowledge in particular research communities (CH. 7, 8, 10). *See also* MUTUAL KNOWLEDGE.

**common sense vs. uncommon sense (expertise)** unexamined but widely accepted assumptions arising out of everyday experience and popular discourse vs. assumptions arising out of the domains of research. *See also* PLAIN LANGUAGE (CH. 9).

**complaint tradition** the cultural practice of publicly deploring the state of the language, announcing its decline from an earlier notion of perfection (CH. 9).

**cultural situation** circumstances that define the relationship between writer and reader; a distinct occasion in a culture. Looking for work and the job interview are examples of cultural situations (CH. 1).

**definite expressions** a noun phrase beginning with "the" or "this," marking the entity as familiar to both writer and reader (e.g., the recipe on the spaghetti box). When used in academic discourse, the definite expression (e.g., the choice-theoretic paradigm) encodes a community of researchers (writers and readers) (CH. 9I). *See also* PRESUPPOSITION.

**definition** a statement clarifying how a term is to be used in a particular context. Definition is a remarkably complex phenomenon, and statements can be clarified by a variety of means. Moreover, the approaches to definition vary from DISCIPLINE to discipline, with some disciplines preferring definitions based on TAXONOMY and others allowing definitions to be derived for the immediate purposes of the argument at hand (CH. 5). *See also* APPOSITION, FORMAL DEFINITION, and SUSTAINED DEFINITION.

**direct speech** reported speech that represents the exact words used by someone else in another context. The simplest form of reported speech is quotation (x said "y"), a verbatim record of another's speech (CH. 11).

**discipline** a particular branch of academic study. A discipline can be construed broadly (history, biology) or narrowly (cognitive psychology, medical entomology).

**discourse action** an action which can be represented by a reporting verb (X describes, X observes, X proposes) or reporting noun (X's description, X's observation, X's proposal). Discourse actions are associated both with CITATION (CH. 3) and the DISCURSIVE *I* (CH. 9), and the choice of the verb can be influenced by the discipline in which a writer is working (CH. 11B).

**discourse community** a group of people  identifiable (or recognizable) not only by their shared values, beliefs, and specialized knowledge about the world but also by the way they talk, or write: their talk embodies the shared values and special knowledge. For example, mountain bikers and developmental psychologists constitute distinct discourse communities because each group exhibits characteristic patterns of communication that its members find meaningful and efficient ("vegetable tunnel" and "yard sale" being useful and economical expressions of experience for the first group, but incomprehensible and irrelevant to the experiences and interests of the second) (CH. 9).

**discursive *I*** the use of "I" to refer to the writer in his or her capacity as a researcher/writer. The discursive *I* may also appear in the plural form, as "we" (CH. 9).

**documentation** a two-part tracking system that aids the reader's movement from REPORTED SPEECH or GIST in the body of the text to the full documentation of sources in footnotes, endnotes, and the "References" or "Works Cited" pages (CH. 11C).

**emphasis** expressions drawing attention to key points, as in, for example, "of particular importance here" or "the point I want to stress here …" (CH. 9).

**end-weight principle** the tendency to shift important material to the end of the sentence (e.g., "It has been routinely argued that the advances in obstetrical knowledge in the eighteenth century undermined the traditional role of the midwife") (CH. 9).

**estimate from a position of limited knowledge** modality and modalizing expressions such as "I think" and "seems" indicate that a statement issues from the writer as knowledge-maker (CH. 10). *See also* KNOWLEDGE-MAKING *I.*

**expert vs. non-expert** generally speaking, the distinction between those who are members of a research community and those who are not. However, the boundaries between the two categories can be contested (CH. 3E).

**failed-then-revised hypothesis** the revisions to one's understanding of a noun phrase as one works through it. For example, as a reader works through the noun phrase "the letter-carrier union representative meeting" it becomes necessary to revise one's understanding of the noun phrase with each successive word (CH. 9).

**feminist reasoning** related to ways of thinking following women's rights movements in the nineteenth and twentieth centuries, feminism sometimes critiques the historically masculinist basis of knowledge-making, and has often insisted on emphasizing the role of the subject in the knowledge-making process (CH. 10).

**forecasts** statements about how the argument will be organized, what readers can expect (CH. 9).

**form** used by many people to refer to something like the overall structure of a piece of writing: someone might say that a statute has a preamble, a series of clauses, and a proclamation — and that is its "form"; or that an essay has a "five-paragraph form" — introduction, one paragraph on each of three points, and a conclusion. "Form" can also be used to refer to words that are repeated. When we hear once again "we are gathered here today" or "let me be perfectly clear," the features we recognize could be called formal (or even formalities). In this book, "form" refers to what we have in mind when we sense both an overall shape *and* a recognizable wording. But, in this book, "form" points mainly to the dimension of genre which is linguistic (made of language) and material (made of paper or electronic signals, colourful or plain, small or big, long or short, and so on). So a postcard's typical *form* is a 15 cm x 10 cm rectangle of cardboard with a colour photograph of a landmark on one side, and, on the other side, a two-part division. One part provides for a handwritten address and postage stamp; the other part is filled with a message describing the writer's experience on a journey, often with mention of weather, accommodation, and characteristics of local people. This definition of form does not permit form to be separated from "content"; instead, it urges us to see form and content as fused (CH. 1).

**formal definition** the classical form of a definition consisting of a single sentence in which the term being defined is the subject, which is followed by a form of the verb "to be" and a subject complement that identifies the general class the term belongs to and then provides characteristics distinguishing the term from all other members of that class. A slightly updated version of the classical example of the formal definition is "A human is a rational animal" (human = the term to be defined, animal = the general class humans belong to, rational = the distinctive feature that distinguishes humans from other animals) (CH. 5).

**generalization** a statement that typifies large numbers of instances (intermediate level of generality), as in "Through the 1980s, the babyboomers were the most relentless consumers the marketplace has ever seen." A typified or generalized action or event can itself become an ABSTRACTION (higher level of generality), such as "materialism," and further specified through details (lowest levels of generality), such as "cars, condos, electronic appliances." Both generalizations and abstractions are products of reasoning (CH. 11A). *See also* LEVELS OF GENERALITY.

**genre** traditionally defined in terms of form and used for categorization, genre has been reconceptualized as involving situation and form (situation + form = genre) and, thus, involves not only the type of communication but also the situation that the communication serves (CH. 1). *See also* FORM and CULTURAL SITUATION.

**genre-specific expectations** readers' often unconscious expectations of specific genres' stylistic conventions, which, among academic readers, reflect disciplinary values and preferred methods for constructing knowledge (CH. 7). A reader of an English paper, for example, expects to see quotations from a literary text that demonstrate or illustrate a writer's statements about meaning. Traditional marking comments, such as the request for more "evidence," often obscure the specificity of these tacit expectations (CH. 7C). *See also* UNITARY VIEWS OF LANGUAGE and GENRE VIOLATION.

**genre theory** dating to Aristotle, genre theory attempts to explain and categorize communication into types based on formal similarities. Recent genre theory rethinks the emphasis on FORM and sees TYPE as developing from the situational needs and habits of communication (CH. 1).

**genre violation** the misapplication of the norms, expectations, or needs regarding communication in one situation to those of another situation. This can occur in writing (e.g., a scholar uses technical terminology when addressing an audience of laypeople) or in reading (e.g., a lay-reader criticizes the lack of "clarity" in a research publication) (CH. 9).

**gist** the target of a method of noting, while reading, that avoids copying and instead aims to capture and transport information nuggets for other uses (CH. 3).

**hypothesis** a statement which is deemed plausible but which is, so far, untested and will be shown to be tested in the course of the article or research study.

**imprint** the mark left on language by salient features of a CULTURAL SITUATION. Recent GENRE THEORY predicts that formal features of language develop from and serve recurring situations. When language is used in a way that becomes typical of situation, it is imprinted by that situation (CH. 1). *See also* TYPE, TYPIFICATION.

**indirect speech** REPORTED SPEECH that represents the words of another speaker by using new words: paraphrase or SUMMARY. Indirect speech, unlike DIRECT SPEECH, involves changes in the wording to fit a new and different context. In academic writing especially, it is often leads to NOMINALIZATION (CH. 2, 9, 11).

**knowledge deficit** the gap in established knowledge — what hasn't been said, what needs to be said, some error in what is held to be true. The knowledge deficit is what justifies the present research project. The location of knowledge deficits often comes with MODALITY and LIMITING EXPRESSIONS (CH. 10, 11).

**knowledge-making** *I See* DISCURSIVE *I* and MODALITY, MODAL EXPRESSIONS.

**levels of generality** the structure of information in a given passage, moving from the highest, most abstract concepts through general concepts down to specific details. Levels of generality can be represented in diagram form, with abstractions appearing at the top, generalized or contextualized at midpoints, and specific details at the lowest levels. The levels diagram reveals relationships among ideas and specific details; it also sketches our experience of reading as we negotiate the big issues, the writer's general claims, and the specific references used to illustrate and demonstrate those claims (CH. 3, 4). *See also* ABSTRACTIONS and GENERALIZATION.

**limiting expressions** terms that place limits on a GENERALIZATION ("in most cases," "a majority of interviewees") (CH. 9).

**listeners' centre of attention** an estimate of the responses of a reader that is based on a writer's own social and cultural expectations and experiences with forms of expression (CH. 7).

**management device** a metaphor for how a reader manages information while reading: a device which detects, organizes, and assigns priority or RELEVANCE (CH. 8). *See also* MENTAL DESKTOP.

**mental desktop** a metaphor for how a reader processes information while reading: a space on which statements arrive, one after the other, as the reader advances through a text (CH. 8). *See also* MANAGEMENT DEVICE.

**messages about the argument** features including the DISCURSIVE *I*, SELF-REFERENCE, FORECASTING, and EMPHASIS that help a reader understand the organization of academic writing (CH. 9).

**methods** procedures by which knowledge has been produced. *See also* QUANTITATIVE and QUALITATIVE (CH. 10).

**methods section** an explicit account of how the researchers produced the knowledge they are now reporting. In the sciences and social sciences, such accounts are often accompanied by the heading "methods" (CH. 10).

**modality, modal expressions** expressions such as "I think" or "seems" that indicate that a statement is an inference from a position of limited knowledge (CH. 10).

**modalize** the marking of statements as being knowledge under construction — usually with the recognition that the knowledge is limited in some way — from a certain location: the speaker's or writer's position in the world (CH. 10).

**moral statement** a statement, sometimes occurring in conclusions, that expresses research imperatives or obligations — what actions "must" be taken, what "should" be done. Moral statements may presuppose their disciplines' beliefs about what is good and bad, and they often connect the interests and activities of research to concerns in the public domain. The presence or lack of moral statements and the types of imperatives and obligations they propose are discipline specific (CH. 11). *See also* SUBJECT POSITION.

**mutual knowledge** an estimate of what can be safely assumed as shared background knowledge.

**narrative** a sequence of events organized chronologically — a story. Narratives are especially difficult to summarize because they tend not to contain higher levels of generality which explain the details and conditions in the story (CH. 4).

**nominalization** the process of word transformation when verbs (actions) and qualities are converted into nouns: "observe," for example, becomes "observation" (CH. 9).

**noun phrase** a phrase consisting of a noun or pronoun along with its modifiers (e.g., "the research," "researchers," "he," "they," "sample-size considerations"). Often in academic writing, noun phrases may consist of strings of nouns that modify subsequent nouns or noun-groupings (CH. 9). *See also* NOMINALIZATION and SYNTACTIC DENSITY.

**objectivity** the attempt to avoid personal bias or the limits of personal perspective and experience in the production of knowledge (CH. 10). *Contrast* SUBJECTIVITY.

**obviousness** an expression of attitude regarding a statement (e.g., "of course") in a given DISCIPLINE or field of research that indicates there is some consensus or common ground with regard to it (CH. 10).

**orchestration** a dialogue of two or more speakers (often of other research publications) arranged by a writer by way of direct and/or indirect reported speech (CH. 6).

**passive construction, passive voice** the grammatical construction whereby the object that a transitive verb acts upon is moved from after the verb to before. For example, "I ate all your Easter chocolate" (the active voice) becomes "All your Easter chocolate was eaten by me" *or* "All your Easter chocolate was eaten." The second form of the passive construction is also an example of AGENTLESS EXPRESSIONS.

**plain language** the use of language designed to be understood by a general readership. When standards of plain language are invoked to criticize the complexities of other kinds of discourse — for example, academic or legal writing — a UNITARY VIEW OF LANGUAGE is in evidence (CH. 9).

**postcolonial (reasoning)** a critical tendency which emerges in twentieth-century discourse to challenge the authority of Western researchers to produce knowledge of other cultures, and which exposes traditional anthropological knowledge as saturated with colonial values (CH. 10).

**position, positioning** a relational stance or perspective negotiated through REPORTED SPEECH and the place from which a writer speaks. REPORTING EXPRESSIONS position writers' proximity to and distance from statements made by others. The development of interpretive abstractions from concrete data positions writers both cognitively and socially as members of a community of writers. *See also* COGNITIVE RESPONSE vs. SOCIAL RESPONSE.

**presupposition** the phenomenon of some propositions being assumed rather than asserted (*see* ASSERTION). Presupposing expressions are those which construct the reader as knowing — as sharing a set of inferences about the world. They include social, political, and cultural assumptions, as well as assumptions about the physical world and the relationship between things and between people. Whereas here certain information is *asserted* — "Babur had an influence on South Asian life writing" — here the same information is *presupposed*: "The influence of Babur on South Asian life writing ..." (CH. 9).

**qualitative** a method of study that focuses on a case study or direct observation of a small sample or group over a prolonged period of time (CH. 10).

**quantitative** a method of study that seeks to set aside biases caused by an individual's beliefs or immediate experience of the world by observing and numerically measuring controlled studies or experiments using as broad a sample as possible (CH. 10).

**relevance theory** the branch of linguistics concerned with studying the contexts which condition readers' understanding and interpretation of language (CH. 8).

**reported speech** a projected representation of another's words, directly or indirectly; we use reported speech whenever we convey what someone else has said. Reporting the statements made by other speakers, the writer positions himself or herself in relation to those statements. Reported speech is an essential component in POSITIONING (CH. 11B).

**reporting expressions, double reporting** expressions that report sources of information: the writer's name, the title of the work, the date of publication, and the reporting verb. Double reporting occurs when summarizers report information used by their source, that is, account for the source's summarizing activity (CH. 3).

**reporting verb** the verb, in a REPORTING EXPRESSION, that names or characterizes the action of another work, and describes the development of the discussion. Summarizers can develop a POSITION in relation to another work in their choice of reporting verbs (CH. 2).

**self-reference** a MESSAGE ABOUT THE ARGUMENT in which a work (e.g., article or essay) or a part of a work (e.g., a conclusion) is referred to directly. For example: "In this essay …" or "By way of concluding …" (CH. 9).

**situation** *See* CULTURAL SITUATION and GENRE (CH. 1).

**socio-cognitive needs** *See* COGNITIVE RESPONSE vs. SOCIAL RESPONSE (CH. 9).

**state of knowledge** a writer's estimate of the degree of stability in a designated area of knowledge: established knowledge, limits of knowledge, the conditions under which it was produced, and the positions from which statements issue (CH. 2, 3).

**subjectivity** the personal (social and cognitive) point of view or experience of the world (CH. 10). *Contrast* OBJECTIVITY.

**subject position** relevant personal (social and political) elements of a researcher's experience of the world that may influence or be relevant to the knowledge he or she produces (CH. 10).

**summarizer's position** the position or perspective developed by a summarizer in relation to reported statements, evident in the way the summarized material is characterized (in the REPORTING VERB) and in the ABSTRACTIONS used to interpret details in the original (CH. 2, 3, 4). *See also* POSITION, POSITIONING, and REPORTED SPEECH.

**summary** reported speech that compresses and may rearrange what another speaker has said or written (CH. 2, 3, 4).

**sustained definition** a strategy whereby a writer locates a phenomenon among other, related phenomena in the world. The sustained attention paid to the phenomenon serves to extend or advance the inquiry (CH. 5C). *See also* APPOSITION/APPOSITIVE and FORMAL DEFINITION.

**symbolic domination** domination which operates not through physical coercion but through psychological/social processes.

**syntactic density** the effect resulting from the capacity of noun phrases to expand by incorporating other sentence elements (adjectives, verbs, adverbs, other nouns) and creating noun "strings" (CH. 9). *See also* NOUN PHRASE and NOMINALIZATION.

**taxonomy** schemes for classifying and ordering phenomena, schemes that depend on naming (using nouns) for things.

**think-aloud protocol** a tool for professional writers and a technique for researching the reader's experience of using a text. The readers read and report out loud what's going on in their mind while reading; the writer gets a chance to watch someone making meaning from what he or she has written. Think-aloud protocols help writers understand the reading process by learning to anticipate and predict readers' responses to their text; their subsequent adjustments follow the reader's experience of the text rather than unitary rules about language usage (CH. 7, 8).

**tradition of inquiry** a scholarly practice, including topics considered relevant and worthy of ongoing inquiry, the preferred methods of inquiry, and the research community's style of citation (CH. 11).

**type, typification** formal features of language use that develop when a CULTURAL SITUATION makes that way of speaking or writing characteristic or typical. TYPIFICATION is the creating of TYPES (CH. 1). *See also* IMPRINT and GENRE THEORY.

**typified group** a term that generalizes and categorizes large numbers of individual speakers or writers as members of an identifiable community (e.g., interviewees, psychoanalytic critics); when used in reporting and framing, the names of particular members are eliminated. *See also* AGENTLESS EXPRESSIONS.

**uncertainty/indeterminacy** expressions which indicate doubt about statements, place limits on generalizations, identify gaps or inadequacies in existing research, and otherwise emphasize that knowledge is under construction. These expressions and tendencies can create a sense of uncertainty or a lack of determinate knowledge about a subject. MODALITY, LIMITING EXPRESSIONS, and REPORTING EXPRESSIONS are all associated with uncertainty (CH. 10). *See also* KNOWLEDGE DEFICIT.

**unitary views of language** the idea that a single set of standards can be applied to all forms of writing or speech. Unitary views of language often manifest themselves in set rules (e.g., never begin a sentence with "and," always place a thesis statement at the end of the first paragraph, never end a paragraph with a quotation) (CH. 7).

# Further Readings

Coe, Richard, Lorelei Lingard, and Tatiana Teslenko, eds. 2002. *The Rhetoric and Ideology of Genre: Strategies for Stability and Change.* Cresskill, NJ: Hampton.

Devitt, Amy. 1993. "Generalizing about genre: New concepts of an old concept." *College Composition and Communication* 44: 357–86.

Freedman, Aviva, and Peter Medway. 1994. "Locating genre studies: Antecedents and prospects." In *Genre and the New Rhetoric,* ed. A. Freedman and P. Medway. London: Taylor & Francis.

Heath, Shirley Brice. 1983. "Chapter six: Literate traditions." In *Ways with Words: Language, Life, and Work in Communities and Classrooms.* Cambridge: Cambridge UP.

Keller-Cohen, Deborah. 1987. "Literate practices in a modern credit union." *Language in Society* 16: 7–24.

MacDonald, Susan Peck. 1994. "Chapter two: Patterns in disciplinary variation." In *Professional Academic Writing in the Humanities and Social Sciences.* Carbondale: Southern Illinois UP.

Miller, Carolyn. 1984. "Genre as social action." *Quarterly Journal of Speech* 70: 151–67.

Myers, Greg. 1989. "The pragmatics of politeness in scientific articles." *Applied Linguistics* 10: 1–35.

Swales, John. 1990. "Chapter two: The concept of discourse community." In *Genre Analysis: English in Academic and Research Settings.* Cambridge: Cambridge UP.

Swales, John. 1990. "Chapter three: The concept of genre." In *Genre Analysis: English in Academic and Research Settings.* Cambridge: Cambridge UP.

Swales, John. 1990. "Chapter seven: Research articles in English." In *Genre Analysis: English in Academic and Research Settings.* Cambridge: Cambridge UP.

# References

Agar, Michael. 1994. "The intercultural frame." *International Journal of Intercultural Relations* 18 (2): 221–37.

Alcock, J.E., D.W. Carment, and S.W. Sadava. 1994. *A Textbook of Social Psychology*, 3rd ed. Scarborough, ON: Prentice Hall.

Allen, Ann Taylor. 1999. "Feminism, social science, and the meanings of modernity: The debate on the origin of the family in Europe and the United States, 1860–1914." *The American Historical Review* 104 (4): 1085–1113.

Anselment, Raymond A. 1989. "Small pox in seventeenth-century English literature: Reality and the metamorphosis of wit." *Medical History* 33 (1): 72–95.

Arnold, Bettina. 1999. "'Drinking the feast': Alcohol and the legitimation of power in Celtic Europe." *Cambridge Archaeological Review* 9 (1): 71–93. Reprinted with the permission of Cambridge University Press.

Bar-Yosef, Ofer, and Steven L. Kuhn. 1999. "The big deal about blades: Laminar technologies and human evolution." *American Anthropologist* 101 (2): 322–38.

Bhabha, Homi K. 1994. "Now newness enters the world." In *The Location of Culture*. London: Routledge.

Bodley, John H. 1997. *Cultural Anthropology: Tribes, States, and the Global System*, 2nd ed. Mountain View, CA: Mayfield. Reproduced with permission of the McGraw-Hill companies.

Bourdieu, Pierre. 1991. *Language and Symbolic Power*. Cambridge, MA: Harvard UP.

Bruggink, Thomas H., and Kamran Siddiqui. 1995. "An econometric model of alumni giving: A case study for a liberal arts college." *American Economist* 39 (2): 53–60.

Buchanan, Neil H. 1999. "Taxes, saving, and macroeconomics." *Journal of Economic Issues* 33 (1): 59–75.

Burgess, Keith. 1994. "British employers and education policy, 1935–45: A decade of 'missed opportunities'?" *Business History* 36 (3): 29–61.

Calhoun, Cheshire. 1994. "Separating lesbian theory from feminist theory." *Ethics* 104: 558–82. Reprinted with permission.

Cameron, Deborah. 1990. "Demythologizing sociolinguistics: Why language does not reflect society." In *Ideologies of Language*, ed. John E. Joseph and Talbot J. Taylor. London: Routledge.

Cameron, Deborah. 1995. *Verbal Hygiene*. London: Routledge. Reprinted with permission.

"Cellucci says Canada reneged on missile plan." <www.ctv.ca>, 7 March 2005. Reprinted with permission.

Chafe, Wallace. 1994. *Discourse, Consciousness, and Time*. Chicago: U of Chicago P.

Chavez, Leo R. 1994. "The power of the imagined community: The settlement of undocumented Mexicans and Central Americans in the United States." *American Anthropologist* 96 (1): 52–73.

Chorpita, Bruce F., Anne Marie Albano, and David H. Barlow. 1998. "The structure of negative emotions in a clinical sample of children and adolescents." *Journal of Abnormal Psychology* 107 (1): 74–85.

Clark, Herbert. 1992. *Arenas of Language Use.* Chicago: U of Chicago P.

Clifford, James. 1997. *Routes: Travel and Translation in the Late Twentieth Century.* Cambridge, MA: Harvard UP.

Coates, Jennifer. 1996. *Women Talk: Conversation between Women Friends.* Cambridge, MA: Blackwell.

Coffey, David J. 1977. *The Encyclopedia of Aquarium Fishes in Color.* New York: Arco.

Counts, Dorothy Ayers, and David R. Counts. 1992. "'They're my family now': The creation of community among RVers." *Anthropologica* 34: 168–70. Reprinted with permission.

Cowan, Ann, Janet Giltrow, Sharon Josephson, and Michele Valiquette. 1998. "Feedback: Its uses, reliability, and design." Paper presented at annual meeting of Canadian Association of Teachers of Technical Writing, Ottawa.

Dasenbrock, Reed Way. 1987. "Intelligibility and meaningfulness in multicultural literature in English." *PMLA* 102: 10–19.

Datta, Saikat, and Prabal Roy Chowdhury. 1998. "Management union bargaining under minimum wage regulation in less developed countries." *Indian Economic Review* 33 (2): 169–84.

Daveri, Francesco, and Ricardo Faini. 1999. "Where do migrants go?" *Oxford Economic Papers* 51: 595–622.

della Paolera, Gerardo, and Alan M. Taylor. 1999. "Economic recovery from the Argentine Great Depression: Institutions, expectations, and the change of macroeconomic regime." *Journal of Economic History* 59 (3): 567–98.

Dixon, John, and Kevin Durrheim. 2000. "Displacing place-identity: A discursive approach to locating self and other." *British Journal of Social Psychology* 39: 27–44.

Douglas, Mary. 1996. "The choice between gross and spiritual: Some medical preferences." In *Thought Styles.* London: Sage. Reprinted by permission of Sage Publications Ltd.

Eckes, Thomas. 1994. "Features of men, features of women: Assessing stereotypic beliefs about gender subtypes." *British Journal of Social Psychology* 33: 107–23.

Ellis, Mark, and Panikos Panayi. 1994. "German minorities in World War I: A comparative study of Britain and the U.S.A." *Ethnic and Racial Studies* 17 (2): 238–59.

Endler, Norman S., and Rachel L. Speer. 1998. "Personality psychology: Research trends for 1993–1995." *Journal of Personality* 66 (5): 621–69.

Englund, Mary. 1981. "An Indian remembers." In *Now You Are My Brother*, ed. Margaret Whitehead. Victoria, BC: Provincial Archives. Reprinted with permission.

Evers, D. Elaine, Charles Sasser, James Gosselink, Deborah Fuller, and Jenneke Visser. 1998. "The impact of vertebrate herbivores on wetland vegetation in Atchafayala Bay, Louisiana." *Estuaries* 21 (1): 1–13.

Foot, David K., and Daniel Stoffman. 1996. *Boom, Bust and Echo: How to Profit from the Coming Demographic Shift.* Toronto: Macfarlane Walter & Ross.

Freeman, Victoria. 2005. "Attitudes Toward 'Miscegenation' in Canada, the United States, New Zealand, and Australia, 1860–1914." *Native Studies Review* 16 (1): 41–70.

Gamoran, Adam. 1993. "Alternative uses of ability grouping in secondary schools: Can we bring high-quality instruction to low-ability classes?" *American Journal of Education* 102: 1–22.

Geschwender, James A. 1992. "Ethgender, women's waged labor, and economic mobility." *Social Problems* 39 (1): 1–16.

Giddens, Anthony. 1990. *The Consequences of Modernity.* Stanford UP.

Giltrow, Janet. 2000. "'Argument' as a term in talk about student writing." In *Learning to Argue in Higher Education,* ed. S. Mitchell and R. Andrews. Portsmouth, NH: Boynton Cook/Heinemann.

Glenberg, Arthur M., Jennifer L. Schroeder, and David A. Robertson. 1998. "Averting the gaze disengages the environment and facilitates remembering." *Memory and Cognition* 26 (4): 651–58.

Greening, Daniel W., and Barbara Gray. 1994. "Testing a model of organizational response to social and political issues." *Academy of Management Journal* 37 (3): 467–98.

Grossman, Herschel I. 1999. "Kleptocracy and revolutions." *Oxford Economic Papers* 51: 267–83.

Halliday, M.A.K., and J.R. Martin. 1993. *Writing Science: Literary and Discursive Power.* Pittsburgh: U of Pittsburgh P.

Hamilton, Gary G., and Nicole Woolsey Biggart. 1988. "Market, culture, and authority: A comparative analysis of management and organization in the Far-East." *American Journal of Sociology* 94, 552–94. Reprinted with permission.

Heyes, C.M. 1998. "Theory of mind in nonhuman primates." *Behavioral and Brain Sciences* 21: 101–48.

Higgs, Robert. 1999. "From central planning to the market: The American transition, 1945–1947." *Journal of Economic History* 59: 600–23.

Hobbs, Peter V., and Arthur L. Rangno. 1998. "Microstructures of low and middle-level clouds over the Beaufort Sea." *Quarterly Journal of the Royal Meteorological Society* 124: 2035–71.

Hom, Alice Y., and Ming-Yuen S. Ma. 1993. "Premature gestures: A speculative dialogue on Asian Pacific lesbian and gay writing." *Journal of Homosexuality* 26 (2/3): 21–31.

Huntington, Henry, and the Communities of Buckland, Elim, Koyuk, Point Lay, and Shaktoolik. 1999. "Traditional knowledge of the ecology of beluga whales (*Delphinapterus leucas*) in the Eastern Chukchi and Northern Bering Seas, Alaska." *Arctic* 52 (1): 49–61.

Hurwitz, Gregg. 2002. "A Tempest, a Birth and Death:Freud, Jung, and Shakespeare's Pericles." *Sexuality & Culture* 6 (3): 3.

Husbands, Christopher T. 1994. "Crisis of national identity as the 'new moral panics': Political agenda-setting about definitions of nationhood." *New Community* 20 (2): 191–206.

Hyland, Ken. 1999. "Academic attribution: Citation and the construction of disciplinary knowledge." *Applied Linguistics* 20 (3): 341.

Jackson, Sue. 2002. "To Be Or Not To Be? The place of women's studies in the lives of its students." *Journal of Gender Studies* 9 (2): 189–197.

Kabeer, Naila. 1994. "The structure of 'revealed' preference: Race, community and female labour supply in the London clothing industry." *Development and Change* 25: 307–31.

Kelm, Mary-Ellen. 1999. "British Columbia First Nations and the influenza pandemic of 1918–19." *BC Studies* 122 (Summer): 23–47.

Kerwin, Scott. 1999. "The Janet Smith Bill of 1924 and the Language of Race and Nation in British Columbia." *BC Studies* 121: 83–114.

Khalid, Adeeb. 1994. "Printing, publishing, and reform in Tsarist Central Asia." *International Journal of Middle East Studies* 26: 187–200.

Killingray, David. 1994. "The 'rod of empire': The debate over corporal punishment in the British African colonial forces, 1888–1946." *Journal of African History* 35: 210–16.

Kolodny, Annette. 1994. "Inventing a feminist discourse: Rhetoric and resistance in Margaret Fuller's *Woman in the Nineteenth Century*." *New Literary History* 25 (2): 355–82.

LaFollette, Hugh. 2000. "Gun control." *Ethics* 110: 263–81.

Lane, D.E., and R.L. Stephenson. 1998. "A framework for risk analysis in fisheries decision-making." *ICES Journal of Marine Science* 55: 1–13.

Lee, Thomas W., and Terence R. Mitchell. 1994. "An alternative approach: The unfolding model of voluntary employee turnover." *Academy of Management Journal* 19 (1): 51–89.

Lesure, Richard. 1999. "Figurines as representations and products at Paso de la Amada, Mexico." *Cambridge Archaeological Journal* 9 (2): 209–20.

Lin, Chia-Chin. 2000. "Applying the American Pain Society's QA standards to evaluate the quality of pain management among surgical, oncology, and hospice inpatients in Taiwan." *Pain* 87: 43–49. Reprinted with permission.

Lu, Min-Zhan. 1992. "Conflict and struggle: The enemies or preconditions of basic writing?" *College English* (December): 891–913.

Lupton, Deborah, and John Tulloch. 1999. "Theorizing fear of crime: Beyond the rational/irrational oppositions." *British Journal of Sociology* 50 (3): 507–23.

MacDonald, Susan Peck. 1994. *Professional Academic Writing in the Humanities and Social Sciences*. Carbondale: Southern Illinois UP.

Masson, Michael E.J., and Mary Anne Waldron. 1994. "Comprehension of legal contracts by non-experts: Effectiveness of plain language redrafting." *Applied Cognitive Psychology* 8: 67–85.

Mayes, Patricia. 1990. "Quotation in spoken English." *Studies in Language* 14 (2): 325–63.

McGuire, John. 1998. "Judicial violence and the 'civilizing process': Race and transition from public to private executions in Colonial Australia." *Australian Historical Studies* 111: 187–209.

Milroy, James, and Lesley Milroy. 1991 [1985]. *Authority in Language: Investigating Language Prescription and Standardisation*, 2nd ed. London: Routledge.

Mistry, Rohinton. 1995. "Prologue: 1975." In *A Fine Balance*. Toronto: McClelland & Stewart. Reprinted with permission.

Muir, Angela. "Kosovo." In *The Oxford Companion to Wine*, ed. Jancis Robinson. Oxford: Oxford UP, 542. Reprinted with permission.

Murphy, Rex. 2000, April 23. *Cross-Country Check-up*, CBC Radio.

Myers, Greg. 1999. "Functions of reported speech in group discussions." *Applied Linguistics* 20 (5): 376–401.

Nash, June. 1994. "Global integration and subsistence insecurity." *American Anthropologist* 96 (1): 7–30. Reprinted with permission.

Neiman, Paul J., et al. 1998. "An observational study of fronts and frontal mergers over the Continental United States." *Monthly Weather Review* 126: 2521–52.

Nemutanzhela, Thiathu J. 1993. "Cultural forms and literacy as resources for political mobilisation: A.M. Malivha and the Zoutpansberg Balemi Association." *African Studies* 52 (1): 89–102.

O'Connor, Denis. 1987. "Glue sniffers with special needs." *British Journal of Education* 14 (3): 94–97.

Olick, Jeffrey K. 1999. "Genre memories and memory genres: A dialogical analysis of May 8, 1945 commemorations in the Federal Republic of Germany." *American Sociological Review* 64: 381–402.

Oliver, Pamela E., and Daniel J. Myers. 1999. "How events enter the public sphere." *American Journal of Sociology* 105 (1): 38–67.

O'Toole, Alice, Kenneth A. Deffenbacher, Dominique Valentin, and Hervé Abdi. 1994. "Structural aspects of face recognition and the other-race effect." *Memory and Cognition* 22 (2): 208–24.

Perrault, Charles. 1969. "Little Thumb." In *The Blue Fairy Book*, ed. Andrew Lang. New York: Airmont, 266–67.

Pratt, John. 1999. "Norbert Elias and the civilized prison." *British Journal of Sociology* 50 (2): 271–96.

Prestwich, Patricia E. 1994. "Family strategies and medical power: 'Voluntary' committal in a Parisian asylum, 1876–1914." *Journal of Social History* 27 (4): 799–818.

Quillian, Lincoln. 1999. "Migration patterns and the growth of high-poverty neighborhoods, 1970–1990." *American Journal of Sociology* 105 (1): 1–37.

Quintero, Gilbert A., and Antonio L. Estrada. 1998. "Cultural models of masculinity and drug use: 'Machismo,' heroin, and street survival on the U.S.-Mexican border." *Contemporary Drug Problems* 25: 147–65.

Raasch, S., and D. Etling. 1998. "Modeling deep ocean convection: Large eddy simulation in comparison with laboratory experiments." *American Meteorological Society* 21: 1786–1802.

Rafter, Nicole H. 1992. "Claims-making and socio-cultural context in the first U.S. eugenics campaign." *Social Problems* 39 (1): 17.

Rauch-Elnekave, Helen. 1994. "Teenage motherhood: Its relationship to undetected learning problems." *Adolescence* 29: 91–103. Reprinted with permission.

Reiger, Kerreen M. 1989. "'Clean and comfortable and respectable': Working-class aspirations and the Australian 1920 Royal Commission on the Basic Wage." *History Workshop* 27: 86–105.

Schieffelin, Bambi B., and Rachelle Charlier Doucet. 1994. "The 'real' Haitian creole: Ideology, metalinguistics, and orthographic choice." *American Ethnologist* 21(1): 176–200. © 1994, American Anthropological Association. All rights reserved. Used by permission.

Schriver, Karen. 1994 [1992]. "What document designers can learn from usability testing." *Technostyle* 19 (3/4).

Scott, Rebecca J. 1994. "Defining the boundaries of freedom in the word of cane: Cuba, Brazil, and Louisiana after emancipation." *American Historical Review* (February): 70–102.

Seymour, Susanne. 1994. "Gender, church and people in rural areas." *Area* 26 (1): 45–56.

Sheldon, Amy. 1990. "Pickle fights: Gendered talk in preschool disputes." *Discourse Processes* 13: 5–31.

Smith, Thomas S., and Gregory T. Stevens. 1999. "The architecture of small networks: Strong interaction and dynamic organization in small social systems." *American Sociological Review* 64: 403–20.

South, Scott J., and Kyle D. Crowder. 1999. "Neighborhood effects on family formation: Concentrated poverty and beyond." *American Sociological Review* 64: 113–32.

Speck, Dara Culhane. 1987. *An Error in Judgement: The Politics of Medical Care in an Indian/White Community.* Vancouver, BC: Talonbooks.

Sperber, Dan, and Deirdre Wilson. 1986. *Relevance: Communication and Cognition.* Cambridge, MA: Harvard UP.

Stockton, S. 1995. "Writing in history: Narrating the subject of time." *Written Communication* 12 (1): 47–73.

Stratman, James F. 1994. "Investigating persuasive processes in legal discourse in real time: Cognitive biases and rhetorical strategy in appeal court briefs." *Discourse Processes* 17: 1–57.

Swales, John. 1990. *Genre Analysis: English in Academic and Research Settings*. Cambridge: Cambridge UP.

Tannen, Deborah. 1990. *You Just Don't Understand: Women and Men in Conversation*. New York: Ballantine Books.

Thurber, James. 1940. "The Rabbits Who Caused All the Trouble." *Fables for Our Time*. In *The Norton Reader*, shorter 8th ed. New York: W.W. Norton, 530.

Tiratsoo, Nick, and Jim Tomlinson. 1994. "Restrictive practices on the shopfloor in Britain, 1946–60: Myth and reality." *Business History* 36 (2): 65–84.

Todaro, Michael P. 1997. *Economic Development*. New York: Longman.

Tuffin, Keith, and Jo Danks. 1999. "Community care and mental disorder: An analysis of discursive resources." *British Journal of Social Psychology* 38: 289–302.

Verkuyten, Maykel, Wiebe de Jong, and Kees Masson. 1994. "Similarities in anti-racist and racist discourse: Dutch local residents talking about ethnic minorities." *New Community* 20 (2): 253–67.

Waern, Yvonne. 1988. "Thoughts on texts in context: Applying the think-aloud method to text processing." *Text* 8 (4): 317–50.

Wassink, Alicia Beckford. 1999. "Historic low prestige and seeds of change: Attitudes toward Jamaican Creole." *Language in Society* 28: 57–92.

Wearne, Phillip. 1996. *Return of the Indian: Conquest and Revival in the Americas*. London: Cassell.

Weinberger, Daniel A. 1998. "Defenses, personality structure and development: Integrating psychodynamic theory into a typological approach to personality." *Journal of Personality* 66 (6): 1061–77.

Wenzel, George W. 1999. "Traditional ecological knowledge and Inuit: Reflections on TEK research and ethics." *Arctic* 52 (2): 113–24.

Willott, Sara, and Chris Giffin. 1999. "Building your own lifeboat: Working-class male offenders talk about economic class." *British Journal of Social Psychology* 38: 445–60.

Womack, Peter. 1999. "Shakespeare and the sea of stories." *Journal of Medieval & Early Modern Studies* 29 (1): 169–88.

Wong, Siu Kwong. 1999. "Acculturation, peer relations, and delinquent behavior of Chinese-Canadian youth." *Adolescence* 34 (133): 107–19.

Zervakis, Jennifer, and David C. Rubin. 1998. "Memory and learning for a novel written style." *Memory and Cognition* 26 (4): 754–67.

# Index